¡Viva la Lucha!

Margie —

¡Viva la Lucha!

Personal Reflections on the Fiftieth Anniversary of
the Mexican American School Boards Association

As told to and transcribed by
Dr. Jayme Mathias

se decide

Edited by
Dr. Mercedes Lynn de Uriarte

© 2020 by Mexican American School Boards Association

Mexican American School Boards Association
P.O. Box 474
Austin, Texas 78767

Printed in the United States of America

ISBN 979-8-60-875414-2

Table of Contents

Foreword

MASBA President Willie Tenorio, Jr.

In the same way that we, as human persons, grow and change, the institutions we create also mature and morph over time—ideally transforming themselves into better systems for meeting the needs for which they were organized and/or for which they continue to exist. The same is true of the Mexican American School Board Members Association (MASBMA)—known today as the Mexican American School Boards Association (MASBA)—an organization of Mexican American/*Chicano*/Hispanic/*Latino*/*Latinx* school board members that emerged in Texas during the civil rights movement.

Dr. José A. Cárdenas, Superintendent of the Edgewood ISD in San Antonio, envisioned MASBMA in 1970—according to an account by Teresa Paloma Acosta. Three years later, Chris Escamilla of San Antonio, Rubén E. Hinojosa of Mercedes, and Gustavo L. García of Austin officially incorporated the organization. By 1990, MASBMA lay dormant.

During four years of inactivity, while memories of MASBMA still lingered, Mexican American trustees gathered with the dream of resurrecting the organization. We salute them: Juan Aguilera of Round Rock ISD, Albert Martínez and Tommy Molina of San Diego ISD, Diana Castañeda of Austin ISD, Theresa Gutiérrez of Victoria ISD, and Louis Q. Reyes, III of Seguin ISD. They united trustees around educational and social justice issues. They and their successors brought structure to the organization, nourished its growth, and enhanced its branding. Their efforts bore fruit in what we know today as the Mexican American School Boards Association.

As our self-identity as a people continued to evolve over the last five decades—from Mexican American and *Chicano*, to Hispanic and *Latino* and now *Latinx*—both MASBMA and MASBA provided opportunities for trustees and superintendents to gather to discuss the issues affecting the Mexican American/*Chicano*/Hispanic/*Latino*/*Latinx* students in our Texas public schools.

It is a great pleasure to serve as President of the Mexican American School Boards Association as we initiate the celebration of our golden jubilee! MASBA demonstrates a renewed focus on closing gaps in our Texas public schools—particularly for the *Latinx* students who comprise the majority in our Texas public schools, and for the English Language Learners who are expected to be 25% of our Texas public schools by 2025. MASBA has grown to serve over 100 Texas school districts and is, for the first time, expanding outside the state. Throughout the years, we have taken stands on a number of issues, most recently on the 2020 U.S. Census, the approval of curriculum for Mexican American Studies in Texas, the extension and expansion of Deferred Action for Childhood Arrivals (DACA), racial violence, and the celebration of holidays like Indigenous People's Day and César Chávez & Dolores Huerta Day. We have established a scholarship endowment, and our scholarship program will serve 220+ students in 2020. Indeed, there's much to celebrate at our golden jubilee conference this year!

I wish to share my sincere appreciation for all who founded MASBMA in the 1970s and guided it through its initial years of growth, for all who breathed new life into MASBA in the 1990s, and for all who continue to support our mission of empowering our Mexican American/*Chicano*/Hispanic/*Latino*/*Latinx* students and those who serve them. Our MASBA Board of Directors clearly recognizes that we stand on the shoulders of giants!

I invite you to enjoy this collection of 50 years of memories, and I challenge you to join our mission of closing gaps in our nation's public schools. As this work makes evident, the struggles are real, and they continue. Hence, the very appropriate title of this work.

As we go forward into the second 50 years of MASBA's history, may we find ourselves more closely united with one another in a common purpose to better serve all the students of our public schools. May we join forces to face the struggles still to come, and proclaim with those in whose footsteps we trod: *¡Viva la lucha!*

Acknowledgements

MASBA Executive Director Dr. Jayme Mathias

In Spanish, we say, "*la unión hace la fuerza*" — unity creates strength. This work is the fruit of many people coming together to share memories of their involvement in the Mexican American School Boards Association (MASBA) during these past 50 years.

When I assumed responsibility for the daily operation of MASBA in October 2017, MASBA possessed scant organizational records. Secretary Willie Tenorio, Jr. of the Hays CISD shared with me meeting minutes for 2017. MASBA had fortunately maintained the services of the same accounting firm since 2013, so we were able to reconstruct five years of membership and sponsorship based on financial records kept for us by Garza | González & Associates of San Antonio. President Armando Rodríguez of Canutillo ISD gave me all the emails he had received and sent during his leadership of the organization. MASBA Director of Operations & Development Sam Guzmán, formerly of the Austin ISD, pulled together hundreds of emails during his service to the organization. Secretary Tenorio succeeded in securing a draft list of all MASBA Presidents since 2000 from Former MASBA President and Executive Director Joe Muñoz, formerly of the Hays CISD. Together, those documents formed the foundation upon which we constructed this work.

An online history of MASBA by Teresa Paloma Acosta indicates that Dr. José "Joe" Cárdenas conceived of MASBA in 1970. We're running with that and celebrating MASBA's golden jubilee in 2020, all the while knowing that the Texas Secretary of State did not formally recognize MASBA until December 6, 1973, when Chris Escamilla of San Antonio, Rubén E. Hinojosa of Mercedes, and Gustavo L. García of Austin filed Articles of Incorporation for the Mexican American School Board Members Association.

I wish to thank all who participated in this project of reconstructing MASBA's 50-year history. We share our deepest gratitude with all who agreed to be interviewed for this history. MASBA Past Presidents Dr. Viola García of Aldine ISD, Óscar O. García, formerly of Ben Bolt-Palito Blanco ISD, Joe F. Muñoz, formerly of Hays CISD, and Brian Godínez of ERO Architects deserve special mention for all

4

the materials they shared, which allowed us to reconstruct in greater detail several years of MASBA's efforts, including MASBA's involvement in securing recognition of *mariachi* as a sanctioned competition of the University Interscholastic League in 2015.

We publish this work in time for our golden jubilee conference on February 20-23, 2020, knowing that it is far from complete. Please consider this compilation the first edition of various works to come. Please allow us to include your voice in the second, third and fourth editions that will lead up to our fiftieth-anniversary celebration in 2023 of MASBA's incorporation in 1973!

Are you willing to be interviewed about your memories of MASBA? Do you possess any MASBA meeting minutes, conference programs, photos, recordings, mementos, etc., that you might share? We would be delighted to include them—and to recognize you in a special way—in future editions!

At present, we have discovered very few MASBA records that predate 2000. We don't possess a single photo or set of meeting minutes from MASBA's first 30 years. If you know any trustee, superintendent, partner or sponsor who was involved with MASBA during the 1970s, 1980s and/or 1990s, we are especially interested in speaking with them!

Unity indeed creates strength, and future editions of this work will be stronger because you. We thank you in advance for your assistance in preserving the memory of the Mexican American School Boards Association!

Adelante marchemos unidos,

Dr. Jayme Mathias
MASBA Executive Director
P.O. Box 474
Austin, Texas 78767
(512) 826-0280
jayme@masbatx.org

A History of the Mexican American
School Board Members Association

Teresa Paloma Acosta

The Mexican American School Board Members Association was founded in 1970 by José A. Cárdenas, superintendent of the Edgewood Independent School District in San Antonio. Although Mexican Americans were a substantial part of the population, they were poorly represented on most public school boards in the state. In the early 1970s, for instance, only around 400 (or 4%) of 10,000 school board members in 1,400 school districts were Mexican Americans.

MASBMA incorporated on December 6, 1973, with financial support from the American Lutheran Church's National Education Task Force *De La Raza*, which, under the leadership of Clemente Sáenz, sought to promote educational opportunities for all public school children.

At that time, MASBMA was governed by a board of fourteen directors and was headquartered at St. Edward's University in Austin. Rubén Hinojosa of Mercedes ISD served as the organization's president and oversaw its operations. Chris Escamilla, an Edgewood ISD board member, became the organization's executive director. Membership was open to board members whose school districts had a sizable percentage of minority students.

On February 8-9, 1975, MASBMA and other Mexican-American organizations sponsored a conference on the education of Hispanics. MASBMA organized similar efforts to implement its goals. It acted as a consultant to the Priorities Committee of the State Board of Education and sought to implement the United States Civil Rights Commission's report "Toward Quality Education for Mexican Americans." In partnership with the Intercultural Development Research Association (IDRA) of San Antonio, MASBMA created and offered a program to train Mexican-American school board members in effective leadership. The program continued through 1987, with funding from IDRA, the Ford Foundation, the Carnegie Corporation of New York, the National Education Task Force *De La Raza*, and other groups.

Numerous MASBMA members became prominent Mexican Americans in Texas, including Austin Mayor Gustavo García, Social Security Administration official Alicia Chacón. State Representative Frank Madla, and José Ángel Gutiérrez, a founder of the *Raza Unida* Party.

By 1992, MASBMA had ceased to exist, apparently due to lack of funding.

Tejana poet, historian, author and activist Teresa Paloma Acosta published this online history of MASBMA in 2010. She is the co-author of the award-winning 2003 work, Las Tejanas: 300 Years of History, *which highlights the previously-uncelebrated contributions of Mexican American women to Texas history. In 1991, she organized the Mexican Americans in Texas History Conference, which resulted in the 2000 work,* Mexican Americans in Texas History.

Early MASBA Legal Documents

On December 4, 1973, Chris Escamilla of San Antonio, Rubén E. Hinojosa of Mercedes, and Gustavo L. García of Austin signed Articles of Incorporation for the Mexican American School Board Members Association. Two days later, the Texas Secretary of State recognized MASBMA as a non-profit organization. The Austin office of García, Morrison & Company served as the initial registered office of the organization.

On September 11, 1975, the Texas Comptroller of Public Accounts issued a letter to García, Morrison & Company, exempting the Mexican American School Board Members Association from franchise tax, effective December 6, 1973.

On September 11, 1986, Lydia M. Pérez of the Austin ISD Board of Trustees filed with the Texas Secretary of State a "Statement of Change of Registered Office or Registered Agent or Both," to name herself, in her capacity as MASBMA President, as the registered agent of the organization, and to transfer the organization's mailing address from the Austin office of García, Morrison & Company, to the principal office of the Austin Independent School District, at 6100 Guadalupe Street, Austin, Texas.

On October 26, 1987, Amancio J. Chapa, Jr. of the La Joya ISD Board of Trustees filed with the Texas Secretary of State a "Statement of Change of Registered Office or Registered Agent or Both," to name himself, in his capacity as MASBA President, as the registered agent of the organization, and to transfer the organization's mailing address from the offices of the Austin Independent School District, to P.O. Box 306, La Joya, Texas.

On October 11, 1993, the Texas Secretary of State issued a letter to the Mexican American School Board Members Association, stating that, because MASBA failed to file the paperwork required of the Secretary of State every four years, the organization's "right to conduct affairs has been forfeited for failure to file the report as of the date of this letter."

Recognition of Founding Members

U.S. Congressman Ciro D. Rodríguez shared the following words in the program of the 2000 MASBA conference.

Recognition of Founding Members
Mexican American School Boardmembers Association

Dr. José Cárdenas, San Antonio, Texas
José Ángel Gutiérrez, Attorney, Dallas, Texas
Rubén Hinojosa, U.S. Congressman, McAllen, Texas
Gus García, City Councilman, Austin, Texas
Chris Escamilla, Edgewood ISD, San Antonio, Texas
Amancio Chapa, President, La Joya ISD, La Joya, Texas
Ciro Rodríguez, U.S. Congressman, San Antonio, Texas

Since the call for equal access to quality education and school finance reform in the late 1960s and early 1970s, and during my tenure on the Harlandale Independent School District in San Antonio, Texas, I have advocated for public education. During this time, the need for active participation by Mexican Americans in the educational arena was recognized. This participation is still needed now. In 1973, along with other education advocates, we formed the Mexican American School Boardmembers Association.

It is because of this vision that we continue to press for an education agenda that recognizes the needs of the disadvantaged and under-served populations of our country. The work to ensure that the rights of Mexican Americans, Hispanics and other minority students are recognized must continue.

Adhering to this creed, I will continue to vote against voucher proposals or other programs that undermine public education. Recently, I voted against legislation seeking to require Limited English Proficient students to request permission to receive Title I services. The good fight for educational reform will continue. As a member of the U.S. House of Representatives, I will continue the good fight.

I thank the founding members of the Mexican American School Boardmembers Association because I learned from you. You have allowed the opportunity for myself and many others in the future to represent the interests of our children's educational potential.

—Ciro D. Rodríguez

"We Decided to Organize"

José Ángel Gutiérrez

Walkouts as Protests Against Racism

I was elected to the Crystal City ISD Board of Trustees in 1970, as a result of the phenomenon of walkouts. In 1967, I helped to found MAYO, the Mexican American Youth Organization. We had 3,000 MAYO members all over the state, so we were strong. Beginning in 1968, we organized walkouts at high schools, and, in some cities, we organized multiple walkouts. In Crystal City, we organized walkouts at the high school, middle school, and elementary school. In Kingsville, we organized walkouts at the high school and middle school. I did 31 walkouts in Texas myself.

Segregation and blatant racism were rampant—and not as politely covert as they are today. Whites would tell you to your face, "You're a Mexican!" We lived in segregated parts of the town. We were pushed out of schools at a higher rate. As young bucks, we said, "We're going to get rid of all this crap," and we decided to organize. We organized people who felt like we did. We were already in college, but we knew that high schoolers and dropouts and gang members felt the same way, so we organized them to do walkouts in their towns. By walking out, these students caused an economic hit for their schools, so administrators quickly came to their knees and asked us to settle.

Because our walkouts not only demanded school reform, but also *Chicano* Studies, Professor Leonard Valverde of California assisted us. We wanted *Chicano* teachers. We wanted to be able to speak Spanish. We wanted to eat Mexican food the way our parents made it—not the white rice with ketchup on top that they call "Spanish rice." In order to have *Chicano* Studies, you need professors, so they hired two or three professors from California and from the University of Texas at Austin to assist us. We were the activists, and the professors supported our efforts.

The Tragic Uvalde Walkout

A tragedy occurred in Uvalde: The kids decided to walk out without our support and protections. We told them, "Don't do this. We don't want you to lose. You're going to get busted, you're going to get suspended and expelled, you'll be sent off to Vietnam, and you'll be dead." They didn't listen, and they walked out anyway. If you go to the Uvalde Cemetery, you'll see the headstones of all the young men who did not survive Vietnam.

A Shift in the Crystal City School Board

Many of us later ran for our local school boards and changed the administrations of our districts. We recognized that the agreements to end our walkouts couldn't be "Indian treaties." Otherwise, those who hurt us and discriminated against us would still be there. We had to get rid of them.

Before 1970, the Crystal City ISD Board — like many other boards — had a singular *mexicano* who worked and voted with the Anglos. In our case, it was Eduardo "Eddie" Treviño.

We'd ask Eddie, "Do you know what you're supposed to do on the school board?"

"No."

"Have you ever gone to any trainings?"

"Los americanos son los que van [The Whites are the ones who go]."

"Why don't you ask for travel money, so you can go to the trainings?"

"No, no puedo [I can't]."

The 1970 election marked a shift for the Crystal City ISD Board of Trustees. We elected three *Chicanos*: Arturo Gonzales, Miguel Pérez and me. Together with Eddie, we, *Chicanos*, became the majority on the board, almost always resulting in a 4-3 vote.

Finding a *Chicano* Superintendent

When Arturo, Miguel and I ran for the school board, we went to see Eddie, and we asked him if he would join us if we won, and he said, "Of course!" We didn't involve him in the election. We kept him at bay. During the lull between our victory and our swearing-in, we talked with him, and he said, "I'm with you. I'll vote with you." I asked him, "Will you make the motion to nominate me as president?" And he said, "I will."

When we took over the school board, we had to find a superintendent. That's when I found out we had only five *Chicano* superintendents in the state of Texas. I said, "My goodness, we need more!" I certainly didn't want to have a *gringo* superintendent. That was one of the reasons for our walkouts!

Training *Chicano* Superintendents, Principals and Teachers

Viviana Santiago and I wrote a grant, and the Carnegie Corporation gave us $1.3 million, and we started a two-year program to train *Chicano* superintendents. We trained 30 superintendents every two years for the next four or five years. That's when we met Dr. José Cárdenas of the Edgewood ISD: He became one of our faculty members. Later, when I left the school board after one term and became county judge for Zapata County, I passed that program on to Tomás Arciniega. He headed the Department of Education at San Diego State University, where we received the credentials for our principals and superintendents.

The National Education Task Force *De La Raza* is sometimes mentioned in connection with MASBA's history. They sponsored two training for us here in Texas. Dr. Cárdenas hosted one in San Antonio in December 1970, and we hosted one in Crystal City in January 1971. Dr. Atilano Valencia of the University of Colorado and ten consultants, including Dr. Cárdenas, made recommendations, including an increase in the number of Mexican American teachers in our district. I'm not sure what else the National Education Task Force *De La Raza* did for MASBA. Dr. Cárdenas later became the director of their southwest regional office, so MASBA may have received funding from them.

I would say the same of the Ford Foundation. They stepped up and funded MAYO and enabled us to create the Mexican American Unity Council, which is still going in San Antonio today, but I'm not sure what they did for MASBA.

Challenges with School Finance

As soon as we started taking over school boards in Crystal City and other places, we realized the fundamental structural problem of school finance in Texas. Dr. Cárdenas and I started talking about this, and he started addressing it with our superintendents-to-be. We knew we had to look at school finance and the way some schools received more money than others. In some districts, administrators would call some schools "academies," simply to justify funneling more money to those schools.

During the Demetrio Rodríguez case, we did a huge march in Austin, and we literally took over the Capitol on the issue of school finance. Cárdenas decided to contact the Carnegie Foundation about funding him to tackle school finance issues. We supported him as our faculty member, funded by the Carnegie Corporation. That's how IDRA, the Intercultural Development Research Association, came to be! Dr. Aurelio "Hershey" Montemayor, from our walkout in Del Río, is still involved in IDRA.

The *Raza Unida* Party

We also started the *Raza Unida* Party at that time. It all tied back to our early activism: We didn't stop with the takeover of school boards; we wanted to take over cities and counties—and the state! And you have to have a partisan political party to run in county and state elections. We said, "We need our own political party! We can't be Democrats or Republicans. *Pues, está bien* [That's alright]: We'll create our own party!"

If you see an old MAYO button, you'll notice it says, *La raza unida* [the united human race]. Mexico's Former Secretary of Education, José Vasconcelos, inspired us with his idea of *la raza cósmica*, a view of humanity that transcended race and nationality. Ignacio Pérez of San Antonio, one of the co-founders of MAYO, came up with *la raza unida*. He said, "We should call ourselves *la raza unida!*" The phrase inspires hope and vision. So *la raza unida* became the slogan on our MAYO buttons. *Somos la raza unida* [We are the unified human race]. Then we made it a political party.

Even during our days with MAYO, we already had that idea of the *raza unida;* we just needed the time to implement that vision as organizers. You can't start talking to people about Plan K or L or M. You have to start with Plan A and move them to B to C to D. The *Raza Unida* Party was no different: At the beginning, we talked about walkouts and the protections of those who participated and were expelled from school. Only later did we start thinking about *la raza unida*.

The Creation of NALEO

Our creation of NALEO resembled our creation of the *Raza Unida* Party. We said, "Why do we have to create all these separate organizations for *Chicano* elected officials — separate organizations for city council members and for county commissioners, and MASBA for school board members?" That's where the idea for the National Association of *Latino* Elected & Appointed Officials came in: All elected and appointed officials have a lot of policy power, and they make budget and personnel allocations. We included appointed officials in NALEO as an acknowledgement of Secretary of State Roy Barrera of San Antonio, the sole *mexicano* appointed to a statewide position at that time.

A Meeting to Organize *Chicano* School Board Members

Quite a few of us got together. At one gathering in the early 1970s, we talked about how we needed to create organizations to do advocacy for our concerns and our interests. I helped pull that meeting together. We divided ourselves into two groups: The school board members and those with school districts met in one corner of the room, and the university faculty met in another corner of the room. Out of that latter group came TACHE — the Texas Association of *Chicanos* in Higher Education.

As a school board member and an academic, I had to choose which group I'd be part of that day. I joined the group of school board members, and that's when we decided to organize the Mexican American School Board Members Association. Those of us in that room were the founders of MASBA. We took part in that initial discussion that led to MASBA's organization. Dr. José Cárdenas, the superintendent of the Edgewood ISD — and one of only five *Chicano* superintendents in the state of Texas — participated in our group. I also remember Dr. Leonard Valverde taking part in our conversation; he was later elected the first president of TACHE in 1975.

There's a reason that Cárdenas got the credit for starting MASBA: As a superintendent, he received a salary and travel money, and we didn't. So, he could travel to any meeting at any time and in any place. For that reason, some people believed him to be the founder of MASBA.

Not the *Chicano* School Board Members Association

We called ourselves *Chicanos* back then. The "Mexican American" part of MASBA's name came later. Someone likely said, "We need to 'soft-pedal' this and not be so blatant in our militancy." I don't recall if we had a discussion on calling ourselves *Chicanos* or Mexican Americans — but we probably did, because why else would it have been named the Mexican American School Board Members Association? We probably followed the lead of MAYO and MALDEF in using "Mexican American" in our name, too.

Early MASBMA Members Who Became Prominent Leaders

Gustavo García of the Austin ISD Board of Trustees would later be part of our MASBA efforts, after his election in 1972. He went on to be part of the Austin City Council under a "gentleman's agreement" that allowed one Black and one Mexican to serve on the council.

U.S. Congressman Rubén Hinojosa of the Mercedes ISD Board served as an initial incorporator of MASBA. We hired Ángel Noé González as our superintendent in the Crystal City ISD. I'm guessing that he brought Hinojosa into our efforts.

U.S. Congressman Ciro Rodríguez participated in our Harlandale walkout and became the first member of the *Raza Unida* Party that we elected to the Legislature, then to Congress.

State Representative Frank Madla, part of the Southside political machine for *La Raza* in San Antonio, is also associated with MASBA's early history.

Chris Escamilla, a former MAYO member, served on the school board in Edgewood, one of four walkout sites in San Antonio. After that walkout, we took over the Edgewood school board and ousted Superintendent Bennie Steinhauser.

Alicia Chacón, the first *Latina* elected to the Ysleta ISD Board of Trustees in 1970, is recognized as an early leader of MASBA. We had a walkout at Ysleta High School, where they suspended several students. As a school board member, Alicia asked for hearings on the reasons these kids walked out and were suspended and expelled. She later became the El Paso county judge.

After I left our school board in 1973, I didn't keep up with MASBA, except through Roberto Alonzo. He participated in a walkout at 14 years old and wanted to become a politician. We put him on our

Crystal City Board as an *ex officio* student representative. He became a state representative and served for over 25 years, and MASBA would invite him to speak all the time. Roberto contributed mightily to MASBA. He went to MASBA meetings, while I went on to other endeavors.

50 Years of Struggles — and Far From Finished

For those of us who started organizing in 1966 and 1967, it's been more than 50 years of struggles and advocacy — and we still have a long way to go. School finance is still an issue, as are the rates at which our students are pushed out of schools. We still need more Hispanic superintendents and principals and teachers. Our college enrollment and graduation rates are terrible. We aren't promoting ethnic studies, like we should. We're still underrepresented across the board — because of gerrymandering and money.

This is an important time of 50-year celebrations. The walkouts started on December 9, 1969, so we just celebrated that 50th anniversary. On January 10, the *Raza Unida* Party celebrated 50 years. This is also the 50th anniversary of the L.A. moratorium anti-war protests — all these celebrations now because we did those things 50 years ago. MASBA arose in the middle of all those struggles, as a result of our decision to organize.

Dr. José Ángel Gutiérrez serves as professor emeritus at The University of Texas at Arlington. After organizing walkouts for the Mexican American Youth Organization (MAYO), he served as President of the Crystal City ISD Board of Trustees from 1970 to 1973, and later as Zapata County Judge. Dr. Gutiérrez played a role in the founding of such organizations as the Mexican American Legal Defense & Educational Fund (MALDEF), the Intercultural Research Development Association (IDRA), the Raza Unida Party, and the National Association for Latino Elected & Appointed Officials (NALEO).

"MASBA Gave Us a Voice"

Amancio J. Chapa, Jr.

Elected in 1971, at the age of 23, I served a total of 22 years on the La Joya ISD Board of Trustees—in three different segments. I served for three terms—nine years—then the mayor of La Joya asked if I would run for mayor. So I resigned from the school board, ran for mayor, and served as mayor of La Joya for one term—a rather boring task in a small city. As soon as my term as mayor ended, I ran for the school board again, got elected, and served another nine years. I later came back to the board and did another four years, stepping down in 2000—before finishing my second three-year term that time—because the district hired my son's fiancée, and I didn't want there to be any appearance of nepotism. Shortly after that, the district asked me to establish a history and cultural research center. I then served as the district's fine arts director for 10 years, beginning in 2002.

Mexican Americans founded La Joya back in the 1920s, and our community had always been 90% Mexican American. We always had Mexican Americans on our school board, but they weren't so outspoken. Before the 1960s, many of our political leaders allied with the very conservative, Anglo Democrats who controlled the county government. In 1965, Leo J. Leo, a very liberal Democrat active in the Political Association of Spanish Speaking Organizations (PASSO), which got the first Mexican Americans elected to the city council in Crystal City, became mayor of La Joya. While I studied at UT, Leo challenged the more conservative *mexicanos* in our community and took control of the school board. Likewise, I remember Dr. Ramiro Casso, a politically-active physician in McAllen, who also belonged to PASSO. Middle-aged *mexicanos* who represented a very liberal wing of the Democratic party and were starting to make some noise within the party, Leo and Casso were the precursors of the *Chicano* movement in La Joya.

In 1965, after I graduated from La Joya High School, PASSO chose me to attend a two-week student leadership conference at St. Edward's University in Austin. The AFL-CIO sponsored the event, and PASSO, the NAACP, and other liberal, Democrat-affiliated organizations supported its political indoctrination, making us conscious of the issues affecting Mexican Americans outside of La Joya. I realized that, having Mexican American teachers, administrators and school board members in La Joya, we didn't suffer discrimination in the same way as others throughout the state.

I participated in the *Chicano* movement at UT, becoming one of the founders of the Mexican American Student Organization (MASO). We got involved with campus politics and spoke out on issues affecting the small number of Mexican American students at UT, as well as what we perceived to be the lack of recognition and attention that the university paid to Mexican American student issues. Before I left UT, we switched the name of MASO to MAYO, the Mexican American Youth Organization.

During those years, I also got involved in Austin politics. In 1972, one year after I returned to La Joya, Gus García became the first-ever Mexican American on the Austin ISD school board. We took a lot of pride in *mexicanos* getting elected, especially in places with smaller Mexican American populations north of the Valley.

At UT, we committed ourselves to come home to our communities and make a difference there. When I got back to La Joya, Mr. Leo contacted me and told me of an upcoming vacancy on the school board. He encouraged me to run for the school board, and, in 1971, I became the second college graduate to serve on the La Joya ISD Board.

Anglos controlled most school boards in the Valley, and they employed Anglo superintendents. When I started going to conventions of the Texas Association of School Boards (TASB), those gatherings seemed lily-White. Over time, larger numbers of Mexican Americans began attending. In the early 1970s, we had the idea of coming together as an organization and achieving recognition from TASB. We chose the name MASBA for ourselves: the Mexican American School Board Members Association. Many of our members came from South Texas or were the sole Hispanic school board members in their districts throughout the state.

I became more involved with MASBA in the mid-1980s, after my stint as mayor. Lydia Pérez, an active and outspoken leader in the desegregation of the Austin ISD, served as MASBA's Chair at the time.

Ann Enríquez served on our MASBA Board from San Elizario ISD, a small district represented by very active and vocal board members in our association and in TASB.

I can't remember the names of others, including a gentleman from a neighboring district to San Elizario, who became a superintendent in the Valley. I recall an outspoken, female police officer, the sole Mexican American school board member in the Lubbock ISD. We also had members from San Antonio school districts, from Edgewood ISD, and smaller Mexican American communities.

When people joined MASBA, we tried to provide as much counseling and support to them as we could. We shared ideas with them on how to deal with the disrespect and treatment they received. We also started coordinating our own state events, bringing in relevant speakers and dealing with subjects that TASB overlooked regarding the education of Mexican American students. One of our main purposes remained interacting with TASB and trying to get them to take notice of the increasing number of Mexican American school board members here in Texas. We also pushed for more relevant speakers and more interesting issues, like bilingual education and the high dropout and pushout rates among Hispanic students.

We came to TASB's attention under the leadership of Orbry Holden, an Anglo TASB Executive Director who identified several Mexican American school board members throughout the state for a special training project. We called ourselves Hispanic Leadership Development, or something like that, and we met on a regular basis in Austin and in different places around the state. He wanted to groom some of us for getting elected to TASB Board positions. White faces filled the TASB Board, with few Mexican Americans, like Tony Gonzales from the Pharr-San Juan-Alamo ISD, serving. We felt that Mexican American school board members didn't have that much visibility within the state association, and Orbry hosted some frank discussions on how we could promote ourselves and mount a campaign to be elected to the TASB Board. He also provided us training to be more effective school board members at the local level. After a few years, some Anglo directors on the TASB Board pressured him to stop the program cold. They complained that he singled out Mexican Americans for preferential treatment with this special program that they hadn't approved. Orbry apologized to us when that program came to an end.

I decided to run for the TASB Board. I enjoyed the support of the majority of school board members in the Valley. I possessed all the right credentials as President of MASBA, as President of the Valley School Boards Association, and as a participant in TASB's school board leadership program for two years. However, I spoke very directly to the TASB Board's almost-entirely-Anglo Nominations Committee about issues pertaining to the Mexican American community. I apparently came across as too strong, and a more middle-of-the-road, Mexican-American attorney from the Harlingen CISD got that position.

Mexican Americans were underrepresented on school boards and also as superintendents. With rare exceptions, all our superintendents in South Texas were Anglos and ex-football coaches from East Texas. They didn't have a real feel for the Mexican American community, and they didn't push for progressive programs. For example, I wanted to make sure La Joya applied for federal monies for the bilingual education of the children of migrant farmworkers and for teaching Mexican American history and other culturally-relevant subjects—and the superintendent at the time didn't understand the need for this. I made sure we didn't renew his contract, and we hired a progressive, Mexican-American superintendent. I wanted to see more progressive teachers and administrators in the district. I even recruited candidates from surrounding school districts whom I met at meetings of the *Raza Unida* Party—people who could impact our community and its politics.

At a conference in Austin, I succeeded Lydia Pérez as MASBA Chair. I had been serving as the Vice Chair, I had enough support to run for Chair, and I got elected. We didn't have a lot of controversies back then, no bitter battles among members, but we had active, vocal people who came into leadership positions.

We'd run into other Mexican American school board members at TASB conventions, but then we decided to host our own annual conferences. Lydia put together a great conference in Austin. It dealt with some very serious topics, like bilingual education, political issues, and the dropout and pushout rates—one of MASBA's chief concerns at that time.

One year, we held our conference in Odessa. The only Hispanic trustee on their board attended. Out in West Texas, things were "behind the times," and she wanted us to take our MASBA conference to Odessa, to show folks that there are Mexican Americans serving on school boards throughout the state. I don't remember if she became a Chair of MASBA. I believe we held that conference on Father's Day weekend. She brought in Mexican American assistant principals and teachers, and they talked with us about how they "walked on eggshells" in their district, and how they had to be really careful. They said, "We don't even want them to find out that we're here talking to you all!"

We also tried to get the attention of the National School Boards Association (NSBA), and we pushed for opportunities at national meetings to interact with other Hispanic board members from different parts of the country. African American school board members had a national caucus, but Hispanic school board members didn't. We finally coalesced and formed the NSBA Hispanic School Board Member Caucus, which I chaired. We had wanted to call it The "National" Caucus of Hispanic School Board Members, but the NSBA would not accept that title.

When I reflect on all those experiences, I realize that MASBA gave us a voice and allowed us to take stands on educational issues affecting Mexican American students here in Texas. MASBA also gave us leadership opportunities that empowered us to emphasize the growing number of Mexican American students in our schools — and the lack of attention and programming they received.

Amancio J. Chapa, Jr. served on the La Joya ISD Board of Trustees for a total of 22 years, beginning in 1971 and concluding in 2000. While serving as President of MASBA, he became the first Chair of the National School Boards Association Hispanic School Board Member Caucus.

"I Had Just Taken Over a Dying Organization"

Jimmie Adame

My friend, Mike García, an activist here in Taft, Texas, concerned himself with things that affected the Hispanic population in our small community. He and I filed a lawsuit against the City of Taft, to create single-member districts. That's where our association and friendship developed.

Mike served on the school board and saw the disparities between our Hispanic and Anglo children in Taft. We grew up in South Texas, where White kids and Hispanic kids went to separate schools, and this segregation continued into the 1980s. One night, while we sat on my patio, Mike encouraged me to run for the school board. I had two small girls, so, as a parent, I cared about their education. That's how my involvement on the school board began. Mike died of leukemia shortly after I got on the board, so we only served for three or four meetings together.

Back then, TASB always held its conferences in San Antonio. We went to those conferences as greenhorn board members from a little Podunk town. I looked around the conference and saw *puros gringos*—all Whites. Very few *mexicanos* served as school board members in Texas. So there we were: an infant group of Hispanic board members in a sea of White experience. How eye-opening, to say the least!

I attended my first MASBA meeting at that conference, at the Henry B. González Convention Center. MASBA President Óscar Hernández of the San Antonio ISD came up to me and two other trustees from my district and said to us: "We're going to have a meeting *con todos los latinos* in such-and-such a room!" Óscar grabbed as many *latinos* as he could for that meeting, and we decided to go.

We conducted business in a small, noisy room next to the kitchen, as waiters bustled around, going back and forth with plates. I've often thought back on that contrast: how TASB catered to the Black Caucus and stuck our humble race beside the kitchen! We accepted what they gave us, without demanding more.

Óscar chaired that meeting. Immediate Past President Amancio Chapa from La Joya ISD sat at the front table, with a colorful necktie. Dr. Luis Gutiérrez wore two "hats," as a board member from one district and a superintendent in another. I can still picture him: He wore round glasses and always looked professional. Those guys led that meeting of some 25 to 30 people. They were part of MASBA since the early- to mid-1980s, and they had no executive director. Board members simply got together and did the business of the organization, as best they could.

MASBA obviously lacked strength and organization. We discussed some of the education issues affecting our kids in a forum that more closely resembled a conversation than a structured meeting. Then they took nominations from the floor for President, and nobody wanted to serve in that capacity. I sat there with two of my fellow board members, and one of them, Art Acosta, said, "I nominate Jimmie for President!" I thought: "I just walked into this meeting, and I don't even know anything about this group!" They said, "It's O.K. We'll help you!" So, in an unorganized gathering, in a noisy room, amid the clanking of dishes, they elected me by a show of hands, without me knowing anybody in the room! At the end of the meeting, everyone scurried out of the room, with no ceremonial sharing of a gavel or anything to sign.

To say that MASBA sputtered after that would be generous. I had just taken over a dying organization that would soon go dormant. In fact, nothing happened after that meeting for three or four years.

Santiago "Jimmie" Adame serves on the Taft ISD Board of Trustees. He was elected MASBA President in 1989, then again in 2001. He participated on the MASBA Board through 2005 and was named MASBA's Executive Director in January 2007.

The Presidency of Those Who Led MASBA
in the 1970s & 1980s

Apart from the aforementioned records filed with or received from the government, MASBA possesses no photos or written records from the 1970s or 1980s.

If you would like to share any photos, meeting minutes, conference programs, mementos, etc. from that time period, for inclusion in Volume II, please email them to info@masbatx.org or mail them to MASBA | P.O. Box 474 | Austin, TX 78767.

Thank you for helping us to reconstruct our history!

"School Finance Stole the Attention from Hispanic Issues"

Kevin O'Hanlon

I became involved with MASBA in the early 1980s. Back then, many active MASBA members also participated in the Equity Center, focusing on the funding inequity between minority and White schools. The Edgewood cases centered around this disparity. The Equity Center and MALDEF represented two sets of plaintiffs in the original Edgewood case: MALDEF represented Edgewood ISD and about five other districts, while the Equity Center represented about 100 districts.

The Edgewood ISD belonged to MASBA, and Superintendent Jimmy Vásquez became involved after his predecessor, Joe Cárdenas, one of the original founder of MASBA, who only went by "José" on paper. Joe served as superintendent of the Edgewood ISD during the 1973 U.S. Supreme Court case of San Antonio Independent School District v. Rodríguez, brought by Edgewood parents. It settled the right to participate in education, but it didn't solve the problem of unequal school finance; it simply said that the parents had the standing to pursue it. That case went back to the trial courts for a decade. The legislature did a few things on school finance, but, by 1983, the state hadn't done enough—resulting in the Texas Supreme Court case, Edgewood v. Kirby.

The Edgewood lawsuits framed the conversation on the purpose and limitations of Texas' public schools. Beginning in 1983, I served as Assistant Attorney General for the State of Texas during the first three Edgewood cases. I filed the original response and remained involved from the first Supreme Court case, through the fourth case. In the end, I essentially wrote the five options that ended up being a part of Senate Bill 7—"Robin Hood"—in 1993.

Parents filed the first Edgewood case and sued for the right to play a role in their children's education. The ruling assured that they did. Other decisions in the 1980s clarified whether a child could be educated if not a U.S. citizen, but it did not solve the problem of inequitable funding. Texas school finance is based on property taxes, which results in rich districts always being more generously funded than poor ones. Although we cooperated with the plaintiffs, it took four years for Edgewood v. Kirby to go to trial.

By the time of Edgewood IV, I served as General Counsel for the Texas Education Agency (TEA), and helped draft the legislation then under scrutiny.

After Edgewood I and II, we realized the structural problem: school district boundaries encompass varying degrees of wealth. Some of it is intentional, and some is accidental—like whether you have oil or gas in your district. If you have oil or gas, you're wealthy, and, prior to Robin Hood, the state did a lot to level it. Regardless, inequity persisted because super-rich districts could do a lot more for a lower tax rate. The Supreme Court insisted that we find a structural solution to the unequal distribution of education funding throughout the state. After Edgewood I and II, we tried to "buy" our way out of the problem: We significantly increased the amount of state funding for the low-wealth districts, but we didn't do anything about the high-wealth districts on the theory that you had to equalize up to the sufficient tax required for public education, but not beyond. We tried that twice. Both attempts possessed substantial increases on a percentage basis, and the Supreme Court deemed them insufficient.

Following that, we created a system of County Education Districts (CEDs), which significantly reduced the disparities and left the districts with some tax base above the county rate. Prior to that, the school district tax rate was $1.50 for every $100 of property value. With CEDs, the state redistributed the first dollar among all the districts in any given county, then districts could keep any taxes they levied above that, without being subject to "recapture." It created absolute equity for the first dollar and probably would have worked in terms of equity, but the Supreme Court ruled that we needed a prior local authorization election to do that. Then "Robin Hood"—Senate Bill 7—came around, and we created the mechanism for the authorization.

We tried it two different ways. For the first attempt, County Education Districts (CEDs), the state took the authorization for part of the tax levy from school districts, without local consent. Those were knocked down in Edgewood III, so we came back and created Senate Bill 7, the cafeteria-style "recapture" system that has been in law since 1993. In May 1993, I helped create the mechanism to "recapture" funds, which the press dubbed "Robin Hood" and framed as a negative, unfair action.

The history of judicial elections in this state is important for the outcome of cases: The decisions in the Edgewood cases, for instance, reflected the composition of the Supreme Court, which, from the first filing to the final ruling in 1993, significantly changed from liberal to conservative.

As a result of the litigation, school districts got a lot more aggressive in terms of advocacy: TASA, TASB, MASBA and the Equity Center got involved in specific advocacy issues. Moreover, school finance equity stole the attention from Hispanic issues, culminating with Plyler v. Doe (1982), which deprived kids of education because of their citizenship. Cases were filed over testing, and a bilingual case resulted in a settlement in the late 1980s. School finance became so all-consuming that it took the wind from other issues, diminishing their visibility.

In 1994, I entered private practice, and, by 2000, representatives of MASBA began inviting me to speak at their conferences. I represented various MASBA member districts, and school board members who served on the MASBA Board came to me for legal advice. I later began to share of my time as Legal Counsel for MASBA.

As strange as it may seem, in light of my career trajectory with the state, I'm an advocate of local control and small government. I believe that school districts should have a more direct and active role with respect to the provision of public education. I support that goal and believe in its importance. The state has a role as a regulator, but not as an operator, of public schools. That is why I am involved in fighting the Texas Education Agency over school takeovers. I worked at the TEA; I know they don't know how to run schools. Running schools is a local responsibility. So, I support the autonomy and independence of local school districts.

MASBA recently showed significant support for the Houston ISD Board of Trustees, in light of the TEA's threat of the takeover of their district. We presented MASBA's resolution on the matter to the federal court, and the judge noted MASBA's support for the district. Long-term, we have a problem that school districts need to fortify the barricades: There's no question that the state's accountability system disproportionately identifies school districts and campuses that serve low-income and Limited English Proficient kids, labeling them as underperforming and setting up their schools for transfer to private enterprises that have no freaking idea what to do with them. It is a destructive perspective that needs to become enlightened.

School district leaders must provide their understanding about what these young people need from educators and the public — essentially more resources. It's about more seat time — and seat time costs dollars. We make a mistake by talking always about money. Our current system takes schools on the front lines of improving the educational opportunities for kids and calls them "failures." Because that's a bad idea, I defend the autonomy of local school districts that are closer to the students and know what they need.

One of my favorite MASBA memories is when MASBA went to war against a racist textbook in June 2016 — and blew it up! The State Board of Education formulated TEKS (Texas Essential Knowledge & Skills) for a Mexican American Studies program. They then put out a call for textbooks, and a rightwing former State Board member published a horrible and stereotypical book, *Mexican American Heritage*, which became the only book headed for approval. MASBA led the charge, and we defeated it.

Going forward, I hope MASBA continues to focus on getting better at educating low-income, Limited English Proficiency students in Texas. That's important for the future economic development of our state — and for their security. We should also advocate for mandatory English/Spanish dual language programs for all students. I've been advocating for this for 30 years. Based on Republican principles, if we think about where the future economic growth of the state will be, it will deal with Mexico and countries south of the U.S., which is a huge economic market. If everyone in Texas spoke Spanish, people south of the *Río Grande* would be comfortable doing business in Texas. That would be a huge, long-term economic development project. So, I am a big supporter of dual language programs and am happy to see MASBA involve itself in such issues.

Kevin O'Hanlon serves as Legal Counsel for MASBA. He acted as Assistant Attorney General for the State of Texas during the first three Edgewood cases, then as General Counsel for the Texas Education Agency for the fourth Edgewood case. His firm, O'Hanlon Demerath & Castillo, has been a gold and diamond sponsor of MASBA for years.

The Early Years of MASBA's Resurgence

Juan Aguilera

I recall the first time I attended a conference of the Texas Association of School Boards (TASB) after being elected to the Round Rock ISD Board of Trustees in 1992. I don't remember seeing any Hispanics at the conference, and I thought, "These people are setting the policy for our Hispanic kids!"

I knew many Hispanic and *Latino* professional associations, like the Hispanic Bar Association and the Hispanic Masters of Business Administration. Naturally, I wondered if there existed a Hispanic, *Latino* or *Chicano* organization of school board members. After that 1992 TASB conference, I began asking around. When I called TASB, they made it clear that they were happy to help in any way, but that they had their own organization. They suggested that I contact Lydia Pérez, a former school board member in the Austin ISD.

In 1993, I thought it might be a good idea to gather together Mexican American school board members. I worked with a New York banking firm, Morgan Stanley, and I suggested that we host a reception for Mexican American school board members to honor State Treasurer Martha Whitehead, who oversaw millions of dollars of investments. The firm essentially said, "Just send me a bill!" The firm's New York office printed and mailed all the invitations for that event. We hosted that reception at a really nice venue: Union Station Dallas. I called the Mexican American school board members I knew, including Dr. Manuel Flores of Corpus Christi ISD. I spoke with ten folks and included their names as co-hosts on the reception invitation. The event drew a significant group, and attendees suggested that we attempt to organize.

The following year, I got my firm to sponsor another reception, and the conversation continued. By that time, we had discovered that a Mexican American School Board Members Association (MASBMA) existed in the 1970s and 1980s. I couldn't find anyone working for the organization, but I remember Jimmie Adame later telling me that he served as President of MASBA in the last 1980s, when it died— probably because no one brought trustees together anymore. So, those of us who attended that 1993 reception decided we would get the organization going again!

We called a meeting in a room we reserved at TASB. We decided we would call ourselves the Mexican American School Board Members Association, to continue the legacy of the organization founded in 1970.

Diana Castañeda of the Austin ISD actively organized people and brought people together in Austin, and she became our first President, until she lost her local election in May 1996. Lupe Zamarripa of Linebarger gave her $5,000 for our efforts—a lot of money back then! Theresa Gutiérrez of Victoria ISD worked closely with her and became President after her.

Around 1996, by default, I became the first Executive Director of the resurgent MASBA. I no longer served on the Round Rock ISD board, so I couldn't serve as a MASBA officer—but I passionately wanted MASBA to succeed. MASBA never paid me, and I wouldn't even let MASBA pay for my hotel rooms. Instead, I financed many things for MASBA—and it took me years to get reimbursed for some expenses.

I printed MASBA invitations on hot pink cardstock, and we distributed them at TASB events. I've always joked, "If you want to get Mexicans together, provide free beer and *nachos*, and they'll come." And they came!

By 1998, our MASBA President, Albert Martínez, asked me, "Why don't we have an annual conference?"

I told him, "Albert, you're crazy! We don't have that many interested people!"

He replied, "No, I really want to do this!"

We took Alberto's lead and organized the first MASBA conference since the 1970s. I understood from my reading of MASBA's history that they held an annual conference in 1975. Fourteen years later, we scheduled the first annual conference of the resurgent MASBA.

No more than 40 people attended that event at The University of Texas at San Antonio (UTSA). To generate name recognition for and interest in it, we co-hosted it with the UTSA Metropolitan Research & Policy Institute. UTSA supported our efforts, renting us their classroom facilities for a minimal price of some $150. Former U.S. Secretary of Housing & Urban Development Henry Cisneros addressed attendees. Other speakers included UTSA President Dr.

Ricardo Romo and Dr. Anthony Trujillo, the Superintendent of the Ysleta ISD.

MASBA has hosted an annual conference every year since that first one in 1999. In those early years, U.S. Congressman Ciro Rodríguez, State Representative Dora Olivo of Houston, and the Castro twins — Julián and Joaquín — visited us.

I knew that TASB had student performances at their conferences, so we hosted student performances at our conferences, too! UTSA had a beautiful auditorium, and we began to showcase our kids. In the *Río Grande* Valley, Roma ISD had a great *mariachi*; their board committed to providing a *mariachi* instructor, where students could earn credit — making *mariachi* more than an extracurricular activity. In fact, those kids received varsity letters for *mariachi*: What a motivation for kids! I've always strongly supported *mariachi* as a way of keeping kids in school, and I always enjoyed seeing the pride of their parents. Our trustees were impressed, too. They would come to the student performances at our conference and say, "This is amazing! This is great!"

We even got famed vocalist Vikki Carr to come to one of our conferences! For four years, I tried getting her, but her secretary kept telling me that Vikki had scheduling conflicts. In the end, they probably said, "This guy won't stop calling!" So, Vikki came. She sat in the audience and politely clapped, and we introduced her as our special guest. Then she created a special memory: She got up on stage and sang with the Roma High School *mariachi*! Those of us there will remember that for the rest of our lives.

One year, when Gus García spoke at our conference, we brought in the *mariachi* of The University of Texas at Austin, in their burnt orange *mariachi* outfits. Texas A&M brought a group of kids, too. They wore jeans, and one of our sponsors donated the money for them to buy *mariachi* outfits. All of that happened because of MASBA!

In those early years, our tight budget never allowed us to spend more than $2,000 on a conference. We didn't have the money. MASBA lacked funds, and we struggled to pull things together on a shoestring budget. We struggled to find sponsors. A young organization, people didn't yet see MASBA as a true force.

I remember some of the challenges of that first conference. My employer expected me to work — while I planned a conference! We organized students to present a talent show. A jazz ensemble from

Aldine ISD called to ask if I could find a grand piano for their performance. Sure! Our President, Albert Martínez, also called me, asking if I could buy him a can of starch. I remember telling him, "Albert, I'm your Executive Director. I'm not here to do your laundry!" Fortunately, we can laugh about it now. Despite those things happening behind the scenes, that first conference came off well, and many people expressed satisfaction with a great conference.

After the reorganization of MASBA, I planned the first five annual conferences myself. Mónica, my secretary at the law firm, helped. Her neighbor donated a box of Fritos®, and she picked up the *pan dulce* for our receptions and breaks. My wife helped, and our daughter, Mari Carmen, too. Our son, Humberto, a high schooler, served as the master of ceremonies for our third conference.

We got some criticism, but I took it in stride and saw it as a positive: that so many people wanted MASBA to succeed! At the debrief of our first conference, for instance, one lady from Crystal City or Uvalde complained that we didn't have someone to put away the Fritos®. I dealt with all sorts of details—while she worried about the Fritos®!

I have the program here from our 2001 conference. That year, San Antonio City Council Member Ed Garza joined us, before being elected mayor of San Antonio later that year. UTSA President Ricardo Romo and Vice Provost Jesse Zapata spoke. Lubbock ISD and Southwest ISD presented sessions on successful practices. We provided an "open mic" session for attendees to share what worked in their districts. We had higher education partners, including UTSA and junior colleges, telling us what we needed to do to prepare our students for college. Bilingual education was a big topic, and public education funding continued to be an issue. We also discussed discouraging retention and drop-out rates. I remember State Demographer Steve Murdock saying that even the most racist person had to recognize that the Mexican American population was growing, so we needed to ensure that they become contributing members of our society.

In those early days, we had an organizational meeting at IDRA. They received a grant to do community training and helped us formulate our mission and vision.

In those early years of MASBA's resurgence, 30 districts joined MASBA. Most of them came from me picking up the phone and calling people I knew. Our MASBA Directors made calls as well.

Then, we came up with the idea of MASBA membership for individuals, because some districts in Texas didn't want anything to do with MASBA. "We're Americans and Texans," they said. "There's no need to separate ourselves with words like 'Mexican American'!" In Corpus Christi, Dr. Manuel Flores served on our MASBA Board, but his local board wouldn't become a MASBA member, so the concept of individual MASBA membership started for those trustees who wanted to be part of MASBA, even though their boards voted it down. My law firm, Escamilla & Poneck, even paid for those who couldn't pay their MASBA dues.

From the start, we had a policy that we would not use school district funds to buy the alcohol at our MASBA receptions. We always had sponsors who covered those costs, and I was adamant about not using school district funds for that. We had some generous sponsors, like Linebarger. I remember one reception when we ran out of chips and salsa, and we needed to order more on the spot. I asked Paul Chapa of Linebarger if he could help us out, and he agreed.

Our MASBA dues haven't increased since 1996, when we told even the smallest districts that all seven school board members could be part of MASBA for only $500. We've always included free conference badges for all school board members of MASBA districts.

Back in 1999, I first looked into the idea of giving board members continuing education credits. I knew from my board service in the Round Rock ISD that school board members could get credits for the workshops and training sessions we attended, so I called the Texas Education Agency, filled out the application, and we gave education credits as an additional membership benefit! Now we could tell districts that we advocated for them and their students — but also that they could attend our conferences for free and receive the continuing education credits that they needed as trustees.

Fortunately, my law firm wanted MASBA to succeed, too. They provided an office space for Richard Garza, MASBA's first paid staff member after its resurgence. The law firm gave MASBA a telephone and use of its copier, and it paid for MASBA's mailings.

I've always felt that MASBA has a story to tell. MASBA was important in 1993, when we didn't have a viable organization for Mexican American school board members, and MASBA remains important today. I've always said that, even if your district only has a single Mexican American student, you need to join MASBA, because

MASBA ensures the success of *all* students. If we don't help our *Latino* students, who are now the majority in our Texas public schools, we're not going to succeed as a state. We need to help them succeed!

There's nothing more important than the education and success of our students—which is MASBA's mission. As trustees, we don't run for our local school boards to lower the tax rate or to improve efficiencies. We do it for the kids and for their success. If we're successful, they'll be successful, too. As school board members, we need to constantly remind ourselves of the power we have to make a big difference!

Former MASBA Executive Director Juan Aguilera is largely responsible for reinvigorating MASBA in the 1990s through the hosting of receptions and the organizing of MASBA's annual conference. He served on the Board of Trustees of the Round Rock ISD. 25 years later, he continues to serve MASBA, now providing pro bono *legal counsel for the organization.*

"We Had to Pull Ourselves Up by Our Bootstraps"

Theresa Gutiérrez

In 1985, I became the first Mexican-American woman to serve on the Victoria ISD Board of Trustees. At that time, the U.S. Department of Justice forced our district to change its board structure, from seven at-large trustees, to a board of two at-large trustees and five single-member district trustees. This allowed for more diverse representation. I served on our local school board, representing the south side of Victoria, for 12 years.

It wasn't easy being the only Hispanic on my board. White members didn't want Hispanics to have a place among them. We didn't get elected to anything, and they didn't prepare us, as Mexican American trustees, to operate on our local school boards.

When I got upset, I made inflammatory statements, especially when other trustees tried to shut me up. I would say, "The Brown wave is coming!" I would tell them, "We just want what you want: We just want a slice of the bread that you have!" And they couldn't stand to be told that.

I would ask my friends, "Why are the other school board members so worried about me? I'm just one Hispanic, among seven trustees. They always have the majority, and they outvote me every time!" I didn't support what the other trustees did, so why should I go along with them?

My board disenfranchised me and had proposed censuring me. MALDEF represented me in a lawsuit against them. The other school board members backed off and didn't try to censure me anymore after that.

In the mid-1990s, Diana Castañeda of the Austin ISD started inviting me to the receptions she co-hosted for Hispanic trustees at TASB events. I wouldn't have gotten involved, if it weren't for her. She said, "I don't think anyone knows about these events." And she was right!

I give all the credit to Diana, a marvelous and devoted woman, for bringing MASBA back to life in the 1990s. She wanted to resurrect MASBA and make its presence known. So, she reached out to me. She said, "You know, Theresa, we need to start doing something, so that our people achieve recognition. We need to advance the cause of our people!" She spoke my language.

Diana and I aspired to the same things. Our goals connected. When she called, I couldn't decline her effervescence and passion for the cause.

When I started driving to Austin, to visit Diana, we shared stories of our experiences serving on our local school boards. We discussed issues affecting the Hispanic community. We became personal friends. I really admired her. A gutsy activist, Diana liked my command of English, saying that I put things in ways that commanded the attention of my audience. We were a good pair.

Because the MASBA formed in the 1970s lay dormant for some time, Diana said, "We're going to have to start from scratch. Whatever we want to do, we're going to have to build it!" So, she started the whole process of building our funds, literally from empty coffers.

Diana possessed a rare ability—perhaps because she lived in Austin—of raising funds for our reestablishment efforts. She always arrived with grandiose plans for us. I said, "Diana, that's all great, but I don't have the capability you have to raise funds!"

She said, "Don't worry about that. I'll take care of it." And she did! Diana was the best fundraiser I've ever seen. She told me, "You take care of the leadership part, you lead the group, and I'll take care of the money."

Diana and I then met Albert Martínez of the San Diego ISD at a Texas Association of School Boards (TASB) conference. Albert got involved with our effort, and we became friends. We all understood the purpose of the old MASBA, we started doing things together, and our coalition of Hispanic school board members began to grow.

During those years, we met at TASB conferences. The Blacks had their caucus at TASB events, so we had ours. We realized that the Blacks had a very strong presence within the state organization, and we played a very small role, at most. So I told Albert and Diana, "If we want to have some recognition at the state level, if we want them to acknowledge us, we're going to have to do things, and we're going to have to get on some of their boards!"

Diana took a leading role in bringing together trustees. She made it her priority to bring people together. She planned gatherings for us. We drove to Austin and met in hotels or at Diana's home. Hispanics from throughout Texas came to discuss issues important to us. Diana wanted me to lead the group, and she supplied anything that we needed financially.

We initially planned to make our presence known and to explore issues that affected Hispanics, including poverty and underrepresentation. We started small, but we dealt with big issues.

Some of those issues remain critical today, including the underrepresentation of minorities. Lawyers and Anglo Americans peppered the TASB Board. More Blacks than Hispanics served on the TASB Board. We struggled to achieve a presence there. Most of the people we dealt with had lots of money and were already influential at the state level. We literally had to pull ourselves up by our bootstraps, because we started out with nothing. We even developed a legislative agenda that included the representation of minorities.

People started noticing us. Even the Blacks thought, "Maybe we should join forces together and make our organizations more powerful." We, however, wanted to maintain our separate identity, because we really catered to the needs of the Hispanic community.

I remember one of our funders, Mr. Zamarripa, a friend of Diana who worked for a law firm in Austin. Diana had so many contacts, and money talks: You can't do anything without money! Diana continued bringing in the money for us.

I assisted those early organizing efforts until I left my local school board in 1997. After 12 years of serving on my board, no one called me anymore, and I felt like I no longer existed. Then our community turned against me: A few years ago, when I applied to fill a vacancy on our local board, a Mexican American discouraged me, saying, "Theresa, don't bother to volunteer. You caused so much trouble while you were on the board." A member of our own community said that to discourage me!

The problem of underrepresentation is still real in the Victoria ISD. Hispanics don't get elected to the at-large positions on our school board. In order to get elected, you need to come from a predominantly-minority, single-member district. In the Victoria ISD, 65% of our students are now Hispanic, and yet only two of seven trustees are Hispanic. It's the same problem we faced over 20 years ago.

The only way we'll change that is to convince our people to make voting a priority. We still haven't instilled in our people how important it is to vote. You don't know how many times people ask me, "Why should I vote? It won't make a difference!" Our vote does make a difference. We have the vote! How hard is it to go vote? How long does it take to go to the polling place and cast your ballot? Yet our people don't do it! I've been so desperate to register voters that I've even gone to taverns, where men are drinking, just to get as many people as possible registered to vote. The bottom line is: We don't vote. If we did, we'd have the representation that we currently don't have.

As MASBA celebrates its golden jubilee, I wish the organization continuity of purpose. We have to continue MASBA's important work, and we have to fight for our people!

Teresa "Theresa" Gutiérrez became the first Mexican-American woman elected to the Board of Trustees of the Victoria Independent School District. In that capacity, she represented the south side of Victoria from 1985 to 1997. She served as MASBA President from 1996 to 1997.

The Presidencies of Diana Castañeda & Theresa Gutiérrez

MASBA possesses no photos or written records from 1996 to 1998, when Diana Castañeda and Theresa Gutiérrez served as Presidents of the organization.

If you would like to share any photos, meeting minutes, conference programs, mementos, etc. from that time period, for inclusion in Volume II, please email them to info@masbatx.org or mail them to MASBA | P.O. Box 474 | Austin, TX 78767.

Thank you for helping us to reconstruct our history!

"We Believed in the Organization"

Lupe Zamarripa

I got involved with MASBA through my good friend, Diana Castañeda of the Austin ISD, who asked me for a donation. We both grew up in East Austin, and initially I helped her out of my pocket because of our friendship. Eventually, I asked our law firm to help, and they agreed to do so, because we believed in the organization and the good people in it. Many of them were our clients.

I saw MASBA as a small organization comprised of working people, most of whom didn't make a lot of money. Out-of-town trips can be expensive for school board members and their families. "We'll take care of dinner," I used to say.

I worked for Secretary of State Mark White, who later became Attorney General, then Governor. White and I attended a LULAC conference in 1975 in Texas City or Galveston. That's where I met Louis "The Godfather" Reyes and other folks who played a role in my professional life. Louis and I remain good friends.

In 1983, I resigned as a Special Assistant to Governor White and joined the law firm of Heard Goggan & Blair. People like to do business with people they know and trust. Many people I'd met during my ten years with Mark White became law firm clients. In the mid-1980s, Heard Goggan & Blair merged with another law firm, and then we merged with Calame Linebarger Graham & Peña, which gave our combined firms a larger presence throughout the state. Linebarger Goggan Blair & Sampson—now called The Linebarger Firm—became more involved with many more school boards. As a partner with the law firm until 2007, I came to know a lot of MASBA members.

Life is about relationships, and my aunt, who largely raised me, once said, "*No seas como el asadón*" (Don't be like the hoe—which goes down the row of crops only in one direction). My aunt attended school for only three days in her life, but she taught me to give back. Furthermore, I've never forgotten where I came from. I always smile when some young whipper-snapper says, "I did this on my own!" A lot of young people don't know or don't realize we are where we are because of the work and sacrifices of LULAC, the GI Forum, and other

Mexican American organizations. They worked hard to open doors for all of us.

Diana Castañeda befriended Theresa Gutiérrez, a member of the Victoria ISD Board. Theresa and her daughters occasionally visited Diana. Taking them to lunch, I became friends with Theresa's family. She even invited me to a superb *enchilada* dinner at her home in Victoria!

Diana introduced me to Sonny, a *mexicano* school board member and constable from Waco. He had been an Army Ranger and now sported a ponytail. I attended a birthday party in his backyard. Unfortunately, he passed away a short time after that.

We believe in MASBA, so when they need help, all they have to do is pick up the phone. Paul Chapa runs the Corpus Christi office, oversees the Austin office, and is a key member of the firm's management committee. He's a big MASBA supporter. Several years ago, the organization needed $5,000 for its banquet. Paul secured the money. This year, we donated $15,000 for MASBA's President's reception. We'll also host multiple dinners during the MASBA San Antonio conference.

1,400 employees work for Linebarger. Of all the firms involved in collecting delinquent taxes and court fee fines, we have the best record of equal employment—including Mexican Americans—in executive positions. John Guevara runs the Brownsville office. Lucy Canales runs the Edinburg office, which is responsible for most of the Valley. Carmen Pérez runs the El Paso office, and Bridget López runs the Dallas Office. Norman Nelson, an African American, runs the Houston office, which collects for hundreds of accounts in Harris County and the surrounding cities and schools. We have *mexicanos* and men and women of all colors who are income partners, capital partners, and on the management committee. In our Houston call center, our collectors are fluent in five or six languages, and our New York office is run by a *mexicana*.

MASBA will play a key role in shaping the future of education in Texas schools. *Mexicanos* will eventually run this state; the numbers are there, and it's only a matter of time. For this reason, MASBA will continue to play a key role in trying to make changes in the educational system that are beneficial not only to *mexicanos*, but to all Texans.

What started as "bread cast upon the waters" has come back many times. The rewards are bigger when you help someone without expecting anything back. I helped my friend, Diana, and it came back to me many times. You never know what will happen when you "cast your bread upon the waters"!

Lupe Zamarripa is remembered for his generosity to MASBA during the early days of its resurgence in the mid-1990s. He served as a partner at Linebarger Goggan Blair & Sampson at the time, and he continues to consult for the firm.

"It Was a Lot of Work When We Started"

Albert Martínez

By the late 1980s, the MASBA of the 1970s had gone dormant. In the 1990s, I remember sitting down in the hotel lobby of a TASB conference—perhaps the Four Seasons in Houston—with Diana Castañeda of the Austin ISD and Theresa Gutiérrez of the Victoria ISD. We talked about the idea of reviving MASBA, of starting it all over again.

Tommy Molina of the TASB Board had something to do with that meeting. He and I served together on the San Diego ISD Board. He had the pulse of what was going on, and he probably knew that this was "right up my alley." He said to me, "Albert, these women are trying to get this deal started, and I'm wondering if you'd be interested." I said, "Yeah, I'll meet with them." I credit Tommy for that encounter.

Tommy didn't attend my meeting with Diana and Theresa. He had other things on his plate during that conference, so he threw the ball into my court. After that initial conversation with Diana and Theresa, we consulted with Juan Aguilera, an attorney formerly on the Round Rock ISD Board, and we started piggybacking on TASB's coattails: Every time TASB had a conference, we hosted our own little *pachanga*, our own little party. We hosted dinners and events to recruit trustees. At the TASB conference in 1995, we said, "Diana, you're going to be our President!" Diana became President, Theresa Gutiérrez became Vice President, and I held some other officer position. Sonny, a Native-American Waco ISD trustee with a ponytail, served as a MASBA officer back then, too. By 1996 or 1997, we had some 90 people attending our events.

Diana led our efforts for a time, then Theresa, and then they elected me President for the next three years. I became the only MASBA President to serve for three years, then we passed leadership of MASBA to Jimmie Adame of Taft ISD.

A dedicated, pedal-to-the-metal woman from East Austin, Diana was a pistol with a hairline trigger. She had the personality of those who marched with the Brown Berets in the 1970s. Theresa worked at a bank and was more conservative and laid back. I was the moderate in the middle of them.

The backbone of MASBA during those early years, Juan Aguilera guided us through the mess and the nightmare of restarting MASBA's 501(c)(3) status. He started off as our advisor, and he became the cornerstone of MASBA! Juan served as our executive director and go-to guy. The mastermind of MASBA, he pretty much singlehandedly carried the organization, with funding from his law firm. Attentive to our needs, he always went the extra mile for us. Juan would grab as many sponsors as he could, and he and his firm would bankroll the rest. He would sometimes pay $2,000 out of his pocket. Because of his generosity, I used to joke with Juan: "One day, we're going to put a statue of you in Travis Park in San Antonio!"

I like to tell the story of one of those early conferences: Juan was busy, trying to get everything ready for our conference at UTSA, and my car wasn't working right, and my clothes were wrinkled, and I started to panic. Juan finally answered my call: "What do you need?" I asked him: "Juan, can you stop by a store and pick up a can of starch, so that I can iron my clothes?" He said, "Albert, you're crazy! I'm trying to make things work, and you need starch? Use water!" We both still laugh about that.

During those early years, Tommy served on the TASB Board and urged TASB to share with us "a piece of their pie." TASB provided us space at their conferences. They gave us recognition and respect. Tommy also served as our *ad hoc* executive director for some years.

We partnered with NALEO and with Dr. Ricardo Romo, President of UTSA. Romo graciously hosted our early conferences at UTSA, across the street from conveniently-located hotels. So, we started having our own conferences, outside of TASB conferences. Henry Cisneros came, as did his father, Colonel George Cisneros. Tony Sánchez of O'Brien Oil, who later ran for governor in 2002, came. They spoke to us, and we offered legitimate classes, where trustees could earn continuing education hours. We dotted our i's and crossed our t's, and the rest is history. MASBA started to grow because people really wanted to go to our free conferences!

I also remember representing MASBA a couple of times in Washington, D.C. President Clinton had cut $33 million from Pell grants, so we traveled to Washington, to meet with his Chief of Staff, Leon Panetta. After that meeting, President Clinton restored the funding!

We had a major challenge with recruiting school districts. Even predominantly-Hispanic districts wouldn't join MASBA. They paid thousands of dollars to be part of TASB, but they wouldn't pay $300 or $500 to be part of MASBA! Because of that, we never grew beyond 25 or 30 districts.

In those early days, radicals tried to infiltrate MASBA, to use the organization for their own purposes. I remember we pushed out one Brown Beret from San Antonio, because MASBA is not a political organization. We advocated for education and policy, while he cried, "Burn the *gringos*!" We were trying to partner with TASB, and we didn't want them to hear that rhetoric and "circle the wagons"!

Some school board members wanted us to fight their battles for them. Theresa, for instance, was the only Hispanic on her board—but we couldn't fight her battles. We couldn't "beat the drum" for our members. Instead, MASBA existed to provide education and ideas, and to bring people together to talk about how we weren't getting our fair share of funding and programs for our Hispanic kids.

We slowly began to transition, from a group known for its *pachangas*, to an organization with a bonified curriculum for school board members. Hispanic students were quickly becoming the majority in our Texas public schools, and we tried to prepare school board members for the coming "Brown wave."

I once tried to get the Black Caucus and MASBA to co-host a conference together. We faced similar issues back in the 1990s. I met with George McShan of the Harlingen CISD, and with the board of the Black Caucus. Nothing materialized back then.

By the time I left MASBA, we were thinking of securing state recognition of *mariachi* by the University Interscholastic League. It would take a few more years for that to become a feather in MASBA's cap—something now available to every school district in the state of Texas!

After those three years as President, I felt burnt out. It was a lot of work when we started! I remember some of the people who led MASBA after me. Óscar García of Ben Bolt-Palito Blanco ISD was one of the best presidents MASBA ever had. Dr. Manuel Flores of the Corpus Christi ISD, a professor at Texas A&M Kingsville, played an instrumental role. He and Dr. Viola García were both from universities. They brought a lot of professionalism to MASBA, and people automatically listened to them.

I now work for Congressman Vicente González, and every time I visit a school district, I ask whether they're a member of MASBA. The organization has had its challenges, but I sense that it's now going strong. I don't see MASBA fizzling out anytime soon!

Alberto "Albert" Martínez joined the Board of Trustees of the San Diego Independent School District in 1993, and he served as President of MASBA from 2000 to 2003. He now works for U.S. Congressman Vicente González.

The Presidency of Albert Martínez

No written records dating to the 1990s have been found for MASBA. The first extant MASBA record is dated January 2000. Records shed light on the following events that took place during the leadership of MASBA President Alberto "Albert" Martínez of San Diego ISD.

On January 28-30, 2000, MASBA hosted its second annual conference, "Hispanic Student Excellence: A Vision for the New Millennium," at the downtown campus of the University of Texas at San Antonio. A document lists all 94 attendees of this conference. Held in memory of Senator Greg Luna (1932-1999), the conference featured the following.

Opening Remarks
Alberto Martínez, MASBA President
Dean Dwight Henderson, UTSA
San Antonio City Council Member Enrique Barrera
Dr. Joe Bernal, UTSA, State Board of Education

Keynotes
Dr. Blandina "Bambi" Cárdenas, UTSA
TEA Commissioner Jim Nelson

Sessions

"Violence in Schools & Community"
Dr. Gilbert García, Southwest ISD
Margaret Dunn, Southwest Texas State University

"Legislative Update"
U.S. Congressman Ciro Rodríguez,
U.S. Assistant Secretary of Education Scott Fleming
State Rep Dora Olivo
State Rep René Oliveira
Senator Leticia Van de Putte (moderator)

"Capital Improvements & Finance"
Enrique Alemán, TEA
Patricia Rodríguez, Southwestern Capital Markets
Lisa Dawn, Moak Casey & Consultants
Raúl Villaseñor

"Community Economic Development"
Amancio Chapa

"2000 Census & Redistricting"
Senator Gonzalo Barrientos
David Méndez, Bickerstaff Heath Smiley Pollan Kever & McDaniel
George Korbel, José Garza & Rolando Ríos, Attorneys

"Vouchers: Local, State & National Impact"
Anna Alicia Romero, IDRA
Annette Cootes, TSTA
Edgewood ISD Parent Representatives

"TAAS/Curriculum Alignment/Drop-out Rates"
Dr. Albert Cortez, IDRA & Al Kauffman, MALDEF

"Bilingual & Cultural Education"
State Senator Carlos Truan
Mary Jean Letendre, U.S. Department of Education
Choco Leandro, Edgewood ISD
Delia Pompa, National Association of Bilingual Education

"School District Financial Audits"
Greg Hartman & Julio C. Massad, MGT of America, Inc.

"School Board Relations"
James Vásquez, Region 19 ESC
Pablo Escamilla, Escamilla & Poneck

On January 29, 2000, Cecilia Ballí published an article titled "Hispanic Educators Told to Anticipate Challenges" in the *San Antonio Express-News*. She wrote of TEA Commissioner Jim Nelson's remarks to 100 MASBA conference attendees on the new Texas Assessment of Academic Skills (TAAS), which would be taken by juniors in 2004. After the lunch, Al Kauffman of MALDEF presented a 1:30 p.m. panel on the TAAS, on dropout rates, and on "the trial he argued on behalf of two civil rights groups and seven minority students." The article continues:

On Friday, U.S. Rep. Ciro Rodriguez, D-San Antonio, and Scott Fleming, the assistant secretary who oversees legislation and congressional affairs for the U.S. Department of Education, summarized the climate of education initiatives at the federal level.

Seven years ago, Fleming said, education hardly was a national priority, "but it's No. 1 poll after poll today."

Recapping the State of the Union address Thursday—and taking more than a few stabs at Republic lawmakers' attitudes on education—Rodriguez and Fleming described an "ambitious plan" proposed by President Clinton.

It would make funds available to rebuild schools, improve teacher quality, replenish a diminishing teacher pool, fix failing schools, and foster bilingual education and dual-language programs.

"As far as I'm concerned, there's too many people taking those jobs that require bilingualism that are not native-born," Rodriguez said.

One conference participant reminded the panelists that the country's educational goals need to be grounded in the reality trustees face in their districts.

When Fleming said lawmakers hope every U.S. classroom will be staffed by a certified teacher by 2004, Jimmy Vásquez, the former Edgewood School District superintendent who now heads the Education Service Center in El Paso, warned the task will require highly innovative approaches and incentives for would-be teachers.

"Otherwise, all we're doing is beating a drum that nobody hears," Vasquez said.

On May 17, 2000, President Albert Martínez (San Diego ISD) convened a **MASBA Advisory Committee** meeting at the law office of Escamilla & Poneck in San Antonio. In attendance were: Juan Aguilera (Acting Executive Director), Norma Osuna (Slaton ISD), Jimmie Adame (Taft ISD), Connie Rocha (San Antonio ISD), David Sosa (Harlandale ISD), Paul Soto (Seguin ISD), Juan Martínez (Southwest ISD), Juan Alvarado (Southwest ISD), Tomás Molina (San Diego ISD), Manuel Garza (former trustee, Edgewood ISD). Absent from the meeting were Ada González-Peterson (El Paso ISD), Rudy Montoya (Austin ISD), Amancio Chapa (La Joya ISD), Manuel Flores (Corpus Christi ISD), David Sublasky (Region 19 ESC) and Carlos Caballero (Region 19 ESC). Juan Aguilera shared copies of MASBA's Articles of Incorporation and discussed the need to pay a $25 fee to reactivate the organization. Tomás Molina presented a Membership Committee report: A dues structure needed to be determined for voting privileges, and "all districts in Texas WILL BE considered as members of the association." Ada González-Peterson and Tomás Molina gave a Funding Committee report: Reactivation of the organization's 501(c)(3) status was necessary for Ada to submit a grant proposal to the Stern Foundation, and organizations responding positively to the idea of in-kind funding of MASBA included UTSA, Texas A&M Kingsville, Texas A&M System, TASB and IDRA. Tomás Molina proposed a dues structure of $.49 per Hispanic student, with a minimum district dues of $500 and a maximum district dues of $5,000. Manuel Flores created a prototype brochure, with attached membership application. Tomás Molina will review TASB bylaws and prepare draft bylaws for approval at the June membership meeting. Attendees agreed to form a "transitional Board of Directors," with two directors from each of six regions, with staggering terms, elected in September. Proposed Board members were:

- ESC 1, 2 & 20: Connie Rocha (San Antonio ISD) and Juan Alvarado (Southwest ISD)
- ESC 3, 13 & 15: Paul Soto (Seguin ISD) and Rudy Montoya (Austin ISD)
- ESC 4, 5, 6, 7 & 8: Joe Longoria (Stafford MSD) and Viola García (Aldine ISD)
- ESC 10, 11 & 12: Rose Herrera (Fort Worth ISD) and Kathleen Leos (Dallas ISD)
- ESC 9, 14, 16 & 17: Norma Osuna (Slaton ISD) and Linda DeLeón (Lubbock ISD)
- ESC 18 & 19: Ada González-Peterson (El Paso ISD) and Carlos Caballero (ESC Region 19)

The Advisory Committee proposed that Albert Martínez (San Diego ISD) remain as President for 2000-2001 and that Jimmie Adame (Taft ISD) be designated President Elect for 2001-2002. A new President Elect and 12 Directors would be elected at the first election in September 2001, with half receiving a one-year term and half receiving a two-year term. The MASBA Board will then be comprised of 15 Directors: a President, a President Elect, an Immediate Past President, and 12 regional Directors. For 2000-2001 only, all Officers and Directors will be deemed to be "paid" members, since no district has yet paid dues. The Board agreed: "since some districts where Hispanics are a minority of the local board may choose not to join MASBA, individual Hispanic board members may join and become part of the association." Individual members will enjoy voting privileges. The Advisory Committee agreed to meet again on June 15, 2000, 7:00 p.m., at the TASB Summer Conference in San Antonio, and a Membership meeting was scheduled for June 16, 2000, 5:00 p.m. at a conference site. The meeting minutes, prepared by Tomás Molina, conclude: "The Advisory Committee meeting was very productive. The input provided by all in attendance will be utilized in the re-organization process. Stay in touch. Networking and communicating with each other will lead to better understanding and coordination in order to accomplish our goals. *Muchas gracias* to ALL *y ADELANTE VAMOS!*"

On June 16, 2000, President Albert Martínez convened a **MASBA Membership** meeting in San Antonio. The agenda included:
- Introduction of Interim Board of Directors
- Report to Members
  o Structure, Finance & History – Juan Aguilera (Acting Executive Director)
  o Membership, Recruitment & Involvement – Tomás Molina
- Mission Statement
- Identify & Prioritize Issues Facing Association
- What Can MASBA Do for Member Districts/Trustees?
- Announce Meeting Schedule
  o September at TASB Convention
  o January Conference in San Antonio
  o April 4 State Hispanic Conference in San Antonio

No minutes have been found for this meeting. A financial report from the meeting shows conference expenses totaling $9,539.49. MASBA had $2,654.49 in its checking account on May 31, 2000, with $826.60 still owed to UTSA for conference expenses. A directory labeled "schoolboard members attending meeting for training credits" shares the following attendees:
- Ramón Abarca, Slaton, Texas
- Eddie Abrego, Olmito, Texas

- Juan Acevedo, Del Río, Texas
- Armín Argullín, Río Hondo, Texas
- Peggy Banales, Corpus Christi, Texas
- Ashley V. Barrera, San Diego, Texas
- León Bazar, Corpus Christi, Texas
- Irene Bustamante, Big Spring, Texas
- Rosa D. Caballero, El Paso, Texas
- Nick Cárdenas, Beeville, Texas
- Gloria Casas, La Feria, Texas
- Al Chavira, Jacksonville, Texas
- Anne Cozart, Fort Worth, Texas
- Lupe DeHoyos, Del Río, Texas
- Héctor Del Toro, Corpus Christi, Texas
- Diana Díaz, Mercedes, Texas
- Héctor Escobar, Ben Bolt, Texas
- John Galván, Mathis, Texas
- Gracy S. García, Alice, Texas
- Higinio García, Alice, Texas
- Lionel A. García, Plainview, Texas
- Mary García, Mathis, Texas
- Óscar García, Alice, Texas
- Roberto García, Clint, Texas
- Viola M. García, Houston, Texas
- Adela G. Garza, Olmito, Texas
- Ricardo C. González, Alice, Texas
- Prax Guerra, Jr., San Diego, Texas
- Roberto M. Lerma, El Paso, Texas
- Alberto Martínez, San Diego, Texas
- Benny Martínez, Premont, Texas
- Juan Martínez, Jr., San Antonio, Texas
- Tomás Molina, San Diego, Texas
- Rudy Montoya, Austin, Texas
- Carlos E. Nieto, Presidio, Texas
- Norma Osuna, Slaton, Texas
- Juan Rangel, Fort Worth, Texas
- Yvonne Sapien-Sánchez, El Paso, Texas
- Rosie Sedillo, Marlin, Texas

- Roberto Sepúlveda, Weslaco, Texas
- Richard Skidmore, San Diego, Texas
- María Eugenia Soriano, San Diego, Texas

Directors received a directory of MASBA Board Members. It lists Alberto Martínez as President, Jimmie Adame as President Elect. 11 of the 12 Directors proposed on May 17 are listed as "Interim Directors," with Carlos Nieto (Presidio ISD) replacing Carlos Caballero (Region 19 ESC). Juan Aguilera and Tomás Molina are listed as Facilitators.

Attached to the 2000 MASBA Board directory is a copy of the organization's vision, mission and objectives. It reads:

Vision:
- Make high-quality public education accessible to ALL
- Increase parental/community participation in public governance
- Improve academic achievement
- Advocate equitable school finance

Mission:
Meeting educational and cultural needs and rights of Mexican American and other disadvantaged and historically-underserved students in public schools through:
- Leadership development
- Public policy analysis
- Political awareness
- Community empowerment

Objectives:
- Encourage and promote parental & community involvement in public school governance
- Identify and highlight model educational programs in schools with high Mexican-American student populations
- Disseminate information on financial resources and access to higher education
- Provide diversity training to all school board members
- Provide educational seminars on Mexican-American student & family issues
- Provide leadership training and mentoring for current & future Mexican-American school board members

On September 16, 2000, President Albert Martínez convened a six-hour **MASBA Board Planning Retreat** at the offices of IDRA in San Antonio. The agenda read:

- Vision/Mission
- Accomplishments & Goals
- Objectives & Activities
- Policy Issues
- Calendar
- Next Steps

Objectives listed for the meeting included:

- To reaffirm the Vision/Mission of MASBA
- To review activities accomplished and establish the goals of the organization
- To develop a plan to increase membership and list strategies to increase participation of school districts in MASBA
- To identify programs, activities and tasks of the association
- To review some policy issues on which to focus
- To list some upcoming events of interest to MASBA and to identify ways to participate
- To agree upon next steps: who, what and by when

On September 23, 2000, IDRA created an egroup for MASBA. Anna Alicia Romero of IDRA owned the egroup, and Dr. Aurelio Montemayor of IDRA moderated it. Members of the egroup included: Jimmie Adame, Manuel Flores, Adela Garza, Roberto García, Viola García, Ricardo C. González, Tomás Molina, Rudy Montoya, Joe Muñoz (San Angelo ISD), Carlos Nieto, Juan Rangel and Roberto Sepúlveda. Members used the egroup to organize a MASBA planning retreat on October 21, 2000.

In September 2000, MASBA hosted a reception, presumably in connection with the annual TASA/TASB conference. A sign-in sheet survives with the names, addresses and telephone numbers of 75 attendees.

On October 21, 2000, President Albert Martínez convened a six-hour **MASBA Board Planning Retreat** hosted and facilitated by IDRA at the Omni San Antonio Hotel. Travel and accommodations were funded by IDRA. Dr. Aurelio Montemayor of IDRA led participants through the following agenda:

- Bylaws
- Officers & Board
- Member List
- Information Dissemination
- Annual Conference
- Website/Egroup
- Policies & the Legislature
- TASB Events
- Next Steps

Objectives listed for the meeting included:

- To review the status of the organization's bylaws
- To formalize the process for election of officers and board members
- To validate the list of current active or interested individuals and expand the list of potential members
- To develop materials for a MASBA mailout to all superintendents
- To continue planning the MASBA annual conference
- To review the website and egroup for MASBA
- To highlight policy issues and a communication plan for the Texas legislature
- To plan participation in TASB events

At the meeting, IDRA presented a PowerPoint presentation entitled "Policy Reform Priorities 2000-2001." Notes taken at the meeting by Viola García suggest the TASB Board had 12 Hispanic members.

On December 2, 2000, President Albert Martínez convened a 3.5-hour **MASBA Board Meeting** at the Omni Austin Hotel at Southpark. The agenda follows.

- Welcome
- Meeting Notes
- MASBA Annual Conference Planning (Juan Aguilera)

- Policy Issues
- TASB Events
- Next Steps

Objectives listed for the meeting included:

- To review notes from last meeting (October 21)
- To continue planning the MASBA annual conference
- To highlight policy issues and a communication plan for the Texas Legislature
- To plan participation in TASB events
- To decide next steps

On December 3, 2000, Tommy Molina emailed MASBA Directors to report that a brochure with membership application and a notice of MASBA's third annual conference had been mailed to all school districts in Texas. He said that MASBA members would now be able to attend the conference at no additional charge. The brochure reads,

Visit us at the following:

- April 25-28, 2002 – Celebrating Educational Opportunities for Hispanic Students (Phoenix, AZ)
- May 17-18, 2002 – Region One Spring Workshop (South Padre Island, TX)
- June 13-15, 2002 – TASB Summer Leadership Conference (San Antonio, TX)
- September 27-30, 2002 – 42nd Annual TASA/TASB Convention (Dallas, TX)

Extant records for 2001 are sparse.

MASBA hosted its third annual conference in January 2001. No records have been found for this event.

On September 22, 2001, President Albert Martínez convened the **MASBA Annual Meeting** at the Dallas Convention Center. The agenda follows:

- Transfer Office of Presidency (Albert Martínez to Jimmie Adame)
- Executive Director's Report (Juan F. Aguilera)

- o Financial Report
- o January Conference
- 2000-2001 MASBA Highlights (Tommy Molina)
  - o January 2001 MASBA Conference
  - o Meeting with Rural Trust Community Schools
  - o Summer Leadership Institute Meeting
  - o Teacher of the Year, Superintendent of the Year
- Election of Officers for 2002-2003 (Jimmie Adame)
- Open Forum

No minutes have been found for this meeting.

If you would like to share any photos, meeting minutes, conference programs, mementos, etc. from 1998 to 2000, for inclusion in Volume II, please email them to info@masbatx.org or mail them to MASBA | P.O. Box 474 | Austin, TX 78767.

Thank you for helping us to reconstruct our history!

"We Finally Got the Wheels on It and Pushed It Down the Road"

Jimmie Adame

The resurgence of MASBA began at a TASA/TASB conference in Dallas. Juan Aguilera had planned a reception at a railroad station across from the Marriott, with an open bar and *hors d'oeuvres*. I told Juan how an organization named MASBA existed in the 1970s. I said, "I remember going to a meeting and being elected President, but nothing ever came of it because it had no structure."

We agreed: "Let's get this organization back together! We need to do this!" We also said, "Let's get something going, and let's not leave this convention until we've exchanged phone numbers and email addresses!" So I put together a sign-in sheet for that reception.

We decided to jumpstart the association, and we made it a point to get together at every TASB function. Diana Castañeda of the Austin ISD and Albert Martínez of the San Diego ISD were involved. Tommy Molina from San Diego also helped get the MASBA machine going. We enthusiastically discussed late into the evening the need for MASBA to exist and flourish. At the beginning, it was a slow and painful crawl, but we finally got the wheels on it and pushed it down the road!

Diana served as our President in 1996. Louis and I remember to this day how she committed us to an exorbitant amount of money, for a group of indigenous dancers from Mexico to perform for us. We didn't have the money, but we ended up paying for their travel, accommodations and meals. I also remember our organizational meeting in May 2000. Pablo Escamilla and Doug Poneck hosted us at their San Antonio office. They allowed Juan to spend some of his time on MASBA business, and Juan's secretary did a lot of the recordkeeping and the stuff that needed to be done. Juan acted as the *ad hoc* Executive Director, thanks to the support of his firm.

TASB conferences weren't strong in the topics that Hispanic board members wanted, so we said, "Let's host our own conference!" Putting a conference together was daunting, to say the least. We stayed at the Radisson, and Dr. Romo of UTSA opened the doors of the college across the street. We had resistance from school boards that didn't want to allow their *Latino* school board members to attend a Mexican American School Board Members Association conference. They said, "TASB is sufficient!"

We said, "*Está bien* [that's O.K.], if your school board doesn't want to become a member, but you want to come, then come, join us!" We spread the word and opened our arms and our doors to anyone.

I became President Elect of MASBA at the TASA/TASB convention in 2000. I served as MASBA President from September 2001 to January 2003 — because we moved our officer elections to our MASBA conference beginning in 2003. After serving as Immediate Past President, I remained on the Board through 2005. Our Board welcomed all who had a burning desire to be part of it. We said, "If you're standing around and want to help, come on in! We'll use you in some way and accept your help."

I lost my local election in May 2006, and MASBA hired me the next month. In January 2007, the MASBA Board hired me as their Executive Director.

We got the ball rolling again for the organization. *Y comenzó el movimiento* [movement began]. MASBA started picking up steam. We believed that MASBA must exist to meet the needs of our *Latino* kids. The case in point was our *mariachi* program. For *mexicanos, mariachi* — with its costumes and instruments — is more important than marching band. We knew that MASBA should push to get together a *mariachi* competition for the state of Texas. The recognition of *mariachi* as a UIL competition wouldn't have happened without MASBA!

My fondest memory of MASBA is the impact that it made in the background on education. We were a small organization, but those associated with us over the years were stout educators with a strong passion for Hispanic students. I'm fortunate to have been associated with MASBA through the years. I hold MASBA dear to my heart, and I see it growing into a sizeable organization that has all the kids of Texas at heart — and Texas is better off because of MASBA!

Santiago "Jimmie" Adame serves on the Taft ISD Board of Trustees. He was elected MASBA President in 1989, then again in 2001. He participated on the MASBA Board through 2005 and was named MASBA Executive Director in January 2007.

The Second Presidency of Jimmie Adame

On September 22, 2001, at the Annual MASBA Meeting at the Dallas Convention Center, Santiago "Jimmie" Adame of Taft ISD was elected MASBA President for a second time. Extant records contain the following history.

On January 10-12, 2002, President Jimmie Adame convened the **fourth annual MASBA Conference**, "Hispanic Educational Excellence: Education is Our Solution" at the downtown campus of the University of Texas at San Antonio. The conference program published the following details.

Reception honoring Sen. Carlos F. Truan, Dean of the Texas Senate

Presentation of Colors by Slaton HS Junior ROTC, Slaton ISD

National Anthem José Cipriano & Javier Castilla
                 Edgewood Fine Arts Academy, Edgewood ISD

Remarks   Jimmie Adame, MASBA President
            San Antonio City Council Member Enrique Barrera
            UTSA President Dr. Ricardo Romo
            UTSA Vice Provost Dr. Jesse T. Zapata
            UTSA Vice Provost Dr. Richard A. Diem

Keynotes   Senator Carlos F. Truan, Dean of the Texas Senate
            Dr. Arturo Almendárez, Deputy TEA Commissioner
            Gus García, Mayor of Austin
            Frances M. Guzmán, IDRA
            Dan Morales, Democratic Gubernatorial Candidate

School Finance Panel
Senator Leticia Van de Putte, San Antonio
Senator Eliot Shapleigh, El Paso
Mary Ester Bernal, San Antonio ISD
Tina Treviño, United ISD
Fred Sánchez, Ysleta ISD

Breakout Sessions

"Empowering Teachers & Students via the AP Initiative"
Daniel O. Escobar, UTSA Office of K-16 Initiatives

"Technology & Parental Partnership"
Lolo Hernández & Jason White, Taft ISD

"Higher Education Preparation"
Dr. Omar S. López, Just for the Kids

"The Role of Education Service Centers Helping School Districts"
Dr. Sylvia R. Hatton, Region 1 ESC
Dr. Patrick G. Pringle, Region 13 ESC
Dr. James R. Vásquez, Region 19 ESC

"Leadership in Your Community"
TASB Past Presidents John McInnis, George McShan,
Troy Simmons & David Sublasky

"Building Stronger Communities through K-16 Initiatives"
Eyra A. Pérez, UTSA Office of K-16 Initiatives

"Identifying Educational 'Best Practices'"
Dr. Omar S. López, Just for the Kids

"Writing Strategies for Limited English Proficient Students"
Amy Hirasaki & Christina Gómez, Aldine ISD

"Board Consensus Building"
Pablo Escamilla, Escamilla & Poneck

"Dropout & Attrition Rates in Texas Public Schools"
Dr. Albert Cortez, IDRA

"Parental Involvement in the Hispanic Community"
Dr. Jesús Chávez, Corpus Christi ISD

"New School Board Members: Getting Over the Learning Curve"
Óscar García & Alberto Byington, Ben Bolt-Palito Blanco ISD

"High Stakes Testing & Its Permanent Impact on Our Children"
Anna Alicia Romero, IDRA

"A Dual Language & Inclusion Program"
Dr. Rebecca A. Palacios & Jill A. Scott, Corpus Christi ISD

"Redesigning Site-based Management"
Jeanette Ball-Reyes, Georgia Neuman,
Teresa Tarte, Arazeli Granado, Southwest ISD

"Changing Public Discourse to Assets & Student Achievement"
Dr. Jaime Chahín, Southwest Texas State University

Entertainment
Carroll Blue Cat Jazz Band, Carroll HS, Corpus Christi ISD
Conjunto Estrella, San Benito HS, San Benito CISD
Edgewood Fine Arts Academy Ensemble, Edgewood ISD
MacArthur Dance Ensemble, MacArthur HS, Aldine ISD
Mariachi Azul y Oro, San Diego HS, San Diego ISD
Mariachi del Sol, San Benito HS, San Benito CISD
Somerset *Mariachi* Ensemble, Somerset ISD
Southwest HS Jazz Band, Southwest HS, Southwest ISD

Masters of Ceremony
Karla Reyna, Ben Bolt HS, Ben Bolt-Palito Blanco ISD
José Cipriano, Edgewood Fine Arts Academy, Edgewood ISD

College Facilitators
Maricela García, Southwest Texas State University
Mari Carmen Aguilera, St. Mary's University
Humberto Aguilera, The University of Texas at Austin

A January 13, 2002 article by Patrick Driscoll in the *San Antonio Express-News* reported that Texas gubernatorial candidate Dan Morales attended the 2002 MASBA conference and "told Hispanic school officials that restructuring school financing and funding children's health insurance should be top legislative goals next year." The article states, "Morales didn't mention his controversial stance against using race-based criteria for college admissions, scholarships and financial aid — a position some in the audience of about 100 later said they don't support." It quotes Pharr-San Juan-Alamo ISD Superintendent Arturo Guajardo, who later served on the MASBA Board: "That's going to hurt [Morales] tremendously. Tony Sánchez is going to harp on that....Either would be ideal for Texas. It's time we have a Hispanic governor." The article also reported: "S. Jimmie Adame, a board member of Taft School District, north of Corpus Christi, said after the luncheon that he differs with Morales on the matter, saying affirmative action still is needed to some extent. However, Adame said he hasn't decided which candidate to support in the election and is eagerly anticipating two upcoming debates before the March 12 primary. One will be in Spanish, which is believed to be a first for a Texas governor's race."

MASBA Vice President Tomás F. Molina later published the following summary of the 2002 MASBA conference.

The fourth annual MASBA conference was held, in partnership with UTSA Downtown, in San Antonio, Texas on January 10-12, 2002.

Over 150 registered participants, school board members, administrators and *"amigos,"* representing over 25 school districts throughout Texas attended.

The conference began on Thursday evening, January 10, with a reception honoring the retiring "Dean of the Texas Senate," the Honorable Senator Carlos Truan.

The following morning, Friday, January 11, UTSA President Ricardo Romo, San Antonio City Councilman Enrique Barrera, and UTSA Vice Provost Dr. Richard Diem welcomed conferees to San Antonio and the downtown UTSA campus. MASBA President Jimmie Adame, Taft ISD, opened the conference with welcoming remarks and introduced the keynote speaker, Senator Carlos Truan.

Senator Truan spoke about his 35-year political career, beginning as a State Representative and following as a State Senator, and his involvement in Texas education reform. He gave historical accounts of the early involvement of MASBA and the Intercultural Development & Research Association (IDRA) in school financing issues. He emphasized the need for involvement and input from local school board members in our political system. He gave several examples of how single individuals can make a big difference in getting things accomplished and ended by congratulating the re-engagement of MASBA and encouraging its growth.

Friday morning sessions continued with excellent presentations by UTSA staff, Taft ISD, Just for the Kids, ESC representatives, leadership ideas by Ex-TASB Presidents, and Aldine ISD.

The Friday luncheon featured Dr. Art Almendárez, Texas' Deputy Commissioner of Education, who spoke about the TEA testing and the changes coming about this and next year.

The Friday afternoon conference session continued with panel discussions and/or presentations by San Antonio ISD, Pablo Escamilla of Escamilla & Poneck Law Firm, IDRA, Corpus Christi ISD, Ben Bolt-Palito Blanco ISD, and a legislative review by State Senator Leticia Van de Putte.

The Friday sessions included participation by individuals and groups from several school districts. The morning opening session included a student ROTC group from Slaton ISD presenting the U.S. flag and a solo rendition of the national anthem by an Edgewood ISD student. The lunch entertainment featured the *mariachi* band from San Diego ISD. The last group conference session Friday afternoon included student group performances. These ranged from an interpretive dance ensemble from Aldine ISD to jazz and "big band" music from Southwest ISD and Corpus Christi ISD, to *mariachi* and *conjunto* music by San Benito CISD. The performances, emceed by students from Ben Bolt-Palito Blanco ISD and Edgewood ISD, highlighted the abilities of the students and were greatly enjoyed and appreciated by all.

The conference continued on Saturday, January 12, beginning with a general session and a keynote address by the Honorable Gus García, the Mayor of Austin, Texas. Mr. García served as a school board member in Austin when MASBA originally chartered in 1970. He preceded as a charter member and first President of MASBA. He gave a historical perspective on the involvement of Mexican Americans in Texas politics and encouraged MASBA to organize, develop a legislative agenda, and pursue activism in our communities. He stated that education is everyone's business and that all children in Texas deserve a first-rate education.

On January 12, 2002, the "**First General Meeting of the Board of Directors for the Year 2002**" took place at the Radisson Hotel in San Antonio. Secretary Aguie Peña took minutes for the meeting. No mention is made in the minutes of President Jimmie Adame; instead, they say the meeting was "called to order by President Juan Aguilera." This is obviously a mistake, and the meeting was likely called to order by President Jimmie Adame or Executive Director Juan Aguilera. Until the organization's bylaws were further refined,

Directors agreed to follow *Robert's Rules of Order* for this meeting and elected Tomás Molina as Vice President, Aguie Peña as Secretary, and Juan Martínez as Treasurer. President Elect Gracy García agreed to appoint committee members, as needed. The following motions passed:

- "That the Board create an executive body to conduct business of MASBA in order to make decisions for the well-being and promotion of MASBA."
- "That the Executive Committee be composed of all of the officers, with the inclusion of the Immediate Past President."
- "That the Executive Committee be given authority to look at getting a fiscal agent to keep finances in trust, who will in turn provide professional accountability for the financial status of the organization."
- "That the Executive Committee review and fine-tune the organization's bylaws and bring a comprehensive draft for full membership approval."
- "That Board members who are not officers and other service center individuals will be allowed membership, in order to promote a more diverse team."

The next meeting of the MASBA Board was scheduled for February 23, 2002 in San Antonio.

On February 23, 2002, President Jimmie Adame convened an eight-hour **MASBA Executive Committee** meeting at the San Antonio office of IDRA. The agenda included:

- Reports
  - o 2001 MASBA Bank Statement & Current Financial Status
  - o 2002 Conference Expenses
  - o Introduction of Bylaws
  - o Review of Articles of Incorporation
  - o Federal & State Non-profit Status
  - o Website
  - o IDRA Presentation
  - o *Latino* Education Coalition
  - o Community Policy Presentation

- New Items for Review
  - ○ 2002 Membership Recruitment Drive
    - ▪ Produce brochure, with Manuel Flores' help (Juan, Jimmie & Richard)
    - ▪ Set up a booth at regional conference & create a MASBA presence (Jimmie, Viola & Juan M.)
    - ▪ Attend ESC monthly meetings & make our presence known
    - ▪ TASB Grassroots workshops (Óscar & Viola already participated)
  - ○ Funding: Grants, Sponsorship, Etc.
  - ○ 2002 Activities for MASBA; Mentoring or Leadership Training, Etc.

Secretary Aguie Peña wrote detailed minutes. The organization had $9,345.07 in its account, with a quarterly $119.71 payment due for the website. Juan Aguilera introduced MASBA's credit card and clarified who would use it. He, Jimmie Adame and Juan Martínez would be the signers on MASBA's bank account. Juan Aguilera and Juan Martínez agreed to develop a budget for the organization. The Executive Committee agreed to continue paying Richard Garza $2,000 per month for his services and agreed to reimburse Juan Aguilera for out-of-pocket conference expenses. Jimmie recommended that MASBA develop a promotional brochure. Óscar presented draft #4 of MASBA bylaws, for possible adoption at the January 2003 Member Assembly. The MASBA website consists of eight pages, with the events page still being empty. Richard will complete the application for renewal of MASBA's 501(c)(3) not-for-profit status. The next MASBA Board meeting was planned for April 13, 2002 at the San Antonio office of IDRA.

No record has been found of a meeting on April 13.

On April 18, 2002, MASBA Administrative Assistant Richard A. Garza wrote the following communication, shedding some light on the post-conference MASBA events of that year.

Dear School Board Trustees & Administrators,

The Mexican American School Board Members Association ("MASBA") would like to update you on the events planned for 2002.

For those who will attend the Region One conference on May 17-18, in South Padre Island, Texas, MASBA will present a discussion session entitled, "Critical Issues Affecting Hispanic Students in the 21st Century." The goal of the presentation is to inform school board trustees about the newly-formed *Latino* Education Coalition and its partnership with MASBA. Issues such as fair funding, quality teaching, dropout rates, and college access will be discussed. MASBA will also host a reception on Saturday, May 18. The reception is open to all.

The Summer Leadership Conference, sponsored by TASB, is June 13-15, in San Antonio, Texas. MASBA will have an afternoon mixer for all in attendance. The mixer will be held at Sunset Station, in front of the Alamodome, on Friday, June 14, between 5:00 and 8:00 p.m.

MASBA will also be present at the 42nd annual TASA/TASB convention in Dallas.

The Mexican American School Board Members Association continues to grow, and we hope your school district will continue to support us.

On June 14, 2002, President Jimmie Adame convened a **MASBA Board** meeting in San Antonio. The agenda included:

- Pending Items (Óscar García)
    - Identifying candidates for the remaining spots on the MASBA Board
    - Naming people to serve on various committees
- Financial Status (Juan Martínez, Jr.)
- Report on MASBA's Participation at Region One Conference (Jimmie Adame & Óscar García)
- Open Topic Discussions
    - Membership
    - Judy Canales Support
    - September 28 Reception at TASB Convention
    - Fifth Annual MASBA Conference

No minutes have been found for this meeting. Later that evening, MASBA hosted a reception, sponsored by SWS Securities, to honor TASB President Carlos Nieto and TASB Past Presidents John R. McInnis & David Sublasky at the Sunset Station Complex, in front of the Alamodome.

On September 19, 2002, President Jimmie Adame convened a **MASBA Board** meeting by conference call. The agenda included:
- Introduction of the Hispanic Border Leadership Institute (HBLI) – Jimmie Adame, Dr. Leonard Valverde & Lili Murray
- Update on September Reception
    o Group meeting at Hyatt Regency Hotel
    o Awards & presentations during reception
- Membership Drive
- Financials
- 2003 Conference Update
    o Sponsorship
    o Recognition and/or awards
    o Topic discussion form

On September 28 2002, MASBA hosted a **reception** at the Hyatt Regency Dallas Hotel to honor Tomás F. Molina, who had served on the San Diego Board of Trustees since 1990 and just completed his service to the TASB Board and TASB's Risk Management Board.

On January 17-19, 2003, MASBA hosted its **fifth annual Leadership & Issues Conference**, "Hispanic Student Success for the New Millennium: A Leadership & Issues Conference to Address the Challenges of Our Mexican American Students in Texas," at the downtown campus of the University of Texas at San Antonio. The UTSA Office of K-16 Initiatives & Honors Programs and the Hispanic Border Leadership Institute co-hosted the event. The conference program follows.

Reception honoring Felipe T. Alanis, TEA Commissioner

Keynotes

Dr. María Hernández Ferrier, Assistant Deputy U.S. Secretary of Education for English Language Acquisition

TEA Commissioner Felipe T. Alanis

Consuelo Castillo Kickbusch, Educational Achievement Services

San Antonio City Council Member Julián Castro

State Representative Joaquín Castro

Senator Eliot Shapleigh, El Paso

Remarks

S. Jimmie Adame, MASBA President

Dr. Jesse T. Zapata, UTSA Vice Provost

Dr. Leonard A. Valverde, Hispanic Border Leadership Institute

School Finance Panel

Senator Leticia Van de Putte, San Antonio

Senator Eliot Shapleigh, El Paso

Breakout Sessions

"Superintendent-Board Member Relations"
Alberto Byington, Óscar García & Nadine Kujawa,
Ben Bolt-Palito Blanco ISD; Tomás F. Molina, San Diego ISD (Ret.)

"Using the IFA Program & Bonds to Finance District Contractors"
Patricia Rodríguez, Southwestern Capital Markets
& Enrique Alemán, TEA

"Early Childhood: First Steps Toward Excellence"
Connie Rocha, San Antonio ISD

"*Bienestar* School-based Diabetes Prevention Program"
Dr. Robert P. Treviño, Social & Health Research Center

"To Improve Student Achievement, a Plan is a Must"
Dr. Leonard A. Valverde, Hispanic Border Leadership Institute

"The Population of Texas: Trends Affecting Education"
Dr. Steve H. Murdock, Texas A&M University

"Mentoring Affirmation Leadership Experience"
Daniel Bueno, City of Alice Chief of Police

"Debt Instruments Currently Available to School Districts"
Víctor Quiroga, Jr., SWS Securities

"School Administrators as Servant Leaders"
Linda Bononcini, Edgewood ISD

"Do We Truly Believe 'All Student Can Learn'?"
Dr. Shernaz B. García, The University of Texas at Austin
Dr. Patricia L. Guerra, SWEDL Lab

"AVANCE: Ensuring that No *Latino* Child is Left Behind"
Dr. Gloria G. Rodríguez, AVANCE

"Family Leadership Institute"
Consuelo Castillo Kickbusch, Educational Achievement Services

"*Latino* Education Coalition"
Anna Alicia Romero, IDRA

"Increasing Student Achievement"
Conrado García, Corpus Christi ISD

"Creating & Maintaining a *Mariachi* Program"
Yamil Yunes, Roma ISD

"Limited English Proficient Youth"
Dr. Alba Ortiz, The University of Texas at Austin

Entertainment
Mariachi Los Patricios, San Antonio Archdiocese

Special Sunday Service
Archbishop Patrick D. Flores, San Antonio

If you would like to share any photos, meeting minutes, conference programs, mementos, etc. from the second presidency of Santiago "Jimmie" Adame, for inclusion in Volume II, please email them to info@masbatx.org or mail them to MASBA | P.O. Box 474 | Austin, TX 78767.

Thank you for helping us to reconstruct our history!

"I Started to Help Get MASBA Off the Ground"

Tommy Molina

Back in the day, Duval County was a hotbed of politics, and politics ran in our family: My dad served on our local school board here in San Diego, then I joined the San Diego ISD Board of Trustees in 1990.

Beginning in 1995, I represented Education Service Center Region 2 on the TASB Board. I remained on that board through 2002, when TASB first started serving all school districts in Texas. I also served on TASB's Risk Management Board from 1996 to 2002. I couldn't run for reelection here in San Diego, and that killed my participation in TASB. That's when I got more involved in MASBA.

After I finished my service to TASB, I started to help get MASBA off the ground. We were in the process of reconstructing or reforming MASBA, which fell through the cracks in the 1980s. Back in the 1970s, they called it MASBMA: the Mexican American School Board Members Association. We decided to rebrand it as MASBA, to make it more sellable. When we tried to reorganize MASBA in the 1990s, we started off with social talk — "beer talk" — people getting together at TASB conferences, with people saying, "We need to get our Hispanic point of view across!" That became our emphasis.

During that time, I reconnected with Juan Aguilera of the Round Rock ISD Board of Trustees. Juan and I have been friends for a long time: I worked as a banker in San Antonio in the 1970s and 1980s, and, before he became an attorney, he sold Xerox® products. We became buddies back then. Then I served on the TASB Board, and he served on the Round Rock Board, so we tried to reorganize MASBA. Juan played a key role in getting MASBA reactivated and regaining our 501(c)(3) not-for-profit status, which had lapsed and faded away when no one paid attention to it. Once we got our non-profit status reestablished, that opened doors for us with respect to funding. Always supportive, Juan provided a lot of preliminary funding through his law firm, Escamilla & Poneck.

I remember when Albert Martínez became our MASBA President. We elected him by acclamation. He served for three years. I filled in as part-time Executive Director. I had opened a real estate office in

San Antonio, and Dr. José Cárdenas offered us office space at the IDRA offices in San Antonio.

We tried to promote MASBA from the angle of the Hispanic student population of Texas, and we called attention to our underrepresentation as school board members. Several Anglo trustees refused to get involved in MASBA. Some would say, "I can't join MASBA: I'm not a Mexican!"

I'd say, "Have you ever eaten a taco? That's close enough! You qualify to be a member!"

To promote membership, I would say, "You don't have to be Hispanic. If at least 20% of your students are Hispanic, you have to belong to MASBA!" That was my pitch. We had districts here in ESC Region 2 with 60 to 80% Hispanic students, but with no Hispanic representation on their boards. That never made sense to me.

Our underrepresentation as Hispanics always concerned me. We've always been under-represented. When I served on the San Diego ISD Board, the Texas student population became majority Hispanic, but Hispanics were not even close to being 50% of school board members in Texas. Our people just don't want to get involved. Even the TASB Board had only two or three Hispanic directors. TASB told me that they don't track the ethnic composition of school board members. I said, "That doesn't make sense. You keep track of all sorts of data for school districts, and you track the ethnicity of our kids, but you can't track the ethnicity of school board members?" So, I received some funding from TASB to promote Hispanic representation in Texas. As a result of that focus, we grew our representation on the TASB Board to some 12 Hispanic directors.

Underrepresentation motivated Dr. José Cárdenas and others to become politically involved in the 1970s: Our state representatives and senators didn't reflect the demographics of our state! I'm not so gung ho on being identified as "Hispanic" or "Mexican American," but Hispanics are underrepresented at all levels of government.

Back when I assisted MASBA, Dr. Manuel Flores, a professor of art at Texas A&M Kingsville, held a student contest to design our MASBA logo. He came from Hebbronville, and we've known one another since high school.

Dr. Viola García served on our Board, too, as did Dr. Robert Sepúlveda, a cardiologist in Weslaco. He served on our TASB Board and also as our MASBA President for one year. Carlos Nieto from

Presidio ISD supported our efforts as President of TASB. We had a good working relationship with TASB, and they helped us out quite a bit. They funded us both with in-kind and cash donations. We scrounged for money, always trying to borrow money from somebody. TASB provided the logistical support for some of our early conferences, and we always wondered whether we might get *un poquito* [a little] from what TASB charged school districts. We never got very far with that idea back in my day.

We tried to involve MASBA in different issues around our Texas public schools. I remember advocating for equitable funding of our Texas public schools. When Cárdenas served the Edgewood ISD in the 1970s, they started calling for equity in school financing. He literally wrote the book on school finance. We have a lopsided system of school finance here in Texas: The state legislature set the maximum of what we can charge in property taxes, but they don't look at the other side of the equation. We have poor counties and school districts that, even if they charged the maximum tax rate allowed by law, still couldn't generate enough money to run their schools! So the state started pitching in. I used to say, "85% of our students will graduate and never come back to San Diego, so it's to everyone's advantage that we invest in their education. They're going to be *your* employees. *You* want them to have a quality education!" When I served on the TASB Board, many people blatantly opposed the funding of minority school districts and were against Robin Hood.

Juan Aguilera, Albert Martínez and I wanted to have an award, so we came up with the Golden *Molcajete* Award. We joked at first—but then we looked at what it symbolizes: The *molcajete* (a stone tool to grind corn) has two parts—the base and the *piedra* (the stone)—which work together. So, for us, the *molcajete* symbolized collaboration.

I tried to get TASB and its executive director, Dr. Billy Williams, and later James Crow, to support MASBA. I left MASBA in 2005, with that as my main accomplishment.

Tommy Molina served on the Board of Trustees of the San Diego Independent School District and on the Board of Directors of the Texas Association of School Boards. In 2000, he co-facilitated a meeting of school board members interested in resurrecting MASBA, and he served as MASBA Executive Director in 2003 to 2005.

"MASBA Has Done a Lot of Good"

Vickie De La Rosa

Beginning in 1970, I worked in public school education for 37 years, then at the university level—at Texas Lutheran University—for five years. I taught math, physics and computer science at the secondary level and moved up the ranks: to campus administration, then to the central office administration. I worked in an early childhood literacy program and served as a coordinator, then as a director, then finally as assistant superintendent of instructional technology—all those years with the Seguin ISD. I have a passion for making sure that all children learn, and I worked very closely with the members of our Seguin ISD Board of Trustees. I learned that most board members are not educators, but most of them have a big heart for kids!

When I started with the Seguin ISD, Hispanics rarely had a voice in the district. When MASBA started to reorganize in the late 1990s, my superintendent invited me to accompany our Hispanic board members to MASBA meetings. One superintendent, Dee Carter, really opened the door to MASBA in the Seguin ISD. As a result, I had good relationships with MASBA board members. I remember attending MASBA's second conference in 2000. The nucleus of Hispanic leaders who gathered for those early encounters impressed me.

Initially, the community really didn't want to give credence to MASBA. People asked, "Why do you need MASBA if you have TASB?" MASBA focused on specific issues, like ensuring our students learned the correct history of our Hispanic community. In Seguin, we'd fight all the time to make sure our kids learned about Juan Nepomuceno Seguín and others.

Many people with many agendas gathered at those early MASBA conferences. In Seguin, for instance, we wanted to have single-member districts. We could have said, "You need to fight with us! We need this!" MASBA didn't get involved in local politics. School board members needed to tackle local issues themselves. MASBA didn't come in and fight our battles, but it provided support to school board members with big hearts, who may not have been too familiar with education issues.

As we continued to raise the bar in education, we talked about high-stakes testing, how the state graded us and our students, and the large number of students who didn't meet grade level. We found ourselves *en un laborinto* [a labyrinth]: *Vas por esta puerta, y vas por allá* [you go in all sorts of directions], and at the end of the day, *puro lonche de lengua*—all you do is talk! The federal government investigated Texas for not allowing the full implementation of instruction for special education students: The state told us we could only identify a certain percent of special education students, so students missed out on services, and it took the federal government 15 years to catch it! I truly honor the people who, from the beginning, organized around these issues. MASBA took up the issues that impacted all students in Texas, and MASBA did a lot to close achievement gaps. I enjoyed attending MASBA's workshops on issues like that.

I'm also into the cultural arts, and I know how artistic and gifted our students are—but back then, we realized that our kids didn't know their own culture. They didn't know their ancestors. We recognized our responsibility to teach our kids about our culture.

In Seguin, I worked with my husband and my sister—who's a bilingual teacher—to begin *Teatro de Artes de Juan Seguín*. We worked with parents, and we got their kids involved in *baile folklórico* and *mariachi*. We also started a *conjunto* program, which MASBA highlighted for years. We got the parents involved in the school system and advocating for their kids.

At first, our district didn't want to do *mariachi*, so we began our own *mariachi* for the kids in the community. It took Seguin ISD decades to institutionalize *mariachi* in the school system. We worked hand-in-hand with our local school board members, and our kids performed multiple times at MASBA conferences. Together, we worked with our Hispanic school board members throughout the state to showcase our kids. Even though the majority of our kids in Texas are Hispanic, the Anglos who ran our schools didn't always see the value in our culture. We had to build bridges, and that's what MASBA did: MASBA built bridges all those years.

I fondly remember the big hearts these individuals had and how they uplifted and showcased our kids. Despite their learning curves as trustees and administrators, they gave up their time for a task with a big time commitment and a steep learning curve. They wanted to make a difference for the kids they served. I don't remember meeting a bad person at MASBA — anyone who didn't have our kids in mind.

I also fondly remember how MASBA brought together Hispanic school board members and administrators from throughout the state. We came from towns and school districts with mostly-White leadership, so when we went to MASBA conferences, we gathered and networked with people from other communities that lacked representation. We could "learn the ropes" from those who had been in the fight for a while. MASBA gave us a perspective beyond our districts and regions. For the first time, we saw ourselves as a statewide group. We came from Brownsville and La Joya and McAllen — from the *Río Grande* Valley and the border towns. We came from Austin and Round Rock and Dallas. We even came from racist towns like New Braunfels. *Empezamos a brotar en pueblos y en escuelas* [we began to spring up in towns and schools] where you didn't think we would be.

As a Hispanic educator, I wanted to see MASBA thrive and become a force on issues like the inequities that persisted in our districts. Many of us who gathered for MASBA events experienced racism and inequities. I lived under the umbrella of racism in Crystal City, where I attended high school. Fortunately, I navigated it and graduated and moved on to a two-year college in Uvalde, an instrumental institution for many Hispanics in our community who didn't have the funds for four-year colleges.

I wanted to be a cheerleader in Crystal City, but the school had a quota of one Hispanic cheerleader. That's why the walkouts started in the school system after I left: Hispanic students realized they were the majority and that, if they voted together, they could win on various issues. It started with a simple issue: Each year, we voted on the most handsome gentleman and the most beautiful lady of the senior class, and a Mexican won! The administration decided not to take that vote into consideration. Instead, they sent the pictures of the top contenders to a movie star, Troy Donahue, for his selection of the most handsome gentleman and the most beautiful lady. He, of course, selected a White guy and a White girl, and we revolted as a student body! After I graduated, issues like that motivated José Ángel Gutiérrez and others to organize. We knew those things weren't right. Those things incited us to continue the fight to make things better.

My husband, Homer, grew up next door to José Ángel. In fact, José Ángel's dad was the doctor in Crystal City, and he delivered Homer! Homer attended the Airport School—the old barracks that used to be the Japanese internment camp in Crystal City.

MASBA always worked to level the playing field and to make a big difference on issues like discrimination. I remember studying physics at Southwest Texas State University, facing the dual dagger of being a Hispanic and a woman trying to trailblaze in math and physics and computer science. Many of my colleagues—mostly White men—didn't accept me, despite my qualifications, choosing instead to hire other White people.

As MASBA celebrates 50 years, I commend all the leaders of this organization for all they did through the years. It's been difficult for MASBA, but MASBA has done a lot of good.

I want to see this organization continue to focus its work and advocacy on *all* children. Let's close the achievement gap and ensure that proper educational practices are put in place. Who are the most important players in the achievement of our students? Our teachers! Let's ensure that they have smaller student-teacher ratios, so that they can better personalize the learning for our students. *Hay que seguir adelante, ayudándole a cada estudiante individualmente y poniendo en efecto las practicas que nosotros sabemos que son las mejores para que los niños aprendan.* We need to empower them to implement best practices, and we need to continue the fight!

Vickie De La Rosa is a retired educator who served the Seguin ISD for 37 years. She attended the annual MASBA conference for many years and enjoys fond memories of the relationships she built with many MASBA members.

MASBA Membership 2001-2004

Extant records contain the following membership information for school year 2001-2002 to school year 2003-2004. Based on their size, member districts paid $500, $750 or $1,000 per year.

Aldine ISD	2001-2004
Anthony ISD	2001-2003
Austin ISD	2001-2003
Ben Bolt-Palito Blanco ISD	2001-2003
Brownwood ISD	2001-2002
Carrizo Springs ISD	2001-2002
Cuero ISD	2003-2004
Dallas ISD	2002-2003
Dilley ISD	2001-2003
Eagle Pass ISD	2002-2003
Edcouch-Elsa ISD	2002-2003
Edgewood ISD	2001-2003
Fort Bend ISD	2001-2002
Fort Worth ISD	2003-2004
Harlandale ISD	2002-2004
Hays CISD	2002-2004
Hidalgo ISD	2002-2003
Ingleside ISD	2001-2002
IRRA Charter Schools, Inc.	2001-2002
Jim Hogg County ISD	2001-2002
La Joya ISD	2002-2003
Laredo ISD	2002-2003
Lockhart ISD	2003-2004
Mathis ISD	2002-2003
Mercedes ISD	2002-2003
Mission CISD	2002-2003
New Deal ISD	2001-2002
Palacios ISD	2001-2002

Pharr-San Juan-Alamo ISD	2001-2003
Port Arthur ISD	2003-2004
Poteet ISD	2002-2003
Progreso ISD	2002-2004
Region 1 Education Service Center	2002-2004
Region 19 Education Service Center	2001-2003
Ricardo ISD	2001-2002
Roma ISD	2002-2004
Round Rock ISD	2001-2003
Sabinal ISD	2001-2002
San Antonio ISD	2002-2003
San Benito CISD	2001-2002
San Diego ISD	2001-2003
San Elizario ISD	2001-2004
San Perlita ISD	2003-2004
Seguin ISD	2001-2004
Slaton ISD	2001-2003
Somerset ISD	2001-2004
South Texas ISD	2001-2004
Southwest ISD	2001-2004
Taft ISD	2001-2004
Tuloso Midway ISD	2002-2004
United ISD	2002-2004
Uvalde CISD	2001-2003
Valley View ISD (Hidalgo County)	2001-2002, 2003-2004
Weatherford ISD	2001-2004
Weslaco ISD	2001-2002
West Oso ISD	2003-2004
Ysleta ISD	2001-2003
Zapata County ISD	2002-2003

Individual members paid $150 each for dues.
Individual members included the following:

Irene Bustamante, Big Spring ISD	2002-2004
Geno Chavarría, Elgin ISD	2002-2003
Dr. Jesús Chávez, Corpus Christi ISD	2002-2003
Lupe De Hoyos, San Felipe-Del Río CISD	2002-2003
Dr. Manuel Flores, Corpus Christi ISD	2002-2003
Lionel A. García, Plainview ISD	2002-2003
Dr. J. Francisco Hidalgo, NALEO	2002-2003
Amanda Martínez, Brownwood ISD	2002-2003
Sal Mena, Jr., El Paso ISD	2002-2003
Eloy Rodríguez, Beeville ISD	2002-2003
Lucy Rubio, Corpus Christi ISD	2002-2003
Nicole Sada, Lockhart ISD	2002-2003
Carmen Zúñiga, Northside ISD	2002-2003
(Unnamed trustee), Devine ISD	2003-2004

"We Were Totally a Volunteer Organization"

Dr. Viola García

I joined the Aldine ISD Board of Trustees in 1992. I began my relationship with MASBA before 2000. I first became involved in MASBA through Juan Aguilera and Tommy Molina. We went to TASB's annual conference and summer leadership institute, and they hosted brief, informal information meetings. I joined the informal get-togethers right away, and became involved in organizing more formally.

I was elected a Director of MASBA when Albert Martinez served as President in 2000. We really struggled during the years I served on the MASBA Board. We created our bylaws, and we tried to organize ourselves and make ourselves known. We had no hired staff and no money to pay anyone. We were totally a volunteer organization. We served in our local districts and at the state level with MASBA. We tried to meet four times a year, all on our own dime. We had very few sponsors, but Escamilla & Poneck and IDRA provided us locations where we could meet. We hosted our conferences with much good will from a lot of wonderful people. A lot of hard work, with many very good people working in the background to support us made this possible.

Dr. Ricardo Romo, President of the University of Texas at San Antonio (UTSA) and a great collaborator, sponsored us. We hosted our MASBA meetings at UTSA's downtown campus. Juan Aguilera and the San Antonio office of his firm, Escamilla & Poneck, also supported our efforts. Juan and his firm likely facilitated our partnership with UTSA. Very committed to helping us, President Romo provided us free use of their facilities. We held our events on weekends, with access to auditorium and meeting room spaces. This fabulous partnership saved us from the expenses of a conference hotel and meeting rooms. It made a very big difference. Of course, Dr. Romo welcomed us, and he provided us university staff and students, to assist us and to get us from place to place.

Our conferences resembled those that MASBA continues to hold today. Some of the issues back then, are still issues today. Concerned for English Language Learners, we hosted sessions on bilingual education and ESL instruction. The Intercultural Development Research Association (IDRA) partnered with us and provided foundational research on best practices. They were also strong in parent development and parental engagement. Many of IDRA's sessions dealt with important aspects of our work as trustees. We recognized back then that the most important partners in our districts are our parents, who are the first teachers of our kids. IDRA helped us understand how to better communicate with parents, to talk about the very important role they play in supporting their children and our schools. Those topics back then remain pertinent today: We're still trying to engage parents, we're still challenged to recruit bilingual staff, and we're still trying to implement bilingual programs in our schools. We also collaborated with the Texas *Latino* Education Coalition (TLEC).

MASBA energized me. The organization really inspired me to continue to work at the state and national levels. During my work with MASBA, I became involved with the Texas Association of School Boards (TASB). I served as a director for TASB for a number of years and eventually became its President. As a TASB officer, I participated in activities of the National School Boards Association, including their annual delegate assembly. I became more aware of issues at the national level, and saw that we're not so different across the U.S.: We struggle to support special needs kids, bilingual students, and kids who don't have medical coverage and wraparound services. Our MASBA members know these challenges.

I hold special memories of various trustees involved in MASBA. My husband, Jorge, and I are from Ben Bolt, which is a very short distance from San Diego, so we felt an immediate connection with Tommy Molina, a very dedicated school board member from San Diego ISD in South Texas. Together with Juan Aguilera, he pushed our organization forward. Tommy also served as a TASB director, so his connections in TASB opened up opportunities for MASBA, led to joint initiatives between MASBA and TASB, and helped pave the road for TASB's sponsorship of MASBA in 2016. The roots of that relationship, laid by people like Tommy Molina and Juan Aguilera, make me very proud to know them.

Manuel Rodríguez of the Houston ISD served as President of MASBA when we struggled without an executive director. In addition to serving as President, Manuel became the organizer of our annual conference. He retained some wonderful speakers for us. He really dedicated himself to elevating the professional level of speakers at our conferences and the quality of conference presentations.

On my living room shelf, I proudly display the Golden *Molcajete* Award that I received from MASBA. What a wonderful and creative award! It's absolutely the most endearing thing to me. It inspires me.

Over the years, through MASBA, I enjoyed getting to know people who work so hard in their communities. MASBA helped me to expand my network of support and friendship. I have appreciated getting to know so many wonderful people across our state, and now at the national level. We're doing hard work, and we're all here to support each other. There are many solid people working with MASBA now, to promote what's best for our kids!

Going forward, my hope is that MASBA might enjoy an even greater membership and that trustees throughout the state might realize that they can join MASBA. If you serve students of color, you need to belong to MASBA or the Black Caucus — and you don't need to be *Latino* or African American to be a members of our associations.

Our *Latino* students and English Language Learners — and those who serve them — need wide support. The need is great, and we cannot sit on the sidelines and think that it's someone else's challenge. Let's continue to learn the things we need to know, in order to better support those students in our districts. Twenty or thirty years from now, those of us who are currently board members will have gone on. Our students will be the workers and the leaders of our communities. We need to educate them to their highest ability, so that they can serve our communities in the most enlightened way they can. They are our future!

Dr. Viola García serves on the Board of Trustees of the Aldine Independent School District. She became an Interim MASBA Director in 2000, was elected to the MASBA Board in 2002, and served as MASBA President in 2003. A Past President of the Texas Association of School Boards, Viola currently serves as Secretary-Treasurer of the National School Boards Association.

The Presidency of Dr. Viola García

On January 19, 2003, prior to the start of the **annual MASBA Member Assembly** at the downtown campus of the University of Texas at San Antonio, MASBA President Jimmie Adame (Taft ISD) announced that his tenure as President had come to an end. He handed over the gavel to Dr. Viola García (Aldine ISD), who presided over the Member Assembly. The agenda of the Member Assembly included the following:

- Call to Order, by President Dr. Viola García
- Approval of Minutes from the 2002 Member Assembly – Aguie Peña
- Treasury Report – Juan Martínez. The organization's bank account contained $11,866.09.
- Report from the Nominations Committee. The following MASBA Officers were elected: President Elect Óscar O. García (Ben Bolt-Palito Blanco ISD), Vice President Raúl "Roy" Navarro (Pharr-San Juan-Alamo ISD), Secretary Norma Osuna (Slaton ISD), and Treasurer Juan Martínez (Southwest ISD).
- Report from the Bylaws Committee. Chair Óscar O. García presented bylaws draft #6 for approval, which were approved as amended, with voting rights granted to the directors of member education service centers.
- Nominations for the MASBA Board of Directors. Óscar O. García noted that some MASBA Directors hadn't been active during the past year. The following Directors were elected:
  - Dr. Manuel Flores, Corpus Christi ISD (exp. Jan. 2006)
  - Juan Alvarado, Southwest ISD (exp. May 2003)
  - Brig Mireles, Round Rock ISD (exp. Jan. 2005)
  - Manuel Guajardo, Texas City ISD (exp. Jan. 2005)
  - Jesse Torres, Lamar CISD (exp. Jan. 2005)
  - Rose Herrera, Ft. Worth ISD (exp. Jan. 2005)
  - Rafael Anchía, Dallas ISD (exp. Jan. 2005)
  - Linda DeLeón, Lubbock ISD (exp. Jan. 2005)
  - Sally Flores, Anthony ISD (exp. Jan. 2005)
  - Carlos Caballero, Region 19 ESC (exp. Jan. 2006)

- Report on Standing Committees. The following people volunteered to serve on standing committees:
  - Program & Member Services: Rose Herrera, Fort Worth ISD, Chair; Dr. Manuel Flores, Corpus Christi ISD; Sally Flores, Anthony ISD
  - Membership & Recruitment: Arturo Guajardo, South Texas ISD, Chair; Héctor Del Toro, Tommy Molina
  - Funding, Budget & Finance: Juan Martínez, Southwest ISD, Chair; Miguel Caballero, Region 19 ESC
  - Nominations: Jimmie Adame, Taft ISD, Chair; Óscar O. García, President Elect; Dr. Viola García, President; Jesse Alcala, Edgewood ISD
  - Bylaws & Resolutions: Óscar O. García, Ben Bolt-Palito Blanco ISD, Chair; Jesús Calvillo, Edgewood ISD; Praxedis Guerra, San Diego ISD
  - Planning & Development: Ashley Barrera, San Diego ISD
- Report on Executive Staff. Juan Aguilera and Richard Garza were recognized as executive staff.
- Other Business
  - "It was stated that MASBA belonged to a coalition with other organizations, such as NALEO, MALDEF, LULAC, etc. It was stated that MASBA must continue to participate with these organizations, to be able to use these ties as a marketing tool."
  - MASBA will hold a reception at the TASB conference in Dallas.
  - All present thanked Richard Garza, who "did most of the legwork for the success of the conference." MASBA will recognize Daniel Escobar of San Antonio College for his hard work in setting up conference workshops and presentations.
  - MASBA has 45 member districts and 15 sponsors this year.
  - "A discussion ensued on the upcoming TAKS test. Members voiced that the test was unproven and being forced on the school districts, and they disagreed with its implementation. The members felt that MASBA should send a strong message to TEA, the legislature, and the governor of Texas on their disapproval of the test. After a long deliberation, the members agreed to submit a resolution on the issue." Dr. Manuel Flores moved that

MASBA file an injunction "to stop the implementation of an unproven TAKS test that experts predict will cause a 45% failure rate among students." The motion passed.
- o The next MASBA conference will be held on January 16-18, 2004 at the downtown campus of UTSA.

On February 14, 2003, President Dr. Viola García convened a **MASBA Update meeting** in Corpus Christi. Those present included: President Dr. Viola García, Tom Molina, Óscar García, Rose Herrera and Jimmie Adame. Meeting minutes provide the following glimpse into that encounter:

- Updates from Executive Director Tom Molina:
  - o Those in attendance reviewed 2002 & 2003 financial summary and a 2004 proposed budget; current net operating funds as of 1/27/2004 are $19,723.70
  - o Tom posted a note on his new role on the TASB leadership webpage; has received several responses from school trustees; some have indicated they will be joining MASBA
  - o Juan Aguilera will write a resolution to open a new bank account and transfer funds
  - o Richard Garza, CPA, from Alice, Texas will do MASBA's 2003 tax report *pro bono*
  - o MASBA Assistant Richard Garza resigned on February 9, will be attending school full-time, and will be available to assist on an as-needed basis
  - o 3-4 people from San Antonio & San Diego have offered to help with MASBA administrative tasks on a volunteer basis
  - o MASBA has received two open tickets from Southwest Airlines, valid through 2005
  - o MASBA has opened a new P.O. Box in San Antonio
  - o Tom has copies of all old bank statements
  - o Viola stated that MASBA will be mentioned in the upcoming issue of TASB's *Lone Star* magazine
- Discussions with IDRA
  - o Tom met with IDRA a couple of times
  - o IDRA may give MASBA some office space

- o IDRA is interested in hosting workshops with MASBA throughout Texas in 2004; they will pay for a mailing to all Texas school districts
- MASBA Website
  - o masbatx.org has been deactivated; masba.net will cost $700 for five years
  - o Gregorio Cortez of San Antonio offered to develop a new website for $7,750, minus $1,000 for placement of his banner on the website for 12 months; monthly maintenance fee will be $70-100; Óscar advised Tom to purchase the domain and accept the proposal; "others agreed, and Tom was given the go-ahead"
- MASBA Logo. Dr. Manuel Flores presented a draft logo by a student: "logo is circular, showing colors, flags, and emblems of U.S., Mexico and Texas, with wording around it"
- Resolution Submitted to LULAC. "Cruz Hinojosa from Galena Park ISD has submitted MASBA's resolution on Mexican Americans in history books to LULAC District 8 Board of Directors, for their support. Directors accepted resolution, and he would be submitting it to national council for their support."
- Position Statement from Linda DeLeón. "Mrs. DeLeón submitted a position letter addressed to the State Board of Education for consideration. The letter addresses the SBEC's rule to permit school districts to hire under-prepared and untrained individuals as classroom teachers for high schools. The letter asks the SBOE to stand with MASBA in rejecting the rule."
- Celebrating Educational Opportunities for Hispanic Students Conference in San Diego, California. Jimmie and Rose will represent MASBA.
- Openings on the MASBA Board
  - o "Diana Maldonado could not accept her position"
  - o "Rafael Anchía of Dallas ISD will become state representative and can no longer serve on his board"

On February 22, 2003, President Dr. Viola García convened a two-hour **MASBA Planning Meeting** at the Warwick Hotel in Houston. The meeting followed the conclusion of a NALEO conference there. The minutes state that "approximately 20 people participate[d], including visiting board members from California." Meeting minutes report the following:

- Feedback on the January MASBA Conference. The Member Assembly should be moved to Saturday afternoon; MASBA Officers should sit together during the Member Assembly and distribute the agenda in advance.
- Financial Report. Treasurer Juan Martínez reported that the organization possessed $12,295.13, with three accounts payable totaling $4,000; the only recurring expenses are Richard Garza's $2,000 monthly salary and "a small fee for maintaining the website."
- Membership. MASBA currently has 30 members.
- Standing Committees. Viola asked that the Bylaws & Resolutions Committee take on a legislative role and draft legislative procedures.
- MASBA Board Directors. Ishmael Flores of Seguin ISD and Lionel García of Plainview ISD were elected to the MASBA Board, with Lisa Hernández of El Campo ISD as an alternate, in the event that Flores can't serve.
- Legislative Resolutions
  o Vouchers. Viola recommended that MASBA take a stand on school vouchers. She presented a sample resolution by TASB, accepted by all present.
  o Advocacy. Tommy Molina shared a draft resolution stating, "MASBA members are elected school board trustees who represent the communities in which they are elected, supporting the needs of the students of their districts by actively seeking, by their involvement, the best means to achieve the best in public education for all students." Richard Garza noted that the *Latino* Education Coalition "had already issued its position on the issue."
  o Public School Funding. Tommy Molina shared a draft resolution on public school funding. "Some felt that MASBA should not take a position on it; others felt MASBA should. After a long debate, the attendees agreed

on the following position: 'MASBA will not support the removal of the Robin Hood plan without an equitable alternative funding solution. As an alternative, MASBA supports the implementation of a state income tax for public education funding.'"

○ <u>Bilingual Education</u>. Tommy Molina shared a draft resolution on bilingual education. "After some debate, the attendees agreed on the following position: 'MASBA supports the continued funding of bilingual education.'"

- <u>Upcoming Conferences</u>. MASBA will try to have a presence at the Celebrating Educational Opportunities for Hispanic Students Conference in Albuquerque in April, the Region 1 Conference on South Padre Island in May, the TASB Summer Leadership Institute in San Antonio in June, the TASB Conference in Dallas in September, and the NALEO meeting.
- <u>Other Information</u>. Norma Osuna shared information on the Texas Border Infrastructure Coalition.
- <u>Next Meeting</u>. The Board agreed to meet again on March 29, 2003 at the IDRA office in San Antonio.

There is no record of a MASBA Board meeting on March 29, 2003.

On April 13, 2003, the **MASBA Board** apparently met. An attendance sheet exists, with the following typed names in this order: Juan F. Aguilera, Richard A. Garza, S. Jimmie Adame, Viola García, Aguie Peña, Juan Martínez, Jr., Rose Herrera, Óscar García, Sally Flores, Manuel Guajardo, Jr., Tommy Molina, Anna Alicia Romero (IDRA).

On June 13, 2003, MASBA and IDRA co-published a **concept paper** for the creation of the Texas *Latino* School Board Network, a $190,000 three-year project to provide "(1) timely information on key issues in education; (2) leadership development; and (3) a sustained network of communication to support success for *Latino* school board members hoping to have a positive impact in the districts they serve." The paper sought funding for a project coordinator ($50,000), training ($19,000), database development ($55,000), communications ($35,000), educational materials ($18,000), and evaluation ($13,000). MASBA and IDRA committed $95,000 of in-kind resources for the project.

On June 20, 2003, MASBA hosted a **reception to honor Octaviano "Tony" González of the South Texas ISD Board of Trustees**, at Steers Steakhouse & Saloon in San Antonio. Southwest Securities and LaMarr Womack & Associates Architects co-sponsored the event. *Mariachi Los Caporales* provided the entertainment. An event program lists the following MASBA Board Officers and Directors:

- Dr. Viola García, Aldine ISD, President
- Roy Navarro, Pharr-San Juan-Alamo ISD, Vice President
- Norma Osuna, Slaton ISD, Secretary
- Juan Martínez, Jr., Southwest ISD, Treasurer
- S. Jimmie Adame, Taft ISD, Immediate Past President
- Manuel Flores, Corpus Christi ISD
- Arturo Guajardo, South Texas ISD
- Brig Mireles, Round Rock ISD
- Rudy Montoya, Austin ISD
- Manuel Guajardo, Texas City ISD
- Jesse Torres, Lamar CISD
- Rose Herrera, Fort Worth ISD
- Rafael Anchía, Dallas ISD
- Linda DeLeón, Lubbock ISD
- Lionel García, Plainview ISD
- Sally Flores, Anthony ISD
- Carlos Caballero, Region 19 ESC

On July 28, 2003, Richard Garza relayed to MASBA Officers and Directors a proposed **Memorandum of Understanding between MASBA and NALEO**. Each organization would recognize the other as a strategic partner on its website and would provide speaking opportunities for members of the other organization.

On July 31, 2003, President Dr. Viola García convened a **MASBA Board meeting** by conference call. Her notes from the meeting indicate that the following persons joined the call: Rafael Anchía, Tommy Molina, Richard Garza, Jimmie Adame, Sally Flores, Juan [likely Juan Martínez or Juan Aguilera], and Bea (whose last name is not listed). Her notes confirm that they discussed the proposed MOU between MASBA and NALEO, reviewed upcoming events of the National Education Leadership Initiative, and spoke of the MASBA

Board's next meeting, scheduled for September 19, 2003, at the Hyatt Regency Dallas Hotel. A MASBA Board directory circulated during the meeting indicates that Jesús Calvillo (Edgewood ISD) had now replaced Arturo Guajardo (South Texas ISD), that Ishmael Flores (Seguin ISD) now served on the Board, and that Rudy Montoya (Austin ISD) and Brig Mireles (Round Rock ISD) no longer served on the Board. The directory lists three "Advisors": "Mr. Tomás Molina, Former School Board Member; Mr. Carlos Nieto, Former TASB President; Mr. Arturo Guajardo, Superintendent of Pharr-San Juan-Alamo ISD and Board Member of South Texas ISD."

In early October, 2003, President Viola García, Jimmie Adame, Óscar García and Juan Aguilera exchanged emails suggesting they would see one another at the October 9-10, 2003 HBLI Seminar in San Antonio. Óscar noted the "need to track the follow-ups Richard is doing on new leads." Viola suggested the need "to discuss a management plan." They share their hope that IDRA will reimburse them for travel and accommodations—something that seemingly didn't happen for their April meeting in San Antonio. Viola's handwritten notes for that meeting include the following:

- $13,000 balance
- July $1,000, August $1,000, September $2,000
- Dallas: $6,100 - $3,221.74
- Richard (March '02)
  - Will receive payment today of $3,000
  - Outstanding bills?
  - Final invoice from Steers & Beers
  - Mileage reimbursement for TASB
  - Do you want to continue hourly pay up to $2,000?
    - Membership recruitment
    - Donors/sponsors
    - Website
    - January conference
    - MASBA files, banner, bags, pens to office
    - Letter of understanding

On December 18, 2003, President Elect Óscar García emailed Executive Committee members, to communicate the following:

- Juan Martínez did not wish to be re-nominated for Treasurer, but wished to remain on the MASBA Board; Ishmael Flores has agreed to serve as Treasurer.
- Jesús Calvillo has resigned from the Edgewood ISD Board of Trustees and is no longer eligible to serve on the MASBA Board.
- The following have agreed to be nominated at the January 18, 2004 Member Assembly:
  o President Elect Roy Navarro
  o Vice President Manuel Flores
  o Secretary Norma Osuna
  o Treasurer Ishmael Flores
  o Directors Jimmie Adame & Juan Martínez
  o Two positions on the Board remain unfilled, for ESC Regions 3, 13 & 15

On December 19, 2003, MASBA Director Rafael Anchía emailed the MASBA Board, to announce that he had filed for the March 2004 primary, to fill the seat vacated by State Representative Steve Wolens.

On January 12, 2003, Juan Aguilera emailed the Executive Committee, to inform them that Diana M. Maldonado (Round Rock ISD) shared her interest in serving on the MASBA Board.

On January 5, 2004, President Elect Óscar García emailed Executive Committee members, sharing the following:

- Santiago "Jimmie" Adame (Taft ISD) will be nominated to fill the seat of Dr. Manuel Flores, who will become an officer.
- Juan Martínez (Southwest ISD) will be nominated to replace Jesús Calvillo.
- Lionel García (Plainview ISD) will be nominated to represent his region.

On January 16-18, 2004, MASBA hosted its **sixth annual conference** at the downtown campus of the University of Texas at San Antonio. A list of 130 registrants exists for this event. A draft schedule for that conference shares the following details.

Keynotes

State Representative Scott Hochberg

State Representative René Oliveira

Albert Kauffman, Harvard University Civil Rights Project

Dr. Sheryl L. Santos, Dean of Education, Texas Tech University

"Texas Public School Finance Update"
by State Representative Mike Villarreal
& Wayne Pierce of The Equity Center

Breakout Sessions

"Dispute Resolutions"
Tomás F. Molina, San Diego ISD (Ret.)
& James R. Vásquez, Region 19 ESC

"Open-ended Discussions, and Trustees as Servant Leaders"
Pablo Escamilla, Escamilla & Poneck

"Legal Issues for School Districts"
Beverly Rickoff, Escamilla & Poneck

"Public Relations & Establishing Rapport with the Media"
Matt Flores, *San Antonio Express-News*
Carlos Guerra, *San Antonio Express-News*
Dr. Manuel Flores, Corpus Christi ISD

"Salary Study Implemented at Edgewood ISD"
Dr. Luis B. González, Our Lady of the Lake University
Mary Regan, TASB
Dr. John Walch, Edgewood ISD

"Creating a Chess Program"
Nida Ruth Soto, Brownsville ISD

"Distance Learning"
Emiliano Alaniz, Taft ISD

"Strengthening Students' Math Skills"
Dr. Jaime Chahín, Texas State University

"Border Literacy Initiative"
Dr. Francisco Hidalgo, Consultant
Dr. Stan Swartz, Foundation for Comprehensive Literacy Learning

"Establishing a Fine Arts Program"
Sarita Salinas, Aldine ISD

"UTSA Office of K-16 Initiatives & Honors College"
Ricardo González, UTSA

"The 'Smart Ruler' to Help Mathematical Equations"
Max Peña, Corpus Christi ISD

"Creating a Successful Baseball Program"
Robert Zamora, South San Antonio ISD (Ret.)
Leopoldo Moncada, Eagle Pass ISD
Steve Castro, Robstown ISD

"Equitable School Finance"
Anna Alicia Romero, IDRA

Student Performances
Carroll High School Madrigal Singers, Corpus Christi ISD
Carver Performing Arts Company, Aldine ISD
Conjunto Juan Seguín, Seguin ISD
Crystal Deluccio & Priscilla Vargas, Edgewood ISD
Guadalupe Dance Academy, Guadalupe Cultural Arts Center
Mostly Mozart, Northeast ISD

Student Masters of Ceremonies
Amanda Cuevas & Priscilla Vargas, Edgewood ISD
Stephanie Barker, Ben Bolt-Palito Blanco ISD

On January 20, 2004, President Dr. Viola García presided over the opening of the **annual MASBA Member Assembly**. After welcoming all, introducing Officers, Directors and Past Presidents, and sharing a review of 2003, she handed the gavel to Incoming President Óscar García.

If you would like to share any photos, meeting minutes, conference programs, mementos, etc. from the presidency of Dr. Viola García, for inclusion in Volume II, please email them to info@masbatx.org or mail them to MASBA | P.O. Box 474 | Austin, TX 78767.

"MASBA Was Looking for Volunteers, so I Volunteered"

Óscar García

I'm originally from Palito Blanco, Texas, and I graduated from high school in the Ben Bolt-Palito Blanco ISD, which serves an area that is 99.9997% Hispanic. Most families have been here for at least a hundred years. *Todos son conocidos* [everyone is known to one another]. Many families descend from the pioneer families of Ben Bolt-Palito Blanco, so many of the people I see at H-E-B or Walmart went to the same high school. Obviously, our entire school board was Hispanic.

We didn't experience discrimination in Ben Bolt-Palito Blanco. *Somos todos raza.* We were all Hispanic here, from the *ranchos* or living on dairy farms. I grew up speaking Spanish because *a la comenzada*, before I went to elementary school, my parents and siblings spoke Spanish at home. When I went to kindergarten and first grade, I picked up English. So, yes, I'm bilingual.

My wife and I moved our family around a bit, but in 1995, we moved back to Palito Blanco, where I grew up. My children were in middle school, so I became involved with the school district. I always wanted to serve the community on the school board. I'm very active with a church in Palito Blanco, but I always intended to run for a school board position here. I did so in 1997 and served for 12 years.

Once I got on the school board, I started to attend TASB's leadership conferences in San Antonio. I saw on one agenda a meeting of the Mexican American School Board Members Association. Curious, I decided to attend. I met Juan Aguilera and Jimmie Adame and others. Every time I went to a TASB conference after that, I made it a point to attend MASBA gatherings. That's how I learned more about MASBA.

MASBA was looking for volunteers, so I volunteered at one meeting: I took on the responsibility of helping with the bylaws. Someone gave me a copy of TASB's bylaws as a template, and I literally sat down and typed the very first draft of the bylaws of our organization. After several meetings, we finalized and approved them. I'm sure they been modified many times since, but that's how our MASBA bylaws came to be.

The leaders in MASBA included Tommy Molina and Albert Martínez of the San Diego ISD, Viola García of Aldine ISD, and Jimmie Adame of Taft ISD. Juan Aguilera, a former school board member now living in San Antonio, served as our part-time executive director. Juan had a big heart for school board activity and for students.

Albert is still around. A good man and always *bien tipo*—always well-dressed, well-groomed and looking good—he cared about the Hispanic communities and school districts in this area.

A tall man—probably 6'3" or 6'4"—and *bien chicano*, very Hispanic, Tommy had a big heart for Hispanic students, and he tried his best to keep the organization alive and lead it. Once he left his school board, he became our part-time executive director. In fact, he held this position when I served as President. I laugh when I think about it: How do you appraise a part-time person who's giving up his free time to work for you, for no pay?

Viola is a distant cousin of mine: Our grandmothers were sisters. She's a brilliant lady. I remember her loyalty and her dedication to Hispanic students. A major school district in the Houston area, the Aldine ISD shared its resources with MASBA—like presentations and student performances at our conferences.

Always very dedicated and loyal, Jimmie dressed sharply and spoke eloquently. He helped us through, despite our financial struggles.

We struggled because we didn't have any money. That's the bottom line. Our members were very loyal and dedicated to the organization, but we never had more than 30 member districts, so we struggled financially.

After I got involved and started to understand the people and objectives of the organization, I started attending MASBA's annual conference each January or February. We had a two-and-a-half-day conference, with musical performances by students.

I introduced MASBA to our local school board, and I started taking my colleagues to the conference and introducing them to MASBA. One of my fellow board members, Danny Bueno—I always confuse him with his twin brother, David—became President of MASBA as well. Danny used to be the police chief, so we called him "Chief," but now he's the sheriff, so everyone calls him *el Sherife*.

Beginning in 2004, I served as President of MASBA for over a year. I followed Viola, and I expected to be president for one year. Roy Navarro from Pharr-San Juan-Alamo School District planned to be my successor, but we got word on the Friday before our conference that he would not be present. We were left scrambling. In the end, we decided that I would announce that I would continue to serve as president. By default, I became my own successor! At that conference, we elected a new vice president and a new president elect, and Manuel Flores of Corpus Christi ISD succeeded me in March 2005.

From my later years in MASBA, I remember Joe Muñoz from Austin, Josh Cerna from Harlandale, Gloria Casas from the Valley, and Irene Galán from West Texas. Of course, Louis Reyes of Seguin ISD assisted us, bringing us the perspective of an old-time activist of the *Raza Unida* Party who helped with voting registration in Crystal City. Juan Rangel of Fort Worth represented North Texas at our meetings, balancing the rest of us from the *ranchos* of the Valley.

MASBA partnered with other organizations, like TASB and NALEO. I served on the NALEO Board for two years. My sister, U.S. Congresswoman Sylvia García, who currently serves on the Judicial Committee, nominated me to serve along with her on the NALEO Board. We attended the National Leadership Institute, and many of us from MASBA attended those conferences as well.

In 2009, after twelve years of service on my local board, I began to miss meetings because my job required me to travel all the time, even overseas. So, one day, after two strong cups of coffee, I wrote an email and hit "send," and my board service immediately ended — as did my relationship with MASBA at that time.

As MASBA celebrates 50 years, my wish is for it to continue to grow and serve the needs not only of Hispanic students, but of all students. MASBA has always been for *all* students!

Óscar García served on the Ben Bolt-Palito Blanco Board of Trustees for 12 years, beginning in 1997. He joined the MASBA Board in 2002 and became President Elect in 2003. Óscar served as MASBA President in 2004 and remained on the MASBA Board through 2006. He is remembered for his role in writing and refining MASBA's bylaws.

The Presidency of Óscar García

On January 17, 2004, President Viola García presided over the opening of the **annual MASBA Member Assembly**. After welcoming all, introducing Officers, Directors and Past Presidents, and sharing a review of 2003, she handed the gavel to Incoming President Óscar García. The remainder of the meeting, under Óscar's leadership, consisted of the following:

- Approval of Minutes of 2003 Member Assembly – Secretary Norma Osuna
- Treasurer's Report – Treasurer Juan Martínez
- Report from the Nominations Committee – Jimmie Adame
  - o Nominations for 2004 Officers
  - o Nominations for Board Members
- Report from Resolutions & Bylaws Committee – President Óscar García
  - o Presentation of resolutions for adoption
- Report from Membership Committee – Arturo Guajardo
  - o Membership drives
- Report from Funding, Budget & Finance Committee – Treasurer Juan Martínez & President Óscar García
  - o Tax-exempt status
  - o Funding drive & corporate sponsorships
- Report from Planning & Development Committee - President Óscar García
  - o Alliances with IDRA, NALEO & *Latino* Education Coalition
  - o 2004 Calendar of Events
- Report from Executive Director – Juan Aguilera
- Recognition of Richard Garza – President Óscar García
- Introduction of New Assistant – President Óscar García
- Other Reports & Business – President Óscar García

The minutes from this meeting are skeletal. 31 member districts comprised MASBA, which possessed $22,293.60 in its account. The organization achieved tax-exempt status and named Tommy Molina, Tomás "Tommy" F. Molina its "official recruiter." The Member Assembly adopted the following resolution, drafted by Dr. Manuel Flores:

> Be it resolved that the Mexican American School Boards Association of Texas supports a resolution that would make the teaching of the contributions of the Hispanics — to include Mexicans, *Tejanos* and Spanish settlers — to the development of Texas and the United States a requirement for all Texas history textbooks, from elementary to middle school and high school. It is our belief that enough research has now been done to include pertinent passages of the contributions of the Hispanics to our state and our nation. It is also our resolve to lobby the state legislature and the Texas State Board of Education to pursue this project with utmost urgency, so that future textbooks will reflect the truth about our culture, our people, and our contributions to the development of Texas and the American Dream. Be it further resolved that this organization will do anything possible to help any state agency or organization, including the Texas Association of School Boards, if it so desires to assist us in this matter, to make the teaching of the contributions of Hispanics to the development of Texas and the United States.

On May 3, 2004, Francisco Hidalgo of the Hispanic Border Leadership Institute emailed Tommy Molina, Óscar García and Juan Aguilera a reply to previous questions concerning a sponsorship request of State Farm Insurance for a yearlong contract for the professional development of teachers in at least ten schools, with a funding commitment of $10,000 to $20,000 for MASBA. The funding request would be made by MASBA and CELL (Comprehensive Early Literacy Learning), a for-profit organization, where MASBA, as the not-for-profit organization, would receive the monies for the initiative and contract with CELL for the provision of services. Francisco had previously provided a draft of the funding request in March 2004.

On June 11, 2004, President Óscar García convened a two-hour **MASBA Board meeting** in San Antonio. The agenda for the meeting included:

- Roll Call. Those present included: Óscar García, Tommy Molina, Juan Martínez, Jimmie Adame, Leonel García, Sally Flores, Roy Navarro, Manuel Flores, Ishmael Flores, Viola García, Arturo Guajardo & Juan Aguilera. Those absent included: Joe Hernández, Manuel Guajardo, Jesse Torres, Linda DeLeón, David Sublasky, Norma Osuna, Carlos Nieto & Rose Herrera. Guests included Joe Muñoz (Hays CISD), Gregorio Cortez (AMGtech) & Víctor Quiroga (SW Securities).
- Financial Report (Tommy Molina & Ishmael Flores). $11,256.52 is the projected balance, after bills. An extension has been filed for 2003 income tax report.
- Status of Budget (Tommy) MASBA's goal is to have $25,000 in its account by 2005. Tommy has applied for an SBC grant to pay for website construction. IDRA has applied for a grant on MASBA's behalf.
- Status of Membership & Fees (Tommy Molina). 40 districts are members.
- Status of June Reception at SLI (Tommy Molina). Víctor Quiroga presented the Board a $5,000 check for this evening's reception.
- Review of South Padre Conference & Reception (Tommy Molina & Óscar García). MASBA and Escamilla & Poneck presented on "Employment Laws Facing School Districts."
- Discussion on Proposal from ICON for School Board Workshop in 2004 (Tommy Molina & Óscar García). ICON has offered to sponsor a cruise ship for MASBA to host training sessions for trustees. Tommy will develop the idea, and Juan will research legal issues.
- Review & Action on Proposal from Border Literacy Initiative (Tommy Molina & Óscar García). Tommy and Juan reviewed the proposal by Dr. Francisco Hidalgo of the Border Literacy Initiative and recommended that MASBA not accept it.
- Review & Action on Proposal to Partner with Association of Hispanic Municipal Officials (AHMO) (Tommy Molina & Óscar García). Arturo Guajardo has recommended this organization. Tommy will follow up.

- <u>Review & Action on Resolution on Hispanics on TEA Executive Staff</u> (Tommy Molina & Óscar García). Tommy will draft a resolution on the lack of Hispanics on TEA Executive Staff, for possible Board approval.
- <u>Status of Resolution for LULAC</u> (Tommy Molina, Óscar García & Cruz Hinojosa). Cruz has submitted MASBA's resolution on the contributions of Hispanics to LULAC.
- <u>Review & Action on MASBA Logo</u> (Tommy Molina, Óscar García & Manuel Flores). MASBA's new logo is on the website and materials, though it hasn't been officially approved by the Board. The Board approved the new logo, shown below, which fades in color from red to white to green.

- <u>Status on MASBA.net Website</u> (Tommy Molina). Gregorio Cortez of AMGtech introduced MASBA's new website, which is ready for launch.
- <u>Status on MASBA Board Positions</u> (Óscar García). Joe Muñoz shared that Joe Hernández could no longer serve on the MASBA Board. Joe Muñoz (Hays CISD) and Andy Govea (Lockhart ISD) were elected to vacant positions. Cruz Hinojosa (Galena Park ISD) replaced Manuel Guajardo. Jesse Martínez (Fort Worth ISD) and Irene Bustamante (Big Spring ISD) were recommended for future Board service.
- <u>Discussion on Request from TASB President Elect Robert Sepúlveda for 2005 Celebrating Educational Opportunities for Hispanic Students Conference</u> (Tommy Molina & Óscar García). Robert has asked that MASBA be "very involved and visible" at the Celebrating Educational Opportunities for Hispanic Students conference in San Antonio on March 3-6, 2005. MASBA will share a presentation and host a reception.
- <u>Preparations for Dallas Conference & Reception</u>. Preparations are underway. Rafael Anchía and Rose Herrera have offered to help.

- Preparations for Annual Winter Conference in January 2005. The conference will be held at UTSA. The dates are not yet chosen.
- Other Items. Manuel Flores suggested that the 2006 MASBA Conference be hosted in Corpus Christi.
- Next Meeting. The MASBA Board will meet again at the TASBA Conference in September.

Later that evening, MASBA hosted a reception to honor 2004 NSBA President, Former TASB President & Harlingen CISD Trustee George McShan at *Casa Río* in San Antonio. According to the invitation, the event featured "*botana*, beverages, *mariachis*."

In September 2004, the **MASBA Board** met, according to the minutes of its January 7, 2005 meeting. The minutes of the January 7, 2005 meeting suggest that another conference call meeting followed the September meeting.

On January 7, 2005, President Óscar García convened a 90-minute **MASBA Board** meeting at the Radisson Hotel in San Antonio. Those present included: Óscar García Jimmie Adame, Juan Aguilera, Ishmael Flores, Manuel Flores, Sally Flores, Leonel García, Viola García, Andy Govea, Cruz Hinojosa, Albert Martínez, Juan Martínez, Tomás Molina, Joe Muñoz and David Sublasky. The agenda consisted of the following:

- The Board thanked Tomás Molina for his service to MASBA
- Those who participated in a recent conference call meeting agreed to move the 2006 MASBA conference to Corpus Christi.
- Treasurer Ishmael Flores shared a financial report as of October 1, 2004, and Tomás Molina shared an update on outstanding pledges.
- The Board discussed ICON's proposal to provide board member training on a cruise ship. The Board expressed concerns and decided to invite representatives of ICON to the Board's March meeting.
- Tomás Molina reported that the SBC denied MASBA's grant application.
- Óscar García stated that many website pages were incomplete or not operational. The contract with AMGtech will expire in

March. Óscar García, Manuel Flores, Cruz Hinojosa and Mónica Escobar volunteered to form a Website Committee. The Board then voted to contract with Mónica for three months of work on this project.

- The Board discussed the idea of charging for the MASBA conference. Manuel Flores suggested charging members a nominal fee. Óscar García suggested using the conference as a small "fundraiser" for the organization.
- MASBA & IDRA will co-present on parental involvement at the Celebrating Educational Opportunities for Hispanic Students Conference.
- Tomás Molina has participated in various TLEC events; TLEC plans to be active during the next legislative session.
- Óscar García stated that he will host the rest of the conference, in light of Roy Navarro's absence and inability to assume the MASBA Presidency. 2005 Officer nominations include: President Elect Manuel Flores, Vice President Jimmie Adame, Secretary Norma Osuna, and Treasurer Ishmael Flores.
- Óscar García proposed the following bylaws revisions for the Member Assembly the next day:
  o "MASBA regions" will be known as "MASBA districts."
  o Past Presidents will serve as at-large members of the MASBA Board, count toward quorum, and have the ability to vote.
  o The Executive Director will be evaluated on an annual basis.
- Óscar García reported that MASBA will create an online database for documenting continuing education credits.
- The Board considered two items in executive session: (1) discussion and action on continuation of employment of the executive director, and (2) discussion on the name of the organization.

On January 7-9, 2005, MASBA hosted its **seventh annual conference** at the downtown campus of the University of Texas at San Antonio. A draft schedule for that conference provides the following details.

Reception in honor of Dr. Viola García
& Congressman Ciro Rodríguez

Keynotes
"Texas *Latino* Education Coalition (TLEC):
Who We Are & What We Do Together" by IDRA

"2005 Legislative Review: What's Cookin' in Austin?"
Dr. Alberto Cortez & Anna Alicia Romero, IDRA

George McShan, Harlingen CISD, NSBA President

Breakout Sessions
"Accessing Higher Education"
TASB Past President Dr. Bonnie Lognion, Humble ISD
TASB President Dr. Roberto Sepúlveda, Weslaco ISD
Past MASBA President Dr. Viola García, Aldine ISD
Superintendent Dr. Guy Sconzo, Humble ISD

"Technology Solutions for Access, Action
& Accountability for At-risk Students"
Dr. Arturo Almendárez, Asst. Superintendent, Corpus Christi ISD
Dr. Katherine Conoly, Special Programs, Corpus Christi ISD

"New Arrivals: What To Do with Non-English-speaking Students"
Molly Tidwell, Elsa Hinojosa & Joe Muñoz, Hays CISD

"*Tejanos*: Pride, Passion & Culture"
Marcos Flores, Mathis ISD
Dr. Manuel Flores, Corpus Christi ISD

"*Latinos* and Sports: Academics & Beyond"
Andrew Borrego, Escamilla & Poneck;
Frank Hernández, Texas State University

"The Fair Funding Lawsuit: What Now?"
David Hinojosa, MALDEF

"Website, Technology & You"
Gregorio Cortez, AMGtech

"Model Parent Program"
Dr. Linda Rodríguez, Aldine ISD

Student Performances
Mariposas Fly, Performing Arts School, Aldine ISD
Ray High School Jazz Band, Corpus Christi ISD
San Diego ISD Choir
Seguin ISD *Conjunto*
Southwest ISD *Mariachi*

On January 8, 2005, President Óscar García convened the annual **MASBA Member Assembly** at the Radisson Hotel in San Antonio. Minutes from the Assembly reflect the following:

- Executive Director Tomás Molina will remain for one more year.
- The MASBA Board has approved hosting the 2006 conference in Corpus Christi.
- In light of the absence of President Elect Roy Navarro, Óscar will continue to host this conference, and the presidency will be transferred at a later date.
- Due to an emergency affecting Secretary Norma Osuna, no minutes were available from the 2004 Member Assembly.
- Óscar proposed the following persons for 2005 MASBA Officers: President Manuel Flores, Vice President Jimmie Adame, Treasurer Ishmael Flores, Secretary Norma Osuna. Jimmie "stated that he accepted the nomination for the sake of moving the organization forward, but that he did not want the members to get the impression that the same people would always serve as officers." Past President Albert Martínez shared the same concern and nominated William "Bill" Moreno for Vice President. Bill accepted, and Jimmie withdrew his name from consideration. The Member Assembly unanimously elected the slate of Officers.
- Óscar announced that, with a bylaws change later in the meeting, Past Presidents would have the right to vote on the MASBA Board. Past President Jimmie Adame withdrew his name from consideration for a Board position, and Louis Garza (Corpus Christi ISD) filled the vacancy. Lisa Hernández

(El Campo ISD) rounded out the slate of officers, unanimously elected by the Member Assembly:

- o Louis Garza, Corpus Christi ISD (exp. Jan. 2007)
- o Joe Muñoz, Hays CISD (exp. Jan. 2007)
- o Andy Govea, Lockhart ISD (exp. Jan. 2007)
- o Cruz Hinojosa, Galena Park ISD (exp. Jan. 2007)
- o Lisa Hernández, El Campo ISD (exp. Jan. 2008)
- o Juan Rangel, Fort Worth ISD (exp. Jan. 2008)
- o Jerome Garza, Dallas ISD (exp. Jan. 2008)
- o Sally Flores, Anthony ISD (exp. Jan. 2008)
- Treasurer Ishmael Flores shared a report on budget & finance.
- Executive Director Tomás Molina stated that MASBA currently has 40 member districts.
- Óscar and Tomás presented the following proposed bylaws revisions, which were unanimously approved:
  - o "MASBA regions" will be known as "MASBA districts."
  - o Past Presidents will serve as at-large members of the MASBA Board, count toward quorum, and have the ability to vote.
  - o The Executive Director will be evaluated on an annual basis.
- Executive Director Molina shared that MASBA will begin to document trustee training hours on the MASBA website.

On March 4, 2005, President Óscar García convened a meeting of the **MASBA Board** at the Hyatt Regency San Antonio Riverwalk Hotel in San Antonio. The following were present: President Óscar García, President Elect Manuel Flores, Vice President Bill Moreno, Directors Louis Garza, Cruz Hinojosa, Juan Martínez, Joe Muñoz & David Sublasky, and Past Presidents Jimmie Adame & Viola García. Minutes from the meeting reflect the following:

- "Óscar García reported that he had spoken with Roy Navarro right after our annual conference in January, and that Roy had asked for more time. Since then, Óscar had attempted to contact Roy several times but had not been able to reach him nor get his decision." The Board elected Manuel Flores as President, effective at the conclusion of the meeting, and asked Óscar to notify Roy of this by certified mail. The Board elected Bill Moreno President Elect.

- Óscar reported that Tomás Molina had resigned as Executive Director. The Board voted to name Juan Aguilera's daughter, Mari Carmen, as Interim Executive Director. Manuel will form a three-member search committee and prepare a recommendation for the Board's June meeting.
- Óscar shared a financial report on behalf of absent Treasurer Ishmael Flores. "At the time of the meeting, MASBA had 13 paid school district members....The account balance was not very healthy."
- "Since the organization did not have a healthy budget at this time, it was decided that MASBA provide a presentation, but would not host a reception" at the Region One School Board Conference. "The decision was later rescinded and modified to include the presentation and to host a reception, contingent on finding a sponsor."
- "It had been difficult to get [Board committees] organized and functioning."
- Óscar "reported that the MASBA website was in dire need of updating." Manuel will speak with a Texas A&M student about this need.
- The Board "decided to kindly decline the [ICON] offer" of board training on a cruise ship "because it would not look right in the eyes of constituents."

If you would like to share any photos, meeting minutes, conference programs, mementos, etc. from the presidency of Óscar García, for inclusion in Volume II, please email them to info@masbatx.org or mail them to MASBA | P.O. Box 474 | Austin, TX 78767.

Thank you for helping us to reconstruct our history!

108

"We Became an Extended Family of School Board Members"

Dr. Manuel Flores

I represented District 2 of the Corpus Christi ISD—a primarily poor district that had no representative on the school board for at least a year and a half. I had kids in school, so I did what any citizen would do: I went and asked the superintendent, "Why don't we have a representative?" I called the school board president, too. They both suggested that no one from District 2 qualified to be a school board member. I thought, "How ridiculous: I'm a college professor!" I decided to run for the school board. After that election, I served on the school board for 12 years, and as President for two of those years.

I first met Juan Aguilera when I attended a social he hosted for Mexican American school board members. Juan has been the lifeblood of MASBA, first as a school board member, then as a volunteer. He believed so deeply in MASBA, and his infectious passion impelled me to join MASBA the next year. I attended an organizational meeting and became involved as a member.

We didn't really have a clear agenda back then, other than to speak up for Mexican American school issues. From the very start, we felt we lacked representation at the state level, with the Texas Association of School Boards. Tomás Molina from the San Diego ISD became our liaison on the TASB Board, helping to legitimize MASBA.

Tomás also got us involved in making presentations at the annual state convention. Tomás asked me to do a presentation at a TASB conference on the history of Mexican Americans in Texas. I said, "Sure, I can do that!" They assigned me to a small room, which fit about 20 people, but then, a week before the conference, a staff member called to say they moved me to a bigger room because of the overwhelming response they had received for my presentation. They scheduled my presentation in an auditorium that seated 300 people. You could feel the electricity in the air of that packed auditorium. The majority of attendees were Mexican Americans, and, when I gave examples, they said, "That has happened to us, too!" With that presentation, we proved we had something valuable to offer to school board members. I felt grateful that so many people listened to our presentation on the needs of Mexican American children.

Tomás was always with us, and Albert Martínez from the San Diego board, too. Jimmie Adame from Taft ISD and Joe Muñoz from Hays CISD were also leaders back then. So we started to be more vocal and more political. Back then, just saying "Mexican American education" was a political act!

We focused on UIL acceptance of *mariachi* as an approved program. We met with the Texas Music Educators Association, the University Interscholastic League, and the State Board of Education, and all of us pushed for *mariachi* to be a UIL event. Everyone told us "no," and we knew it would be difficult.

One night, some of us attended a reception celebrating the ethnicities of Texas at the Hemisfair, and we heard a small, family *mariachi* group. We spoke with them after the event, and their daughter told us how her school did not allow a *mariachi* program, instead marking her absent for representing her school at *mariachi* events. She testified with us before the UIL Board, which marked the beginning of UIL acceptance of *mariachi* programs.

We had *mariachi* programs in the Valley and in San Antonio, but they weren't approved. Now, they are, and it all started with a resolution at our annual MASBA Member Assembly in Corpus Christi, which attracted 200 people from the Valley, San Antonio, Austin and Houston. Joe Muñoz and Juan Aguilera deserve the credit for pushing UIL recognition of *mariachi*, one of our greatest accomplishments.

We also became involved in the issue of Mexican American Studies. In 2004, professors from The University of Texas — our auxiliary MASBA members — started a movement to launch a Mexican American Studies curriculum. Dr. Emilio Zamora spearheaded it. In MASBA, we listened to his idea and created a counter-proposal, which we called the *Tejano* Heritage Project. Tomás Molina, Albert Martínez and I pushed for it and made presentations on *Tejano* history. I received permission to work with those UT professors to start a *Tejano* heritage curriculum — which has come to pass. Dr. Zamora and other professors took their Mexican American curriculum and our *Tejano* curriculum and came up with a course of study, which they presented to various publishers. At the same time, the *Tejano* Monument project started: Some wealthy Mexican-American ranchers and bankers decided that we needed a *Tejano* monument on the Texas State Capitol grounds!

Beginning in 2007 or 2008, MASBA advocated that *Tejano* studies be included in the curriculum of our public schools. In Mary Helen Berlanga, the only Mexican American on the State Board of Education, we found a real ally in this. We presented our ideas to her and supported her. She came to one of our conferences and made a passionate speech, saying, "I need your help to change the textbooks in Texas!" We responded, "We're with you!" Tomás Molina and Joe Muñoz testified, and all that led to us having more information in our children's textbooks about Mexican Americans and *Tejanos*.

With the leadership of Tomás Molina and Juan Aguilera, things just happened. Joe Muñoz helped to bring us together as family. He hosted annual socials and dances for us, to bring us together and build relationships with one another. Manuel Rodríguez from Houston also helped with that sense of family. In essence, MASBA became the extended family for Mexican American school board members, and we became an extended family of school board members from throughout Texas. When I went to Houston or to the Valley, I made a point to visit the school board members I knew from those places.

Under the leadership of Juan, Tomás and Joe, we became a "satellite" of TASB in many ways. Before then, some considered MASBA just a group of school board members of Mexican descent, who liked to have nice parties with *mariachis*. TASB leadership used to come to our parties, but, after that, they started coming to our conferences, too. The demographics of our Texas public schools were changing, Mexican Americans were quickly becoming the majority in our Texas public schools, and we were preparing TASB and the state of Texas for the future of Texas education. We sponsored speakers and forums that made us legit. We said, "We're going to be the majority of the students in our Texas public schools; you have to be ready for this, and we're here to help you!"

I served as Vice President of the organization when Roy Navarro, our President Elect, didn't attend the Member Assembly where he would assume the presidency. Somebody had to lead the meeting. Juan Aguilera told me, "You need to take over." So I stepped up. The next month, the MASBA Board asked me to serve as Acting President through the next Member Assembly. I was then elected President for a full term.

We also created MASBA's first, real logo. We contracted a young man, Richard García from Corpus Christi—he's now a tattoo artist—to design it. We didn't want a logo with a sleepy Mexican or a *charro* or even a *Tejano*; we wanted a professional logo that portrayed MASBA as a forward-moving organization. We wanted it to be red, white and green—the colors of the flag of *México*. We also said it needed the state of Texas in there somewhere. So Richard came up with a simple design of two arrows, where the colors fade into one another. It signified that we're not going back anymore. The green arrow showed that we are moving forward for our Mexican-American children, and the state of Texas was depicted on both A's.

Tommy Molina doesn't like to boast, but he conceived the unique idea of the Golden *Molcajete* Award, a symbol that connected us with our Mexican-American culture. He told the story that during a visit to Market Square in San Antonio, he saw a *molcajete* and said, "We can do this!" He took it back to his hotel room and sprayed it gold. He may have rarified the story, but the Golden *Molcajete* became the most prestigious award of our organization. We used it to recognize our own people: our superintendents and politicians and principals. It gave us more legitimacy as an organization.

School boards throughout the state refused to fund their trustees to be part of MASBA. They would say, "Why do we need MASBA? We have TASB, and we're all Texans!" Tomás Molina worked hard to try to change that. We also had the challenge of gaining legitimacy and acceptance, not just as a group of Mexican Americans who get together and had a good party—because Juan made sure we had great parties—but we had the challenge of becoming legitimate players in the education of Mexican American children.

Despite those challenges, we persisted. We maintained visibility. We took pride in our heritage as Texans and as Americans. We saw our job as helping to make others—trustees and students—proud of who they were!

Dr. Manuel C. Flores served on the Corpus Christi ISD Board of Trustees for 12 years. He joined the MASBA Board in 2003, became MASBA President in March 2005, and served in that capacity through January 2007.

The Presidency of Dr. Manuel Flores

Dr. Manuel C. Flores assumed the presidency of MASBA on March 4, 2005. In January 2006, he was elected to his own term as MASBA President. Manuel served in this capacity through circa May 2006, when he was not re-elected to his local school board.

No extant records have been found for that period.

If you would like to share any photos, meeting minutes, conference programs, mementos, etc. from the presidency of Dr. Manuel C. Flores, for inclusion in Volume II, please email them to info@masbatx.org or mail them to MASBA | P.O. Box 474 | Austin, TX 78767.

Thank you for helping us to reconstruct our history!

Moving the Needle for MASBA

Joel López

MASBA Conferences in the mid-2000s

In 2006, Dr. Manuel Flores of the Corpus Christi ISD first drew me into MASBA. I ran my own business, and my wife, Sylvia, and I visited Corpus Christi ISD. We went out to breakfast with my brother, and he talked about MASBA.

As President, Dr. Flores helped MASBA flourish. He brought NALEO and Bonilla & Bonilla to the conference, as well as Mary Helen Berlanga, the State Board of Education representative from Corpus Christi. Dr. Flores re-energized MASBA and inspired many people to move the needle for MASBA. Lucy Rubio of the Corpus Christi ISD Board also enthused people about getting involved in MASBA.

As a result, my company, JDL Lighting, became a sponsor of the 2006 conference at the old Holiday Inn on Ocean Drive in Corpus Christi. MASBA's budget could handle that hotel. That's where I met Manuel Rodríguez and Juan Rangel. I remember sitting with Juan at the conference, and we took a liking to one another.

The next year, in 2007, the MASBA conference returned to Corpus Christi, this time to the Omni. I spoke with districts in the El Paso area about lighting projects, so I invited school board members to the 2007 MASBA conference. That's how MASBA started engaging folks from the El Paso area.

I remember sponsoring Manuel's farewell as president that year, when he handed the baton to President Elect Joe Muñoz. That year, MASBA hosted an event at the Texas State Aquarium in Corpus.

You've probably heard rumors of a big party that we hosted in the presidential suite of the Omni at that 2007 MASBA conference. I had rented the presidential suite, where MASBA members played loud *mariachi* music. Before long, the security knocked on the door. Chief Bueno from Alice opened the door. The security officer was annoyed and threatened to kick them out. Then they came to my room, because I was responsible for the suite. The officer said, "Mr. López, we're going to boot those people out!" People in MASBA still make fun of me because I hurried up to the presidential suite — in my pajamas! — and asked them to turn down the music. They took the party down to the second floor.

Back then, I met all the people who are now the "senior statesmen" of MASBA. Chief Bueno of the Ben Bolt-Palito Blanco ISD and Joe Muñoz were *compadres*. I remember Dr. Viola García of Aldine ISD, Jimmie Adame of Taft ISD, Josh Cerna of Harlandale ISD, Irene Galán-Rodríguez of Big Spring ISD, Sam and Diane Mullen of the Mullen Group, Kurt Hixson, and Diana Maldonado, who later became a state representative. I also remember Joe's President Elect, Cruz Hinojosa, who lost his local election in the Galena Park ISD, so the Board voted for Joe to continue as President for another year.

Conference attendance waxed and waned over the years. Participation fell at the McAllen conference in 2014, which almost exclusively hosted members from the *Río Grande* Valley. The 2015 conference in Austin, during the Legislative Session, seemed a complete debacle, with 30 people in attendance. MASBA rebounded the last two years, and we've had ten times that number.

The Creation of an Interlocal Agreement

In 2014, when Chief Bueno served as President, I built an interlocal agreement for MASBA and put it "out on the street." We did an ESCO project for Ben Bolt-Palito Blanco ISD, and we gave the district a scholarship check for $27,000. Always a class act, Chief Bueno spoke really nicely about me. When he took the microphone, he always spoke in Spanish first, then in English. He carried himself that way, with complete integrity and a passion for MASBA.

I remember the conflict in forming that interlocal agreement. Some members of MASBA's Executive Committee insisted that MASBA not compete with TASB. They asked, "Why not compete with TASB?" During that time, various vendors wanted to create cooperatives.

The idea of the interlocal fell apart, but it seems the idea contributed to TASB stepping up to fund MASBA in a significant way beginning in 2016. I urged TASB to invest big bucks in MASBA. I told MASBA not to sign an agreement until TASB upped the ante. What TASB ended up giving MASBA is "a drop in the bucket" for them; I believe they should be investing a million dollars a year in MASBA! Then it could be a much bigger organization and do many more educational things with more dollars in the coffers.

Music at MASBA Events

Roger Velásquez & the Latin Legendz started playing for MASBA in 2014. Roger had a close relationship with MASBA. He promoted MASBA wherever he played, and, when we went to his concerts around the town, he pointed us out and identified us as his good friends from the Mexican American School Boards Association — which is why I always wanted to bring Roger back to MASBA events.

Executive Director Joe Muñoz brought in other *Tejano* groups, but those bands never played the variety of music that Roger does. At the 2015 MASBA conference in Austin, MASBA brought in David Lee Garza *y Los Musicales*. They brought in Ram Herrera for another event. For their conference in the Valley, they paid a fortune for *Grupo Mazz*. In my opinion, none of those groups worked out as well as Roger. When we went back to Roger, we had to put tables and chairs in the hall — because so many people came to hear him!

I've always been interested in the music at MASBA events. As vendors, we're putting money into MASBA, and it doesn't need bands with name recognition. I would tell the MASBA Board, "We're just trying to have a little *pachanga* [party] here. We're not trying to have a concert!"

MASBA's *Mariachi* Competition

Joe Muñoz and Juan Ortiz of *Campanas de América* played a major role in putting together MASBA's *mariachi* competition. They raised the sponsorships and hosted the competitions at places like the Edgewood ISD fine arts facility. Student groups submitted tapes and hoped to be selected for the finals. Maclovio Pérez of WOAI Channel 4 promoted the competition. A couple from Kingsville and Alice, Manuel and Lucinda González, sponsored the competition for three years. Those phenomenal, televised competitions generated media attention. I remember when Edinburg CISD won, when Robert Peña of the Edinburg CISD Board served on the NALEO Board. 200 to 300 people enjoyed the fierce competition at that event! With the establishment of the *mariachi* competition, everything started "clicking" for MASBA.

Raising Money for Scholarships: The MASBA Golf Tournament

As President, Gloria Casas really pushed the MASBA scholarship program. I remember when ERO Architects jumped into the game, and Brian Godínez of ERO and I had a challenge at the podium to drive scholarships. That's when we created the golf tournament to help MASBA. I've always been enthused about creating scholarships so that kids can continue their education. I believe that we should follow them through college and bring them back—like MASBA did at its 2019 conference in Austin. Those kids were very eloquent speakers. We were really in touch with the students. After all, most of us worked with MASBA because we wanted students to succeed!

In 2015, under Chief Bueno's leadership, we created MASBA's first golf tournament. Louis Reyes helped pull it off. I worked for Johnson Controls then, and they donated $7,500. I asked the Executive Committee for seed money to pay the expenses of a golf tournament. I got pushback: Some Board members misunderstood the idea and thought that we would take away MASBA vendors and have them direct their gifts toward a golf tournament, rather than to MASBA. As a result, we got subcontractors of Johnson Controls to support the golf tournament. Southwest Foodservice Excellence and Linebarger Goggan Blair & Sampson agreed to help, too. The first year, we had six teams, and Johnson Controls ended up paying out of pocket for a lot of expenses—like the golf course, the trophies, and the food.

The second year, ERO came back, and we raised $3,000 toward scholarships. I remember that Brian Godínez gave a speech at the tournament.

In 2017, we raised almost $12,000 for scholarships. We didn't want to compete with MASBA, so we hosted the golf tournament in the morning. Then we'd display the trophies for the golf tournament at the opening reception of the MASBA conference later that evening.

Manuel Rodríguez became concerned that we were using the MASBA name to fundraise, so we created a non-profit called LASSO, the *Latino* Academic Scholarship & Scholastic Organization, to give back to MASBA. MASBA staff members shared their time with LASSO, planning the golf tournament for us and getting dollars to support MASBA scholarships. I remember going to golf courses with Kurt Hixson, the administrator of the golf tournament, to put up signs and to drum up teams to participate.

The relationships between MASBA and LASSO fell apart in 2018, when those who brought in money for LASSO were no longer part of the MASBA staff. We didn't host a golf tournament in 2018.

Partnership with the Texas Talent Musicians Association

That year, Frank Salazar of the Texas Talent Musicians Association (TTMA) — the producer of the *Tejano* Music Awards — approached me, wanting to partner with a non-profit like MASBA, in order to raise funds for an organization with a scholarship program. We announced that partnership between MASBA and the TTMA at MASBA's 2019 conference in Austin. Nothing has become of it, but I have the TTMA's commitment to MASBA, and it seems the desire is still there.

Looking Toward the Future

It's always been my dream to see MASBA grow. Based on our demographics and who we are in the state of Texas, we should be a lot bigger — and I look forward to supporting MASBA for many years to come!

Joel López is a longtime champion and supporter of MASBA. His company, JDL Lighting, first began supporting MASBA in 2006. He has since championed MASBA sponsorship by the companies he has served, including Johnson Controls and ABM.

MASBA's Role in the Recognition of *Mariachi* as a UIL Event

Joe Muñoz

I served on the Hays CISD Board of Trustees from 1999 to 2010, and some of my fondest memories during those years are connected with MASBA. I got involved with MASBA and joined the MASBA Board in 2003, to represent the Central Texas region. In January 2006, I served as Vice President, when Dr. Manuel Flores of Corpus Christi ISD served as President. A few months later, Manuel lost his re-election campaign in his local district, so, according to our MASBA bylaws, I moved up to President and inherited the remainder of his term. My "trial by fire" as MASBA President began in May 2006! In 2007, the Member Assembly elected me to my own one-year term as President.

At the same board meeting that Manuel and I were elected as President and Vice President, our MASBA Board discussed the fact that the University Interscholastic League (UIL) didn't recognize *mariachi* in the same way that it celebrated other musical talent. I vividly recall that board meeting on January 13, 2006: We were at the Emerald Beach Hotel in Corpus Christi. We talked about how our students, who were predominantly *Latino*, also went to *mariachi* competitions during school hours, and, because these competitions weren't sanctioned by the UIL, they were being punished by having to make up for missed class time by staying after school or going to Saturday school suspension. This affected many students throughout Texas. We wanted a level playing field for them. We wanted *mariachi* to be a UIL-sanctioned event in the same way that band, jazz and choir are. *Mariachi* requires the same talent, dedication and focus. *Mariachi* is also a recognized component of *Latino* culture. So, our MASBA Board passed a resolution at that meeting in Corpus Christi, mandating our MASBA President to work with the UIL to gain recognition of *mariachi* as a UIL-sanctioned event.

Manuel Flores and I assembled a small group to travel to Austin and approach UIL with the idea. We invited MASBA Legal Counsel Juan Aguilera, MASBA Director Manuel Rodríguez of Houston ISD, Belle Ortiz, Executive Director of the Texas Association of *Mariachi* Educators (TAME), and Belle's husband, Juan, who had created the first college *mariachi* ensemble in the nation, in the early 1980s, at Texas A&M University Kingsville. We also invited Gerald Babbitt, Director of Music at Hays CISD, who possessed credibility with Richard Floyd of UIL. In the summer of 2006, we testified with UIL-Music. They turned us down.

We continued to gather research on high school *mariachis* in Texas, and we approached the UIL Music Ensemble Committee in the summer of 2007. This time, we took a young lady from Boerne ISD who had to attend Saturday school due to her participation in *mariachi* during school hours. We were all given three minutes to speak at the public hearing. When that young lady spoke of her experience of being punished, she captured the hearts of the UIL Music Ensemble Committee and, when she hit the three-minute time limit, there wasn't a dry eye in the room. They gave her additional time to finish her story, and resounding applause ensued. At that moment, I turned to Juan Aguilera and said, "I think they're going to recognize us!" You can imagine our excitement later that fall, when we received notification that the UIL was willing to pilot a *mariachi* program through MASBA! The UIL had entrusted us with bringing this program to fruition.

The UIL formed a committee of experts. I served on that committee as the representative of MASBA. I relied heavily on the expertise of our friends at TAME. We heard all sorts of opinions on how a *mariachi* contest needed to be structured, and we discovered we had another hoop to jump through: our own people! They are very strong-willed and have a heart to do the right thing, but it immediately became obvious that, though we all wanted to "get across the street" — we all wanted to get this program off the ground — there were a lot of ideas on how we'd "cross that street." Many negative voices made consensus difficult. People said, "We've tried that before" and "It'll never happen!" We hurdled all those negatives, and we finally formulated a plan. We asked *mariachis* to share a CD of their music, and a panel of judges decided who would be part of the competition. All ensembles that advanced to the competition paid an entrance fee of $250.

While others waited to see what would happen, eleven schools took a "leap of faith" that first year. They submitted a CD for consideration by the five judges who met at Our Lady of the Lake University in San Antonio in December 2009. After listening to the 11

CDs, the judges selected nine groups to advance to the stage at MASBA's first Texas High School *Mariachi* Championship in January 2010. We were elated!

We secured the Edgewood ISD Performing Arts Theatre—a beautiful symbol of MASBA coming full-circle since its founding by the Edgewood ISD superintendent in 1970. San Antonio meteorologist Maclovio Pérez participated in that first *mariachi* competition and served as our first emcee. I pled my case to State Farm, and they went out on a limb to sponsor us with a substantial amount of money, allowing us to rent the venue, create signage, feed and provide a stipend for the judges, and pay for the recording equipment. We designed some really nice medals for the kids—just as nice as the medals that they received at any other UIL-sanctioned event. We created a colorful logo that resembled the UIL logo, something the participating students would be proud to sport. We hosted our first *mariachi* competition, a new experience for us all, and, though some people were waiting to see us fail, it worked out well that first year!

The next year, we had 19 schools submit CDs, of which 11 advanced to our 2011 *mariachi* competition. We only had *mariachi* ensembles from 2A to 5A districts; no 1A or 6A districts submitted CDs. State Farm sponsored us again.

The third year, we held area contests where judges advanced *mariachi* ensembles to the final competition. We hosted those regional contests in Odessa, at Economedes High School in the Edinburg CISD, and at Trimble Tech High School in the Fort Worth ISD. 26 high schools participated, and the winners advanced to our 2012 *mariachi* competition in the Southwest ISD, in San Antonio.

A trustee from the Southwest ISD attended our MASBA Board at our January 13, 2006 meeting in Corpus Christi, and he played a key role. He and Sylvester Vásquez, who served as President of the Texas Association of School Boards in 2011, were pivotal in moving our *mariachi* competition to Southwest ISD. The hospitality there was golden, and we now had a full-fledged auditorium down the hall from the cafetorium where students could gather to meet the college *mariachi* ensembles that set up booths to recruit high school students for their universities and their ensembles. Now we began to expose young people to college! The colleges began recruiting our students for their universities and for their *mariachis*. The college *mariachis* came together for the finale at that competition, our high school students learned that they could use their *mariachi* talents beyond high school, and many of those kids went on to play *mariachi* at the colleges they attended. Even today, some of those kids recognize me from the pep talks I gave them backstage during their high school *mariachi* competition!

I miss our MASBA *mariachi* competitions. The hard work was definitely worth it. I especially enjoyed speaking with the groups before they went on stage. I'd tell them, "No matter how this turns out, give it your best, wear your *trajes* [outfits] proudly and represent your school!" I felt so proud when they came off the stage, gleaming, and the judges had difficulty determining the winners from all the incredible talent on stage!

MASBA's Texas High School *Mariachi* Competition grew steadily. By the fourth year, we had 33 schools submit CDs, and 19 advanced to our 2013 *mariachi* competition at the Edgewood ISD performing arts center. We had a new sponsor that year: Manuel and Lucinda González, whom we referred to in our signage as G², from Tomball, Texas. Manuel and Lucinda Gonzalez were very caring and supportive of our cause. It's not every day, people come to us and offer their financial support and more importantly — their love!

In 2014, we hosted four competitions for 42 schools, and, in 2015, we hosted three competitions for 50 schools. Then politics became involved.

The 84th Texas Legislative Session convened in 2015 and reviewed the UIL. We wanted to bring attention to the UIL's hesitance to take up *mariachi*, so we spoke with legislators who cared about MASBA's goals. They made phone calls and hosted meeting to push recognition of *mariachi* as a UIL-sanctioned event.

Until then, UIL support for *mariachi* seemed halfhearted. I had the sense that they really didn't welcome the idea. I remember that Belle and Juan Ortiz and I went to the office of UIL Executive Director Richard Floyd, who told us, "I believe in what you guys are doing, and we support you." I responded, "Talk is cheap." I told him I wouldn't leave without a press release that we could publish to our website, saying that the UIL supported *mariachi*. A few minutes later, he returned with a signed letter of endorsement, which made our dream of UIL recognition for *mariachi* a reality!

The UIL recognition of *mariachi* in January 2016 was bittersweet: From the beginning, we wanted *mariachi* to earn that status and enjoy the resources of the UIL, but we also had to give up what we had created. We knew that MASBA would no longer be associated with *mariachi* in the same way, and that UIL taking over *mariachi* was the proverbial "nail in the coffin" of our connection to it.

We did our job, and the competition that MASBA created with 11 schools that took the stage at our first MASBA *mariachi* competition in 2010, has now become a competition of more than 100 schools each year!

Joe Muñoz served on the Board of Trustees of the Hays Consolidated Independent School District for 10 years. He served as President of MASBA for nearly two years and as MASBA Executive Director from 2010 to 2014. Joe oversaw the planning and execution of the Texas High School Mariachi *Competition for six years, through 2015, at which time the University Interscholastic League recognized* mariachi *as a sanctioned UIL event.*

The Presidency of Joe Muñoz

Outside of Joe's leadership of the Texas High School *Mariachi* Competitions, few written records have been found from the time of his presidency, from 2006 to 2009. Joe became MASBA President circa May 2006, when Dr. Manuel C. Flores was not re-elected to his local school board. He was then elected to his own term as President at the 2007 Member Assembly. He recalls that MASBA President Elect Cruz Hinojosa of Galena Park ISD communicated just prior to the 2008 Member Assembly that he would be unable to serve as MASBA President, leaving Joe to lead the organization for an additional year, through the 2009 Member Assembly.

A January 10, 2008 press release by President Joe Muñoz states that a press conference would be held on January 10 at the Omni Austin Hotel at Southpark "to announce that *mariachi* will be recognized as a separate, independent category of Medium Ensemble in University Interscholastic League (UIL) competition, beginning with the 2008-09 school year." Richard Floyd, Texas State Director of Music at The University of Texas at Austin, said, "This change will align *mariachi* with show choir, jazz ensemble and other comparable performance mediums."

A January 14, 2008 press release by Executive Director Jimmie Adame states that MASBA held its tenth annual conference. It reads: "The conference kicked off with the announcement that *mariachi* will be recognized as a separate, independent category of Medium Ensemble in University Interscholastic League (UIL) competition, beginning with the 2008-2009 school year. This news was supported throughout the conference with performances by students from Hays CISD, La Joya ISD, Kingsville ISD and Houston ISD. In fact, Saturday afternoon's activities were conducted at the Performing Arts Center in Hays CISD, with a variety of *mariachi* and choral performances. Keynote speakers Ray Martínez, retired Texas Ranger; Gonzalo Barrientos, long-time Texas Senator from Travis County; and Dan Arellano, author of *Tejano Roots: A Family Legend*, enlightened conference attendees. Breakout sessions included: 'Preparing At-Risk Students for the 21st Century,' and 'Board Monitoring System,' by representatives from Midland ISD and Houston ISD, respectively, were very instructive."

If you would like to share any photos, meeting minutes, conference programs, mementos, etc. from the presidency of Joe F. Muñoz, for inclusion in Volume II, please email them to info@masbatx.org or mail them to MASBA | P.O. Box 474 | Austin, TX 78767.

Thank you for helping us to reconstruct our history!

"We Called It the MASBA *Mariachi* Competition"

Juan Ortiz

My wife, Belle, "the Mother of *Mariachi* Education," introduced me to MASBA and got me involved in the Texas High School *Mariachi* Competition. Belle was the first teacher in the United States to offer *mariachi* as a school course for credit, in the Santa Fe School District. California had *mariachi* at UCLA back in 1961 to 1962 — they called it UCLAtlán — but students didn't receive credit for their participation.

In 1969, Belle began the *mariachi* program at Sidney Lanier High School in the San Antonio ISD. She was recruited from an elementary school where she led a choir called *Los Tejanitos*; she also had *baile folklórico* dancers and guitarists. The principal at Lanier told her, "I want you to have the same programs, but at the high school level." Belle agreed, but only if she could offer her courses for credit; she wouldn't offer them as clubs, extracurriculars, or after-school activities! She introduced a course in *baile folklórico*, not only from *México*, but also from Russia and South America.

In 1977, Texas A&I Kingsville recruited me to offer the nation's first *mariachi* university course for credit. In 1980, Belle recruited me to become the *mariachi* director for the San Antonio ISD, and together we founded the Texas Association of *Mariachi* Educators (TAME). TAME had become dormant, but when MASBA's Executive Director, Joe Muñoz, called us with the idea of hosting a high school *mariachi* competition, we knew we had to revive TAME!

Belle and I knew the leaders of the Texas Music Educators Association (TMEA), so we introduced Joe to them. They helped us bring together *mariachi* directors from throughout Texas. We started pulling together our ideas for a MASBA *mariachi* competition. Belle contacted all Texas schools with *mariachi* programs. The TMEA provided the space for us to bring together *mariachi* teachers from throughout the state, to create the scoring for our competition, based on our ideas from band, orchestra and other UIL competitions.

Joe suggested that MASBA spearhead the effort and provide credibility for the competition. TMEA listened to us because of our tie to MASBA. We said, "If you don't listen to us, you're discriminating against *mexicanos*, and you're discriminating against our culture!"

So TAME got its second legs, MASBA brought legitimacy to our efforts, and the TMEA agreed to advocate for us before the University Interscholastic League (UIL). In the end, the UIL said, "We're going to give y'all a chance." They warned us not to expect UIL recognition quickly, noting that it took years for jazz to achieve that status. *No hombre*, our first *mariachi* competitions brought together thousands of kids from hundreds of schools. UIL had no idea there would be such record-breaking interest in *mariachi!*

I served as the coordinator of the Texas High School *Mariachi* Competitions. I secured the judges and timekeepers and those who worked in the tabulation booth. TAME wasn't fully functioning again by the time of the first competition, so we called it the MASBA *Mariachi* Competition, and we used MASBA's rules for the event. Bands sent their recordings, and we convened regional groups of judges to listen to the recordings. Those judges eliminated many groups, and the finalists were selected to perform at the Edgewood ISD Performing Arts Theatre. We separated the groups by the size of their school: 1A through 5A, and, by the end of the competition, we bestowed on one group from each category the title of State Champion. We did that for six years.

Those competitions signified more than *mariachi*. *Mariachi* is simply a tool to maximize students' academic opportunities. Music is in our students' blood, and *mariachi* allows them to showcase every facet of the fine arts. Students who participate in *mariachi* must be good musicians and vocalists. If they don't know Spanish, they have to learn it. They have to be theatrical and put on a good show. *Mariachi* enhances the enrollment at our schools!

Mariachi may have become a UIL event without MASBA, but MASBA definitely sped up the process by at least ten years. MASBA members spoke to their legislators, and this expansive effort made it happen. It was the synergy of Joe, MASBA, and the foundation that Belle and I laid in the 1970s. We were blessed to see the fruit of the seed we planted!

Juan & Belle Ortiz played an instrumental role in securing recognition of mariachi *by the University Interscholastic League. Belle is known as the "Mother of* Mariachi *Education," and Juan served as co-coordinator of MASBA's Texas High School* Mariachi *Competition for six years.*

"We Wanted These Kids to Know Our Beloved *Mariachi*"

Manuel & Lucinda González

Manny: We learned about MASBA through Joe Muñoz. I've known Joe since we were eight years old in Kingsville, Texas. We were in the same class, we had all the same friends, and we graduated the same year. So, Lucy and I have been friends with Joe and his wife, Debbie, for a long time. In 2012, when Joe served as Executive Director of MASBA, he told us about the organization, and we were impressed. During one phone conversation, he also told us that State Farm, the title sponsor of MASBA's Texas High School *Mariachi* Competition in 2012, would no longer sponsor the event, and the competition might cease to exist. The next competition was scheduled for February 2013. We knew that Joe wanted to secure UIL approval of *mariachi*, but he didn't ask us for anything; we were just having a conversation as friends. Later that night, Lucy and I were talking about that conversation, and she asked, "Why don't we sponsor it?"

Lucy: When we hung up after that call, we just couldn't shake it off. We had these images of young students with big dreams and hopes and aspirations. We couldn't let the *mariachi* program disappear! The thought of that inspired us.

Manny: We didn't wait until the next morning; we called Joe and Debbie back that night, around 11:00 p.m., and we said, "Joe and Debbie, we've decided to sponsor the event for the next three years!" Lucy and I have been married for 38 years, and we made some good decisions in 2012, leaving us with some resources, and this cause was perfect for us: We're both from South Texas, we both descend from *México*, we love *mariachi* music, and we both felt we had to help these kids! An undocumented immigrant from Mexico who became a U.S. citizen in the 1950s, my dad worked hard to achieve the American Dream. He didn't listen to *Tejano* music, so, growing up, we heard a lot of *norteño* and *mariachi* at home. You couldn't help but appreciate it!

Lucy: *Mariachi* became part of my life when I married Manny. The instruments are beautiful, and, as *Latinos*, we really get into it, with all the *gritos*. When we began sponsoring the competition, we said that G² sponsored the event. That's me: I'm Lucinda González González. It's been my brand since the day I got married. My friends call me Lucy G².

Manny: I have it tattooed on my ring finger: LG²!

Lucy: Anytime we pour concrete or build something, Manny puts a G² on it.

Manny: G² is part of her brand, and I'll do anything for her, so we injected the G² brand into MASBA! The *mariachi* medals, though, said "Manuel & Lucinda González."

Lucy: We only attended MASBA's *mariachi* events the three years that we sponsored them, but they were overwhelming: to see such a crowd and know that we made a difference!

Manny: There were hundreds of people there!

Lucy: They were there because we helped out in a way. I fought back happy tears when they recognized us on stage.

Manny: We sponsored it for three years. We told Joe we weren't interested in sponsoring a "one-and-done" sort of thing. We said, "Let's have a goal and treat this like a real effort — and our goal is to get UIL approval." We didn't go to all the semi-finals because they were all over the state, but hundreds and hundreds of people poured into the auditorium for the finals. There were hundreds of kids — the most beautiful kids you've ever seen — dressed up and so very proud of who they were that day. The colors, the music: Talk about chills!

Lucy: They sounded like adults, like seasoned *mariachi* musicians. Their pride shone through their voices and instruments!

Manny: *Mariachi* began in *México*, so you're obviously going to have a lot of Mexicans or Hispanics in *mariachis*, but there were also White kids, Black kids, Asian kids. It was as diverse as disco and rock and funk and metal and rap and hip-hop in other parts of the world. *Mariachi* just needs its chance!

Lucy: The young women caught my attention: They would sing with the most powerful voices and then, when they received their medals, they were the shyest, sweetest, most humble young people—two completely different people! They were definitely proud: proud of themselves and proud of their culture. You could see the difference in their self-esteem.

Manny: Their faces glowed. Those kids were learning teamwork and coordination with others. For the *mariachi* competition, you needed at least 17 or 19 in your group—and everyone had to practice: If you had a "weak link," the entire group would sound bad. Everyone must perform to the utmost highest of standards, so they pushed one another to make one another better.

Lucy: You could see the unity among them. For me, that unity is so important. They supported one another and were there for one another. Their parents couldn't stop smiling! Their parents, grandparents, *tíos*, *tías*, siblings and friends showed amazing support.

Manny: Each group of parents would scream out when their children played, and a lot of parents thanked us.

Lucy: Ever so grateful, they approached us, wanting to shake our hands.

Manny: That was probably the most memorable part of the competition! Joe acknowledged all who participated: the kids, the directors and instructors, the judges. He really included us and allowed us to give the kids their medals. We really didn't need all that acknowledgement: We wanted these hundreds of kids to know our beloved *mariachi* and to have it expressed in their schools.

Lucy: We also got backstage, where they were warming up and practicing and were so excited to soon be going on stage!

Manny: You'd see them in their *mariachi* outfits, standing straight and very respectful and disciplined: the young ladies beautifully-dressed and in their makeup, and the young men like little studs in their manly outfits — and then, when they're out of costume, they're just regular kids getting an education. It was cool.

Lucy: Being involved for three years, it was somewhat heartbreaking to see the seniors leave, and to not see their sweet faces the next year. We got attached to them.

Manny: We'd see a student one year and wonder the next year, "Are we going to see her again?" "Are we going to hear him again?"

Lucy: But he or she had graduated and moved on to college! I got attached to them. They were so sweet: Some of the girls would ask if they could hug me.

Manny: We got a lot of kid-hugs. It was awesome. After the first year, we really looked forward to the second and third years. The first year, we only invited our daughters to the event, but the next two years, we invited all our friends and family, who came from all over.

Lucy: The crowds kept getting bigger...

Manny: ...and there were additional bands the third year, with more middle school bands performing. It grew over those three years.

Lucy: It was nice to see that!

Manny: I'll never forget the *mariachi* competition in 2013: It happened to be right around my wife's birthday, and Rolando Molina — the assistant director who taught me trumpet in the seventh and eighth grade — brought his wonderful King High School *mariachi* from Kingsville to play for Lucinda's birthday celebration that night at the *mariachi* bar at *Mi Tierra* Restaurant.

Lucy: I had no idea they were going to do that!

Manny: It was the icing on the cake!

Lucy: It was very special.

Manny: UIL approval of *mariachi* was somewhat bittersweet. We wanted to get *mariachi* approved. MASBA experienced a leadership change in 2014, and we tried to get other MASBA folks involved, to push forward the effort. Lucinda and I were concerned that no one picked up the ball on moving *mariachi* toward UIL recognition. The MASBA efforts seemed to be fading a bit, and we didn't see the same drive in folks. We figured if no one at MASBA had the desire to do this, Lucy and I would take the lead and get it done. We have some rapport with folks in the Legislature. We approached State Representative Richard Raymond of Laredo, who is a dear friend, and we told him we needed help getting face time with the UIL leadership, Dr. Kent and Dr. Harrison. We wanted to explain MASBA's efforts and what we were trying to accomplish. Richard facilitated the effort and helped push recognition of *mariachi*. He coordinated several meetings beginning in February 2014, with Dr. Harrison, then with Dr. Kent. We explained to them the merits. It took until December 2014 for us to get the entire process "packaged" and to "put a bow on it." In October, we had a meeting with Joe Muñoz, Executive Director of MASBA; Rudy Orona of the MASBA Board; Noé Sánchez, President of the Texas Association of *Mariachi* Educators; and with Belle and Juan Ortiz of the Texas Association of *Mariachi* Educators. MASBA had wanted to transition the competitions from MASBA to TAME. We didn't know the politics; we just wanted Dr. Kent to approve it — and he did that in the Fall of 2014. He developed a committee to transition it from MASBA and TAME to the UIL. A lot went on behind-the-scenes. They asked Lucinda and I to be part of that committee, and we said, "We're not experts in *mariachi* music. Let's put this in the hands of experts. Let the *mariachi* educators be the ones to govern this!"

Lucy: We met our deadline: We had said that we would sponsor the competition for three years, and, at the end of it, the UIL recognized *mariachi!*

Manny: We were really pleased that it got done. Richard went to the last event, to address the crowd—and he even began to sing *mariachi* music!

Lucy: He got a hold of the mic and performed *El Rey*!

Manny: To show our gratitude for him, we purchased a handmade *vihuela*—a small guitar—from Mexico for him, and we presented it to him that day.

Lucy: It was a very nice gift.

Manny: That's the story of our involvement in MASBA's *mariachi* competitions. We are very proud of our efforts and participation and will always hold this as one of our utmost accomplishments. The UIL competitions continue. In fact, the 2020 UIL State *Mariachi* Festival will be held in Edinburg on February 21-22—the same weekend as MASBA's golden jubilee conference!

Manuel "Manny" & Lucinda "Lucy" González sponsored MASBA's Texas High School Mariachi Competition from 2013 to 2015.

"Focused on the Kids"

Maria Leal

When my children attended schools of the Mission CISD, I became involved in the band boosters and the Boys & Girls Club. I believed our children needed more attention. We had a tiny band whose uniforms were as old as Moses, so we went before the school board and pleaded for new uniforms. I realized then that we could go before the authorities to advocate for our children's needs.

I ran for the school board twice, unsuccessfully both times because I'm not a native of Mission--I've only been here 45 years! Born and raised in Corpus Christi, it took me a while to become a "native" in Mission. I was elected in 1995 for the first time and served four years, including one year as president of the board. I became very involved in visiting campuses to directly assist our children: We helped them read and study. After four years, I lost the election in 1999.

In 2001, Hidalgo County Judge Eloy Pulido appointed me to serve on the South Texas ISD Board of Trustees. I did that for 17 years. During that time, I also served on the TASB Board for 12 years, beginning in 2002.

I've always said that all people are leaders: Some lead from the front, some lead from the middle, and some lead from the back. Those who lead from the front often let the prestige go to their heads and lose touch with the bottom layer of people. That's not for me. I'm more successful changing opinions on things that need to be considered.

I fought for diversity within TASB, and I spoke Spanish at TASB meetings, so that people would understand that many people in this world speak other languages. James Crow and I enjoyed some deep conversations on the need for greater diversity. One day, I asked him, "Jim, how can an organization that represents all of Texas, which is primarily Hispanic, have White people in all key supervisory positions. That isn't right!" My goal to have more equity and diversity in those things needed help. He said it didn't happen because TASB's employees hardly ever left; TASB retained its employees, so there usually weren't any employment opportunities. When the governmental relations position opened, Jim flew down to the Valley to speak with me and Gloria Casas, to let us know that he tried very hard to recommend a Hispanic for that position, but that he couldn't locate anyone.

Back when I served on the Mission CISD Board in the 1990s, we went to the Region 1 conferences on South Padre Island. MASBA always hosted a reception as part of those gatherings, so we attended.

Eventually, Viola García, a very faithful MASBA member, invited me to join the MASBA Board. Three years later, in 2009, I became MASBA's President. I followed Joe Muñoz. After one year as his Vice President, I didn't feel ready to be President. We didn't have anyone who could explain the responsibilities of our MASBA Officers. After Joe served as President for two years, I served as President, with Manuel Rodríguez as my Vice President.

When I became President, MASBA was unorganized and always at the brink of having no money in the bank. Our Treasurer never gave us a financial report, and we weren't always able to account for all monies. When I was President, I couldn't sleep the night before our conference; I was up until 5:00 a.m. worrying that we didn't have the money to pay for the event! Sam and Diane Mullen saved us and lent us the money we needed for that conference.

I spent a lot of time trying to change things, and I'm happy things have changed since then, and that we now have an Executive Director who takes his work seriously.

I dreamed that MASBA might be an organization that educates Hispanic board members on the needs of all children. There are some people who don't care about our children. We are responsible for outcomes. We have to make sure they have opportunities. The education of our children is never going to be equitable—and everybody knows that tragedy. MASBA members should be learning. *Deja todo del* party *atrás.* I love music, and I used to dance all the time, but we, as MASBA members, need to be about learning more about education needs, instead of just getting together to party. I would tell the guys that we needed to spend on scholarships an amount equal to the amount that we would pay for the bands at our events. If we can spend $7,000 on a band, then we can spend $7,000 on scholarships! I'd say, "You can have your party, but we need to get money for the kids first!" I like to believe that I helped MASBA get its house in order and get focused on the kids. As a result, my efforts helped MASBA's scholarship program to begin a few years later. My dream for MASBA is a bigger, better scholarship program for our children, who have worked really hard and are really deserving.

I'm older, and I act like a mama — so I remember one year, during our MASBA celebration of Hispanic Heritage Month, they gave me an owl trophy. I always appreciated that.

As MASBA celebrates its fiftieth anniversary, I challenge all school board members to be faithful to the cause. Don't let MASBA be like any other club that you're part of. Give it your all, and let's make MASBA the most worthwhile organization there is!

María Leal served on the Board of Trustees of the Mission Consolidated Independent School District for four years and has served on the Board of Trustees of the South Texas ISD for over 18 years. She joined the MASBA Board in 2006 and became MASBA President in 2009. She simultaneously served on the Board of Directors of the Texas Association of School Boards for 12 years.

The Presidency of María Leal

On August 22, 2009, President María Leal convened a **MASBA Board** meeting. Meeting minutes report the following:

- In attendance were María Leal, Manuel Rodríguez, Josh Cerna, Gloria Casas, Juan Rangel, Brian Godínez, Jimmie Adame & Juan Aguilera. Guests included Cynthia Rocha of Education Achievement Resources, Joe Madrigal, and retired educator Élida Madrigal.
- Josh Cerna presented samples of a brochure to be shared at the TASB/TASA conference
- The tentative theme of the 2010 MASBA conference is "*Tejanos in History & Bilingual Education*"; next year is MASBA's 40th anniversary
- A new brand is needed for MASBA; ERO has offered to assist
- Cynthia presented on her Family Leadership Institute
- Brian Godínez facilitated a strategic planning workshop

On October 24, 2009, MASBA President María Leal convened a **MASBA Board** strategic planning meeting. Brian Godínez of ERO Architects facilitated the encounter. The agenda included the following items:

- Findings from first workshop in August
  - Organization WANTS
    - We want to take a stand on issues and be heard
    - We want our Mexican-American children to not be left behind
    - We want to be a recognized Mexican-American voice for educational issues
    - We want to increase Mexican-American board members throughout the state
    - We want school boards to have a reason to join
    - We want to be identified as viable and credible Mexican-American leadership organization
    - We want respect from NSBA and TASB
    - We want our membership more committed, more unified and increase it

- We want acknowledgment from the State
- We want to increase funding to the organization
- Core VALUES
  - Have *corazón*
  - Commitment to education
  - Foster achievement
  - Provide a family environment
  - Foster unity
  - Advocate change
  - Provide opportunities
- Organization Targets
  - Mexican-American school board members
  - School districts
  - Children
  - Grants, funders and donors
  - Media
- Organization Strengths
  - Growth of Hispanic students & population
  - History and legacy
  - Board structure
  - Established base of members
  - Recognized Annual Conference
  - Jimmie Adame
  - TEA partnership for credit hours
  - Resource and history with vendors
- Organization Challenges
  - #1 – Membership and participation declining
  - #2 – Lack of cohesive vision and plan
  - #3 – Board membership not aligned and participating
  - #4 – Organization structure disjointed
  - Value proposition fading
  - Do not have a paid staff
  - High school dropout rate
  - Low awareness and credibility
  - Lack of sustained finances
  - Communications are lacking and disjointed
  - By laws outdated
  - Financial instability – lacks sustainability
  - Resources limited
  - Compete with TASB and regional organizations

138

- Objective Recommendations & Strategic Questions
  - Discussion of MASBA's 4 Pillars of Sustainable Growth: message, program, membership, finance
    - 1. Increase role & awareness of MASBA's advocacy
      - The Vision Committee (Manuel & Sam) will develop a new vision, mission & value message to reinvigorate the organization.
    - 2. Increase participation of Mexican Americans on school boards
      - The Impact Committee (Juan & Gloria) will develop an affordable plan for training school board members to have more impact in their communities
    - 3. Increase MASBA membership
      - The I Am MASBA Committee (Josh & Lisa) will develop a membership plan to inspire school board members to join MASBA
    - 4. Increase MASBA's financial position
      - The Paca Committee (María & Jimmie will develop a financial plan to increase MASBA's financial stability

On January 21, 2010, President María Leal opened the **12th Annual MASBA Conference** at the Hyatt Regency San Antonio Riverwalk Hotel. The conference agenda shares the following:

General Sessions Dr. Steve Murdock
Robert Jaklich, Superintendent, Harlandale
Marty DeLeón, Legislature Issues

Breakout Sessions

"Superintendent Evaluation"
Paul Vranish, Superintendent, Tornillo ISD

"Is Your District Prepared for a Disaster?"
Choice Facility Partners

"Immigration & Nationality Law"
José R. Pérez, Foster/Quan, LLP

"How History & Culture Affect Architectural Design"
Eli R. Ochoa & Manuel Hinojosa, ERO Architects

"Does Your District Qualify for Assistance with School Construction Programs?"
Juan Aguilera, Escamilla & Poneck
Lisa Dawn-Fisher, TEA

"The Why, What & How of Bilingual Education"
Dr. Rudy Rodríguez

"Advances in Public-private Facility Planning Construction & Finance Solutions for Cash-strapped School Districts"
Timothy Merriweather, Bannister Group
Eli R. Ochoa, ERO Architects
Gilbert Gallegos, Broaddus Associates

"Recommendations in Policy & Practice for the Improvement of Educational Services for Hispanic Youth in Texas"
TBD

"The 2010 U.S. Census
and Redistricting of Single Member Districts"
Rolando L. Ríos, Attorney at Law

"VIVA! Vital Information for a Virtual Age:
Developing Community Health Literacy"
Superintendent Marla M. Guerra, Lucy M. Hansen,
Sara Reibman, Ann Vickman, South Texas ISD

"A Board Member's Guide to Bonds & Investments"
First Public

TBD
TASB Risk Management

"Governance Do's & Don'ts"
Tony Reséndez

If you would like to share photos, meeting minutes, conference programs, mementos, etc. from the presidency of María Leal, for inclusion in Volume II, please email them to info@masbatx.org or mail them to MASBA | P.O. Box 474 | Austin, TX 78767.

Thank you for helping us to reconstruct our history!

The Presidency of Manuel Rodríguez, Jr.

Few written records have been found from the presidency of Manuel Rodríguez, who served as MASBA President from January 22, 2010 to January 22, 2011.

On June 11, 2010, President Manuel Rodríguez convened a meeting of the **MASBA Board** at Pat O'Brien's in San Antonio. A subsequent press release announced that the Board invited Co-Executive Director Joe Muñoz to assume the position of Executive Director. Draft minutes relate the following:

- In attendance were President Manuel Rodríguez; Immediate Past President María Leal; Vice President Juan Rangel; Secretary Rudy Rodríguez; Directors Danny Bueno, Gloria Casas, Josh Cerna, Irene Galán, Viola García, Pete López; Co-Executive Director Joe Muñoz; Webmaster Kurt Hixson; and Guests Héctor Ybarra, Art Reyna & Terry Simms.
- Sam Guzmán & Legal Counsel Juan Aguilera were absent.
- The Board approved $1,000 for 1,000 MASBA pins and asked Joe to research the cost of MASBA ribbons to be worn at TASB conferences.
- Manuel appointed Rudy Rodríguez, Viola García & Brian Godínez to work on branding & marketing recommendations.
- Kurt reported that he mailed 5,000 newsletters.
- Josh is still working on the 2011 conference agenda.
- Joe reported that State Farm is interested in sponsoring the 2011 *mariachi* competition and that the San Antonio Livestock Show & Rodeo is interested in hosting future *mariachi* competitions.

On August 8, 2010, President Manuel Rodríguez signed a one-year agreement for the services of Attorney Juan F. Aguilera as MASBA General Counsel, for one dollar.

On September 24, 2010, President Manuel Rodríguez convened a meeting of the **MASBA Board** at the Houston Convention Center. The agenda follows:

- Adjourn to Closed Session – Juan Aguilera
- Guests: Carolyn Boyle & Darci Hubbard of Texas Parent PAC
- Possible Action Items
    - o Minutes from Last Meeting – Sam Guzmán
    - o Treasurer's Report – Rudy Rodríguez
    - o Approval of Bid for Shirts – Joe Muñoz
    - o Calendar Dates for TASB & MASBA Conferences
    - o 2010 TASB Conference Presentation Update – Manuel Rodríguez & Rudy Rodríguez
    - o 2011 MASBA Conference Update – Josh Cerna
    - o Vendor/Sponsorship – Kurt Hixson
    - o Membership – Rudy Rodríguez & Kurt Hixson
    - o *Mariachi* Update – Joe Muñoz
    - o Executive Director Contract – Juan Aguilera
    - o Executive Director's Report – Joe Muñoz
    - o Budget Consideration
    - o Webpage/Newsletter Update – Kurt Hixson
    - o Legislative Agenda Review & Update – Art Reyna
    - o Moving MASBA Conference to Austin on Odd Years, Beginning in 2013 – Manuel Rodríguez

MASBA Executive Director Joe Muñoz shared a press release for the January 22, 2011 Texas High School *Mariachi* Competition at the Edgewood ISD Performing Arts Theatre. It states, "For the past two years, State Farm has been the proud and exclusive sponsor for this event." The winners of the 2A to 5A categories will be "invited to showcase their talents at the San Antonio Livestock Show & Rodeo *Día de Vaquero* on Sunday, February 13, 2011."

If you would like to share any photos, meeting minutes, conference programs, mementos, etc. from the presidency of Manuel Rodríguez, for inclusion in Volume II, please email them to info@masbatx.org or mail them to MASBA | P.O. Box 474 | Austin, TX 78767.

Thank you for helping us to reconstruct our history!

142

"Blessed to Have Been Part of MASBA"

Brian Godínez

In 2007, I became involved in MASBA through Manuel Hinojosa, a partner ERO Architects who came up with the brilliant idea that our firm would throw an after-party for all who attended the Region 1 Spring Conference for school board members at South Padre Island. He and his brother, Rick, owned Doubleday Bar of Champions, a bar and grill in Port Isabel. They had hosted a successful reception for Region 1 conference attendees the previous year. He asked if I could put on my "marketing hat" and make it bigger, better, cooler and neater. That's how I met Louis Reyes, Manny Rodríguez and all the board members from the *Río Grande* Valley. Jimmie Adame served as MASBA's Executive Director. I called Jimmie, and we organized the May event as a MASBA Region 1 joint event hosted by ERO, our architectural-engineering firm named for our founder, Eli R. Ochoa.

I took responsibility for planning the event. Our staff organized the food and planned a BBQ dinner, door prizes, casino tables and a karaoke contest with prizes. Manuel and Eli gave me *carte blanche*, and we hosted a great Saturday night party. The next day, I sat down with Louis Reyes and a couple of board members to plan the next year's event, and I started to learn about MASBA and how we could support its mission.

Louis found out that I'm a strategic planner and a meeting facilitator with a marketing background, so he invited me to lead a planning session for MASBA the next fall. We hosted that meeting at Juan Aguilera's office in San Antonio. I still remember the faces around the table: Louis, Manuel Rodríguez, Sam Guzmán, Viola García, Gloria Casas and María Leal. I led an all-day planning retreat on MASBA's future, and we created a strategic plan. That's how I learned about MASBA and its mission, vision and history — and I was "hooked." I now found myself involved in an organization with a true purpose and meaning, linked to a rich history and making a difference with K-12 studies on our Mexican-American culture. MASBA had already celebrated its 25th anniversary, and they kept asking me to participate and stay involved. Our firm got involved as an annual sponsor as well. We grew the event at Port Isabel. I then got involved in the MASBA's annual conference and SLI event. We decided to host an annual MASBA reception at the TASA/TASB convention. As our firm's involvement escalated each year, we provided a combination of monetary contributions, scholarships and in-kind marketing services.

Kurt Hixson invited me to assist with MASBA's marketing including the long-term brand planning of MASBA. I ended up leading a few strategic work sessions for the MASBA leadership. I recall that we had a few healthy debates about one very important issue: MASBA's identity. We asked how connected MASBA should be to the words "Mexican-American" or to the colors of the Mexican flag. Legacy board members wanted to retain the history and connection to the heritage of our Mexican roots, and younger board members didn't feel as strongly connected to the words "Mexican-American" or the colors of the Mexican flag. At a few meetings, there were good debates to drop "Mexican-American" from the organization's name, and/or change the colors of the MASBA logo.

At ERO, we volunteered our marketing services to come up with a new identity for MASBA and to design a more contemporary logo for the organization. The current MASBA logo honors the past and forges ahead to the future. It preserves the colors of the Mexican flag, and it displays that MASBA's focus is on our students and the ultimate  goal we have for them: to graduate! Mar Rivera, our art director at ERO, designed the new logo. The MASBA board reviewed various versions at two or three meetings, and we unveiled the new modern logo at a MASBA/ERO reception at TASA/TASB on October 2, 2015. The logo inspires a sense of history and pride, with a bright future in mind. The graduate symbolizes accomplishment and is slanted toward the right, to symbolize moving forward into the future.

MASBA introduced our 100%-Hispanic-owned firm to school districts with Hispanic school board members throughout the state, and our firm helped elevate MASBA and its mission during a high-growth period for MASBA. We helped increase MASBA membership, and MASBA provided a way for us to give back to the communities we serve — and others we could someday serve.

I felt fortunate to be actively involved in the growth of MASBA, as our firm grew and received projects outside the *Río Grande* Valley: in Houston ISD, Seguin ISD, El Paso ISD and Austin ISD. I remember the MASBA board members who encouraged us to submit our qualifications and compete for projects in their districts. I owe Manuel Rodríguez a special debt of gratitude: I wouldn't have submitted for school projects in the Houston ISD because I didn't think we were strong enough or had the ability to compete against the architecture giants in the Houston market—but Manuel said, "Listen, when these projects come out, you go for them. Don't be a wimp! Get out there and fight for yourself. Be proud of what you have accomplished!" That five-minute conversation changed my life and the history of ERO. Every time I think of MASBA, I think of Manny Rodríguez, and I'll never forget him for as long as I live. God bless him.

More recently, we were fortunate to be selected for the new, modern T.A. Brown Elementary School in the Austin ISD. We believe that our ability to compete in Austin, Houston and El Paso as successfully as we have, is related to the credibility that we've received from our association with strong organizations like MASBA.

Some years ago, we decided to start touting our work and our pride of being an architectural firm owned by Mexican-Americans and our ability to weave our Hispanic culture into the design of many of our schools. Our project in the Austin ISD seemed to be ERO's destiny: to be invited into the multicultural community that T.A. Brown represents and to build such a dynamic, modern elementary school in honor of a man who did so much for the Austin community. I believe that these last 13 years of being involved with MASBA helped to open opportunities for us and to pursue these projects with more pride as Mexican-Americans. When you're surrounded at MASBA's conferences and events by 300-400 board members who are proud Mexican-Americans or Hispanics, you can't help but feel good about our ancestry and our impact on Texas.

I ended up creating a strong bond with several of MASBA's board members. I watched good executive directors come and go throughout the years. I saw strong boards with strong visions, and experienced many highs and lows of MASBA's successes and challenges.

I enjoyed seeing MASBA's accomplishments, especially the raising of more awareness of Mexican American Studies in our schools. I have seen how MASBA closes the achievement gap between our Mexican-American students and other student groups. I saw MASBA educating school board members and joining forces with others to advocate in front of the legislature for Mexican-American students. Fortunately, I participated in much of these accomplishments.

I remember setting up a lunch for MASBA board members during a TASA/TASB conference in Houston. At ERO, we decided that we wanted to be a bigger sponsor of MASBA the following year, so I told them, "I want to create a bigger sponsorship level. I want to be the Adamantium Sponsor of MASBA!" During that conversation, we came up with the idea of the ERO Dream Scholarship to help students. We wanted to be able to give scholarships to high school students who were making the transition to college, but who didn't have the financial ability to close financial gaps. We did that for four or five years: LASSO provided its scholarships, and ERO provided its Dream Scholarships to the students of MASBA member districts. We were always connecting with school board members, so this scholarship program gave us the opportunity to be more connected to students.

I remember at one MASBA conference, I went on stage and made a corporate challenge: I picked Joel López out of the audience, since he led the LASSO scholarship program, and I said, "Whatever LASSO donates, we'll match!" I invited other corporate sponsors to match it, too. We playfully competed to raise money for scholarships, and I ended up matching Joel's level of giving for that year.

We were also proud to create MASBA's Hispanic Heritage Awards for three or four years. TASA/TASB always hosted its annual conference during Hispanic Heritage Month, so we created some cool *alebrijes* — brightly-colored, Mexican sculptures of fantastical animals. The first year, we created them ourselves: colorful-looking creatures of *papier-mâché* and wire! The MASBA Board chose the recipients of the Hispanic Heritage Award, then I would choose the animals that best suited their personalities. Later I found an *alebrije* artist in Oaxaca, and she created the awards for some years after that. What a fond memory of MASBA coming up with great ideas and allowing ERO to participate and elevate its brand and be associated with such a strong organization!

I want to believe that ERO's affiliation with MASBA directly impacted our growth, and that it went both ways. We are grateful and blessed to have been part of MASBA and to celebrate so many milestones that ERO and MASBA generated together. Eli, Octavio, Jerry, our staff, and I will be forever thankful for this amazing blessing.

Brian Godínez is a partner with ERO Architects, a longtime MASBA sponsor. He has generously shared of his time and talent with MASBA, facilitating strategic planning sessions for the MASBA Board and bringing great creative talent to the organization's events and marketing & branding efforts.

The Presidency of Joshua Cerna

Joshua "Josh" Cerna of the Harlandale ISD served as MASBA President from January 22, 2011 to January 21, 2012 .

A MASBA brochure during President Cerna's leadership of the organization published the following information:

Vision Statement

The Texas public education system accurately represents the cultural and historical contributions of individuals and the Mexican-American community, as a resource so that students can better understand the heritage of their descendants.

Mission Statement

The Mexican American School Board Members Association serves as the leading advocate of a quality public education system in Texas, that represents the land, people and history of the Mexican-American culture.

History

In 1970, a group of courageous Mexican-American school board members founded an organization to serve as an advocate for minority children during the transition of the civil rights era and see to it that these children were not taken advantage of through legislation, governance, policy or regulation, in order to comply with the desegregation of the nation's public school system.

Today, 40 years later, MASBA honors the legacy of our founders, and we stand united to provide leadership, vision and support for a growing number of school board members who represent school districts with demographic profiles represented by a large number of Mexican-American students.

School districts are challenged with this unprecedented growth and in many cases lack the understanding of how powerful our culture thrives in the lives of Mexican-Americans families, combined with the challenge of not speaking English.

MASBA understands these challenges and can assist school board districts as a whole, or as individuals, to present, discuss and

148

promote the advancement and relevance of the Mexican-American culture in your district and its impact in your local education system.

MASBA is an organization committed to help school board members come together and help each other understand the needs of its students in a changing district. We encourage the discussion of these tough issues and are here to support and educate other school board members on legislative issues and introduce policy and programs for your school district.

Current Initiatives
- Resolution against Social Studies Curriculum
- Immigration
- SB1070 Resolution
- *Mariachi*

On March 30, 2011, President Josh Cerna convened the **MASBA Executive Board** at the Wyndham Garden Austin Hotel. Meeting minutes report the following:
- Present were: President Josh Cerna, President Elect & Treasurer Juan Rangel, Immediate Past President Manuel Rodríguez, Vice President Sam Guzmán, & Executive Director Joe Muñoz. Secretary Gloria Casas was absent.
- Officers heard a presentation on an energy partnership from Mikal Abdullah of HMR Business Solutions & Robert Peña, Jr. of Texas Energy Consultants. They moved to receive a formal, non-binding proposal.
- The 2012 conference will be hosted at the La Quinta San Antonio Riverwalk Hotel; June 3 will be the cut-off date for breakout session application.
- The Executive Board toured the Wyndham, to consider it as a possible site for MASBA's 2013 conference.
- Joe is working with Eli Ochoa, Brian Godínez & Manuel Hinojosa to plan the Region 1 reception on April 30 at Doubleday Bar of Champions.
- The 2011-2012 Texas High School *Mariachi* Competition will host five area contests (in Grand Prairie ISD, Edinburg CISD, Houston ISD, Ector County ISD & Southwest ISD), with the state finals at the Edgewood ISD Performing Arts Theatre.

- The SLI South *Pachanga* is confirmed for June 10 at the La Quinta San Antonio Riverwalk Hotel.
- "Josh Cerna & Joe Muñoz have been authorized by the Executive Board members present to talk to Escamilla & Poneck Attorney Juan Aguilera about his plans to continue on serving as MASBA Legal Counsel."

On June 10, 2011, President Josh Cerna convened the **MASBA Board** at the La Quinta San Antonio Riverwalk Hotel. The meeting minutes report the following:
- Roll Call – Joe Muñoz, Executive Director & Gloria Casas, Secretary
- Financial Report – Juan Rangel, Treasurer
- President's Update – Josh Cerna
  - o Committee Assignments
  - o Recruiting dates/location/travel
- Executive Director Update – Joe Muñoz
- Website & PR Update – Kurt Hixson
- Legal Update – Juan Aguilera
- Legislative Update – Art Reyna
- Update on 2012 Convention
- Update on 2013 Convention
- Update on *Mariachi* Competition
- Update on 2014 Convention – Trisha Watts, McAllen CVB
- Energy Presentation – Robert Peña, Jr., Texas Energy Consortium

On September 30, 2011, President Josh Cerna convened the **MASBA Board** at the Austin Convention Center. The agenda listed the following:
- Roll Call – Executive Director Joe Muñoz & Secretary Gloria Casas
- Financial Report – President Elect & Treasurer Juan Rangel
- President's Update – Josh Cerna
  - o Committee Assignments
  - o Discussion on MOU to collaborate with IDRA, NAACP, LULAC, TCEP for litigation over school equity
  - o Recruiting dates/location/travel

- Executive Director Update – Joe Muñoz
- Website & PR Update – Kurt Hixson
  - Dobermann Marcomm contract for 2012-2015
- Legal Update – Juan Aguilera
- Legislative Update – Art Reyna
- Update on 2012 Convention – Joe Muñoz & Josh Cerna
  - Request from President Elect Juan Rangel for a presentation by Dr. Rosanna Boyd, President of National Association of Bilingual Ed
- Update on 2013 Convention
- Update on *Mariachi* Competition
- Update on 2014 Convention – Trisha Watts, McAllen CVB
- Update on *Mariachi* Competition
  - The following area competitions are planned: 1A-3A (Southwest ISD), East (Houston ISD), West (Ector County ISD), North (Fort Worth ISD), South (Edinburg CISD) & Central (Southwest ISD)
  - The finals competition is scheduled for January 28, 2012 at the Edgewood ISD Performing Arts Theatre
- Energy Presentation – Robert Peña, Jr., Texas Energy Consortium
- Dinner Discussion on Possible Agreement with Jason Choate's Business
- New Business
  - Discussion on Town Hall Panel – Vice President Sam Guzmán
  - Discussion on Creation of MASBA History – Past President Manuel Rodríguez
  - Request from Jesús Cantú Medel from *Museo Guadalupe Azatlán* to fundraise at MASBA Conference – Past President Manuel Rodríguez

On January 20, 2012, President Josh Cerna convened the annual **MASBA Member Assembly** at the La Quinta San Antonio Riverwalk Hotel. The agenda listed the following:

- Roll Call – Joe Muñoz, Executive Director & Gloria Casas, Secretary
- Financial Report – Juan Rangel, Treasurer
- President's Update – Josh Cerna

- Executive Director Update – Joe Muñoz
- Website & PR Update – Kurt Hixson
- Legal Update – Juan Aguilera
- Legislative Update – Art Reyna
- Update on 2013 Convention – Joe Muñoz
- Update on *Mariachi* Competition – Joe Muñoz
- Elections

No minutes have been found for the meeting, but two unsigned resolutions were prepared for Josh's signature. The first reads,

> "Resolved, that in light of our current Texas economic and demographic challenges and the complexity of financing public education, improvements in school funding be established with an attitude where education is found as the highest priority; ... this attitude begins within the leadership of Texas school districts and Texas education professional organizations and together, we respectfully share one unified message to all involved: Make Education a Priority."

The second, titled "Adequate Funding of Early Childhood Education," reads,

> "Resolved, that Texas legislative officials support legislation that enables more school districts to offer high-quality full-day pre-kindergarten programs; and, be it Resolved, investing in our children's education (including a more extended program of early schooling) is an investment in the future economic vitality of Texas."

If you would like to share any photos, meeting minutes, conference programs, mementos, etc. from the presidency of Joshua Cerna, for inclusion in Volume II, please email them to info@masbatx.org or mail them to MASBA | P.O. Box 474 | Austin, TX 78767.

Thank you for helping us to reconstruct our history!

"We Turned MASBA Around and Started Making Money"

Juan Rangel

Beginning in 2000, I served on the Fort Worth ISD Board of Trustees for 13 years. All Fort Worth ISD trustees represented single-member districts, except the White, at-large president, whose election for 110 years largely depended on money. You had no chance of being the Fort Worth ISD board president if you were a minority. Several state representatives drafted legislation to change our Fort Worth ISD board composition, but it failed. As a result, we changed our board composition, to allow a single-member-district trustee to serve as president. This change occurred mid-term, so some trustees, like me, served an extra year — which is why I served 13 years.

In 2011, I became the first *Latino* board president in the 115-year history of the Fort Worth ISD. Historically, our board always had a *Latino* member. Before then, the Fort Worth ISD also always had a White superintendent. During my leadership as board president, we hired the district's first African-American superintendent, Walter Dansby, in 2011. That's the kind of power we wield as trustees, when we work together and don't vote against one another.

When I served on the board, several school board members had schools named after them — even while serving on the board. I've never had a school named for me, despite being the first *Latino* president of the board. The politics of school naming in Fort Worth are interesting. I served as board president for six or seven months because other board members conspired to push me out of that position. They curtailed my term, saying, "It's someone else's turn now!" And so we had a Black school board president after me.

During that same time, I also served as President of MASBA, and the MASBA Board considered writing a letter to my Fort Worth ISD Board about the dirty politics going on, but MASBA carefully sidestepped those politics.

I didn't know much about MASBA's impact until my second term as a trustee. I was elected as a regional representative on the MASBA Board for four or five years before becoming MASBA's President in 2012.

When I took over as President, economic stability became my main concern. Joe Muñoz was the Executive Director. He and I turned MASBA around and put it "in the black." Before then, we had gone through some turbulent years financially.

During my time with MASBA, the organization began to experience a turnaround. I'm a marketing and management consultant. I worked with Kurt Hixson on MASBA's marketing dynamic. We reworked his contract, to define his responsibilities. He previously had a contract that wasn't a contract; we simply assumed that Kurt would always be with us. I said, "We're going to do this the right way. We're going to make this a business transaction and more than you just being a friend of MASBA." As a result, we really started pushing the marketing of MASBA. We knew we needed more money, we needed more membership, we needed to have more dynamic conferences. We needed to become an impact machine — an organization that made a difference. So we turned MASBA around and started making money. We were able to finally pay for our conferences. Before, we could not. You've probably heard horror stories of people lending us money. Vendors would lend us money, because we had nothing. You can't do business that way!

So, my focus became marketing. Meanwhile, our dealings with the IRS admittedly slipped. The challenge arose of verifying that we were a legitimate, certified 501(c)(3) not-for-profit organization. We weren't filing our annual IRS Form 990 at a time when the IRS was coming down hard on many non-profits throughout the country. The same happened to the United Hispanic Council of Tarrant County, when I served as their president; their non-profit status was shaken up, too. When you're working as a volunteer, sharing your time with three or four boards, the demands overtake you. Then, fortunately, we found an accountant, Garza | González & Associates, to "get us solid," as they say. They've served MASBA ever since. Gloria Casas gets the credit for making us legitimate in that respect.

After those challenges, I was ready to be done as president. I didn't want to serve another term, but MASBA needed leadership and guidance to fortify our work to make MASBA financially sound, so I stayed on as Immediate Past President. What a time that was! We had money again. Before that, we didn't have money, and no one could tell if or how much money we had in the bank.

While I was President, my whole effort was to push MASBA to become successful, acceptable, attractive, and more well-known. We wanted MASBA to be a powerhouse in Texas, and we wanted to ensure its legacy — that it would last another 10 or 20 years.

Due to politics, I lost my local election in 2013, but I continued to be active in MASBA for two or three years afterward.

I deeply respect our current MASBA President, Willie Tenorio. He is one of the most genuine and admired people I know. He is a courteous, kind man, with no time for backstabbing — even though he's been a victim of that kind of stuff. He's solid. He knows a great deal of our history. We're good friends, and, like me, he believes we have to lift MASBA to its highest level of respect and impact.

When I first got on the board, I recognized our past presidents, to draw cohesiveness and unity to our efforts as *Latino* leaders. It's important for us to know our history and to recognize our achievements. It's like knowing your grandparents and great grandparents. I commend MASBA on pulling together this work on its history. MASBA has its nose in the right direction. My hope is that MASBA might continue to be a pristine organization, an organization with a history that can never be matched by any other organization. If we brought our power together, no organization in the country could match our power. We would be unbelievably powerful!

Juan Rangel served on the Fort Worth ISD Board of Trustees for 13 years. He joined the MASBA Board in 2005 and served as Treasurer, Vice President, and President Elect. Juan became MASBA President in 2012 and continued to be active as Immediate Past President.

The Presidency of Juan Rangel

Juan Rangel of the Fort Worth ISD served as MASBA President from January 21, 2012 to January 19, 2013.

On February 10, 2012, MASBA Executive Director Joe Muñoz convened **a meeting co-hosted by MASBA and the Texas Association of** *Mariachi* **Educators** at the La Quinta San Antonio Riverwalk Hotel to discuss the 2012-2013 Texas High School *Mariachi* Area Contests and *Mariachi* Championship. A reception followed.

On February 17, 2012, President Juan Rangel convened a meeting of the **MASBA Executive Committee & Staff** at TASB Winter Governance in Corpus Christi. The meeting agenda follows:
- Roll Call – Joe Muñoz, Executive Director
- Minutes from Last Meeting – Martín Cepeda
- Treasurer's Report – Juan Rangel & Ron McVey
- Executive Director Update – Joe Muñoz
  - Shirts & Table covers
  - Vendors
  - Golf tournament
- MASBA Conference 2013
  - Manuel Rodríguez, Chair
  - Breakouts/Agenda
  - Vendors
  - Banquet
- Membership – Kurt Hixson
  - New Memberships
  - Board Members' Role
  - Renewals
- Vendor Sponsorships
  - Renewals
  - New Sponsors
  - Board Members' Role
- *Mariachi* Competition – Joe Muñoz
  - 2012 Results & 2013 Dates
  - *Mariachi* Budget

- Newsletter
- SLI – Joe Muñoz & Kurt Hixson
- Webpage – Kurt Hixson
- Legislative Update – Art Reyna
- IDRA – Juan Rangel

On June 15, 2012, President Juan Rangel convened a meeting of the **MASBA Board** at the La Quinta San Antonio Riverwalk Hotel. The agenda follows:

- Roll Call – Executive Director Joe Muñoz
- Treasurer's Report –Ron McVey (Mercedes ISD)
- President's Update – Juan Rangel (Fort Worth ISD)
  - o Committee Assignments
- Executive Director's Update – Joe Muñoz
  - o *Mariachi* Marketing Proposal – GTO Advertising
- Website / PR Update – Kurt Hixson
- Legal Update – Juan Aguilera
  - o IDRA Memorandum of Understanding
  - o ERO Architects Memorandum of Understanding
  - o Texas Rangers Update
- Legislative Update – Art Reyna
- 2013 Convention Update – Manuel Rodríguez
- 2014 Convention in McAllen
- 2015 Convention in Austin
- 2016 Convention in San Antonio
- MASBA Board Vacancies
  - o Replace Juan Garza (Kingsville ISD)
  - o Replace Martín Cepeda (Hidalgo ISD)
  - o Fill unexpired term of Secretary
- Update on *Mariachi* Competition – Joe Muñoz
  - o Area Competitions in Fort Worth ISD, Southwest ISD & Edinburg CISD
  - o Finals at Edgewood ISD Performing Arts Theatre

On September 28, 2012, President Juan Rangel convened a meeting of the **MASBA Board** at the Austin Convention Center. The agenda and minutes relate the following:

- Roll Call – Executive Director Joe Muñoz & Secretary Irene Rodríguez
- Financial Report – Treasurer Ron McVey
- President's Update – Juan Rangel
  - o Committee Assignments
  - o Appoint Directors to Open Board Positions
  - o Closed Session: Executive Director Contract
    - ▪ The Board voted in open session to extend the Executive Director's contract for six months
- Executive Director's Update – Joe Muñoz
- Website / PR Update – Kurt Hixson
- Legal Update – Juan Aguilera
  - o IDRA Memorandum of Understanding
  - o ERO Architects Memorandum of Understanding
- Legislative Update – Art Reyna
- 2013 Convention Update – Manuel Rodríguez, Kurt Hixson & Joe Muñoz
- 2014 Convention in McAllen
- 2015 Convention in Austin
- Update on *Mariachi* Competition – Joe Muñoz
  - o Area Competitions in Fort Worth ISD, Southwest ISD & Edinburg CISD
  - o Finals at Edgewood ISD Performing Arts Theatre

On January 17, 2013, President Juan Rangel opened the **Annual MASBA Conference** at the Austin Doubletree Hotel. The agenda for the conference shares the following:

General Sessions

"The White House Initiative"

"*Tejano* Monument"
Dr. Emilio Zamora, The University of Texas at Austin

Panels
"Legislative Roundtable"
"MASBA, the Organization, Yesterday thru Today:
A Roundtable Discussion"

Breakout Sessions

"Educating English Language Learners (ELLs) in Texas Schools:
Basic Concepts of Bilingual/ESL Education
and Issues of Fair Funding"
Dr. Rudy Rodríguez, Denton ISD
Dr. Albert Cortez, IDRA

"The Importance of Diversity in Construction"
Anita Uribe Martin, Bartlett Cocke

"Avoiding Landmines When Procuring
High-dollar Health Insurance & Construction Services"
Winnie Domínguez & Mike Saldaña,
Walsh Anderson Gallegos Green & Trevino

"Supplemental Employee Benefits"
Steve Orta & Kevin McCarthy, First Public

"Advancing College Readiness"
NALEO

"Common Financing Tools & Bond Election Campaign Tips"
Víctor Quiroga, Southwest Securities

"Public/Private Partnerships:
Financing Options for Future Growth"
Eli Ochoa & Brian Godínez, ERO Architects

"How to Set up a Middle School *Mariachi* Program, Part I"
Dr. William Gradante & Dr. Michael Ryan, Fort Worth ISD

"Technology 101 for Trustees"
Juan Cabrera, O'Hanlon McCollom & Demerath

"Implementing Injury Prevention for Staff Makes Cent$"
Clem Zabalza, TASB Risk Management

"How to Set up a Middle School *Mariachi* Program, Part II"
Dr. William Gradante & Dr. Michael Ryan, Fort Worth ISD

"New Affordable Health Care Act
and its Impact on Texas School Districts"
Holly Murphy, TASB Legal Division

"Improve Academics, Stop Bullying In Schools"
Víctor Salazar & Trevor Romain

"Building Success with Your Team"
Sylvester Vásquez, Dr. Lloyd Verstuyft & Jeanette Ball,
Southwest ISD

"Collective Memory: *Chicanos* & Mexican Americans"
Dr. China Medel

"What Every Student & Adult Needs to Know about Technology"
Reggie Cajayon, Texas School Safety Center,
Texas State University

"Lining up the Stars on STAAR:
A Focused Look at Community Impacts of High-stakes Testing"
Dr. Ángela Valenzuela & Patricia D. López,
The University of Texas at Austin

"The Battle of Medina"
Dan Arellano

"Real-time Solutions for Bullying in Our Schools"
Tim Porter, Appddiction

Student Entertainment
Fort Worth ISD Fine Arts

Entertainment
David Lee Garza *y Los Musicales*

La Campana Award
Dr. Sylvester Pérez, San Antonio ISD

On January 19, 2013, President Juan Rangel convened the annual
MASBA Member Assembly at the Wyndham Garden Austin. The
agenda follows:
- Roll Call – Joe Muñoz, Executive Director & Irene Rodríguez,
  Secretary (Big Spring ISD)
- Financial Report – Ron McVey, Treasurer (Mercedes ISD)
- President's Update – Juan Rangel (Fort Worth ISD)
- Legal Opinion on Unfilled President Position – Juan Aguilera
  & Juan Cabrera
- Election of Officers: President Gloria Casas (La Feria ISD),
  President Elect Danny Bueno (Ben Bolt-Palito Blanco ISD),
  Vice President Louis Reyes (Seguin ISD), Secretary Gloria
  Peña (Arlington ISD), Treasurer Juan Rangel (Ft. Worth ISD)

- Election of Directors: Corando Garza (Kingsville ISD), Willie Tenorio (Hays CISD), Marty Reyes (Ysleta ISD), Lori Moya (Austin ISD), Josh Cerna (Harlandale ISD)
- Consideration of Event at SLI North in Fort Worth
- Executive Director Update
  - June 7, 3:00 p.m. Board Meeting
  - June 7, 6:00 p.m. to midnight *Molcajete* Reception, followed by dance with Ram Herrera & the Outlaw Band
- Membership/Sponsorship Update – Kurt Hixson
- Legal Update – Juan Aguilera & Juan Cabrera
- Legislative Update – Art Reyna
- New Business:
  - The Member Assembly approved drafting a letter to the TEA Commissioner in support of the El Paso ISD Board of Trustees
  - The Member Assembly approved appointing a committee to oversee teacher training
  - The Member Assembly approved creation of a Scholarship Committee chaired by María Leal & Gloria Casas

If you would like to share any photos, meeting minutes, conference programs, mementos, etc. from the presidency of Juan Rangel, for inclusion in Volume II, please email them to info@masbatx.org or mail them to MASBA | P.O. Box 474 | Austin, TX 78767.

Thank you for helping us to reconstruct our history!

"We Got MASBA on the Road to Recovery"

Gloria Santillán Casas

In 1994, I became the first woman to be elected to the La Feria ISD Board of Trustees. I first got involved in MASBA after Viola García, whom I met at TASB's Summer Leadership Institute in San Antonio, suggested that I should join MASBA. So, I started attending some of MASBA's events. In January 2006, I joined the MASBA Board, and I served MASBA for the next nine years.

I never intended to be on the MASBA Board or to be an officer — and certainly not President. That was a big job! I simply wanted to learn and become a better board member in the La Feria ISD. María Leal, a South Texas ISD trustee who served as MASBA President in 2009, finally talked me into becoming an officer.

In 2013, I became President of MASBA, essentially by default: President Elect Sam Guzmán of the Austin ISD stepped down after he stopped serving on the Austin ISD school board. Next in line to serve as President, I accepted the position and decided to do my best to lead the organization and serve its members. I figured, *"Ya que me echaron al agua, ¡voy a nadar!"* ["Since they threw me into the water, I'm going to swim!"]

It's still difficult to believe that MASBA survived some very turbulent years. MASBA, like all organizations, had its ups and downs. As President, I didn't want MASBA to merely continue treading water, so I made some necessary changes.

In 2010, when Manuel Rodríguez became President, MASBA was "in the red," and Manuel managed to get some funding coming in. But by the time I became President, MASBA had lost its 501(c)(3) not-for-profit status. When I found that out, I almost had a heart attack! We worked to get it back. Mike García and Juan Cabrera were very helpful. They gave me a lot of advice on what we needed to do. Juan Aguilera helped us, and we managed to get our status back.

A lot of things happened during my presidency. We had a series of serious and tough meetings in San Antonio, at which I insisted to see things in black-and-white. I wanted us to be transparent. I, along with other members, needed to know what was going on and why we were in such a condition, in order to start taking necessary corrective steps. Consequently, we hired an accountant to put some structure into our finances and books, and to properly account for our funds going forward. My good friend, Marty Reyes of the Ysleta ISD, stayed at my side during this time, lending words of wisdom, guidance and emotional support. While recognizing that MASBA is a non-profit, we were beginning to run it more like a business.

That year, not because of me, but because of many of us who worked together, we managed to get MASBA going in the right direction. Manuel Rodríguez was a great leader and mentor. Like family, we used to talk for hours about how to keep moving forward and never give up.

As President, I set out to establish a scholarship program. I got a lot of help, including from Manuel. The program really got established in a significant way with the help and work of people like Brian Godínez, Sam Guzmán, Kurt Hixson and Louis Reyes. I am very pleased to know that the program has continued to grow. We also continued strong strategic alliances with organizations like IDRA, MALDEF, TLEC and others.

We became a major and prominent member and leader in the legislative struggles at the Texas Legislative Sessions and the battles over school finance issues and many other concerns that affected our school districts, particularly those with high Hispanic student demographics.

Another major milestone was the UIL sanctioning of *mariachi* music education in our public schools. The *mariachis* in our schools were already good; now they enjoyed the opportunity to showcase their magnificence! Joe Muñoz led us to achieve this accomplishment, and we were assisted in bringing this endeavor to fruition by State Representative Richard Raymond.

MASBA is what it is today largely because of our accomplishments in those years. I assure you that MASBA wouldn't exist today as you know it, if it wasn't for programs and initiatives established back then. Let's give credit where credit is due.

It was an honor and privilege to be part of MASBA and to serve as President. MASBA is near and dear to my heart for many reasons, including the fact that one of its founders is a good friend of mine: the former U.S. Congressman from the *Río Grande* Valley, the Honorable Rubén Hinojosa. He previously served as a school board member of the Mercedes ISD, and he and other visionaries, like Dr. José Cárdenas from the Edgewood ISD, gave us a great gift: MASBA! They had the foresight and vision fifty years ago to get together and create and establish what is now considered an institution. The MASBA conference at which we honored Congressman Hinojosa was one of the most memorable conferences we have had.

Our challenge now is to live up to the vision they had and the reasons why they felt MASBA was necessary then — and indeed is still necessary now. Have we lived up to that challenge, and will we continue to do so going forward? I think that we have, but still have a long way to go. For example, MASBA needs to find a way to stand on its own two feet in terms of its leadership, independence and finances. We can do it by continuing to work together, keeping the faith, and never forgetting what our founders had in their minds and hearts when they founded MASBA.

Gloria Santillán Casas serves on the La Feria ISD Board of Trustees. She was elected to the MASBA Board of Directors in 2006 and became MASBA President in 2013. She also served on the Board of Directors of the Texas Association of School Boards from 2004 to 2016.

The Presidency of Gloria Santillán Casas

On February 15, 2013, MASBA Executive Director Joe Muñoz convened **a meeting co-hosted by MASBA and the Texas Association of** *Mariachi* **Educators** at the La Quinta San Antonio Riverwalk Hotel to discuss the Texas High School *Mariachi* Area Contests and *Mariachi* Championship. The meeting agenda follows:

- Welcome – Noé Sánchez, TAME President
- TAME Report – Belle Ortiz
- TAME Treasurer Report
- MASBA Report – Joe Muñoz, Executive Director & *Mariachi* Coordinator
  - ○ Sponsor – G^2
  - ○ List of Issues
- North Area Competition: continue or not, vs. combine or not
- Central Area Competition
- South Area Competition
- Finals: propose change from Edgewood ISD to Southwest ISD
- Judges – Juan Ortiz & Joe Muñoz
- Middle School Competition: Texas A&M College Station – Roy Lozano

In May 2013, President Gloria Casas convened a meeting of the **MASBA Executive Board** at the Region 1 Conference at South Padre Island. The agenda for the undated meeting follows:

- Possible Partnership with community college board members, State Board of Education members & NALEO – Gloria Casas
- Financial Report & Discussion on Fund Balance – Juan Cabrera
- Current & Projected Financial Status – Joe Muñoz & Juan Rangel
- Review of Selection Process for Golden *Molcajete* (September) & *La Campana* Award (January)
- Report on 2014 Conference – Manuel Rodríguez, Joe Muñoz & Kurt Hixson
- *Mariachi* Update

- Update on MASBA Strategic Plan – Joe Muñoz & Gloria Casas
  o Ernie Nieto will host at his ranch in Martindale
- Bylaws Review & Update – Juan Cabrera
- Update on SLI Fort Worth – Gloria Peña
- Update on Continuing Education Credits – Manuel Rodríguez
- Update on Scholarship Initiative – María Leal
- Creation of Standard News Release for *Mariachi* Initiative – Joe Muñoz & WFAA Dallas
- Development of June 2013 Board Agenda – Joe Muñoz & Juan Cabrera
- MASBA Presence at the Legislative Session – Louis Reyes

On June 8, 2013, President Gloria Casas convened a meeting of the **MASBA Board** at the San Antonio Marriott Rivercenter Hotel. The agenda and meeting minutes reflect the following:

- Roll Call – Joe Muñoz, Executive Director
  o Those present were President Gloria Casas; President Elect Danny Bueno; Vice President Louis Reyes; Directors Manuel Rodríguez, Willie Tenorio & Marty Reyes; Executive Director Joe Muñoz; Staff Kurt Hixson; MASBA Attorneys Juan Aguilera & Juan Cabrera.
  o Those excused were Treasurer Juan Rangel; Directors Viola García, María Leal, Corando Garza, Lori Moya, Gloria Peña; and MASBA Legislative Attorney Art Reyna.
  o Larry Pérez was absent.
- Gloria appointed Marty Reyes as Treasurer, and the Board elected Irene Galán (Big Spring ISD) to fill the seat vacated by Josh Cerna
- Treasurer's Report – Juan Rangel (Fort Worth ISD)
- Minutes of Last Meeting: Gloria Peña (Arlington ISD)
- President's Update - Gloria Casas (La Feria ISD)
- Committee Assignments
  o Nomination Committee: Gloria Casas & Juan Cabrera
  o Legislative Committee: Louis Reyes (Seguin ISD)
  o Scholarship Committee: María Leal (South Texas ISD)
- Executive Director's Update - Joe Muñoz
  o Standard News Releases
  o July 22 Meeting with TAME in San Antonio

- June 19-21 SLI South
  - Music by Marcos Orozco *y Grupo Rebelde*
  - The Board agreed to table the idea of a gathering at SLI North in Fort Worth
- *Mariachi*
  - Donations Update: Manny & Lucy González of G^2 committed a second $25,000 to host the competition during the 2013-2014 school year
- Website / PR Update – Kurt Hixson
- Vendor/Scholarship Update: Kurt Hixson & Juan Cabrera
- Legal Update – MASBA Legal Advisors Juan Aguilera/ & Juan Cabrera
- Possible Bylaws Change to Allow State Board of Education Members to Join MASBA – Juan Cabrera
- Possible Bylaws Change to Allow Community Colleges & Others to Join MASBA – Juan Cabrera
- Report on Fund Balance Proposal – Juan Cabrera
- Legislative Update – Art Reyna, MASBA Legislative
- Presentation – Dr. Edelmiro Escamilla, Construction Science, Texas A&M University College Station; the Board approved working with him on an initiative to change perceptions of careers in the construction industry
- Presentation: Dr. Jan P. Seiter, Huston-Tillotson University; the Board approved having Dr. Seiter work with Hays CISD and Seguin ISD and to report on her work at the September 28 Board meeting
- Closed Session: Vote on Executive Director Contract (tabled)
- TASB Update – Viola García (Aldine ISD)
- Update on 2014 MASBA Convention in McAllen
  - Manuel Rodríguez, Chair
  - Information on Call for Presenters
- Old Business: Juan Cabrera reported that Rudy Colmenero, CPA has filed MASBA's delinquent tax reports and is filing for MASBA's Certificate of Reinstatement with the Secretary of State; he is hopeful that MASBA will soon be reinstated

On July 22, 2013, MASBA Executive Director Joe Muñoz convened a **meeting co-hosted by MASBA and the Texas Association of** *Mariachi* **Educators** at the La Quinta San Antonio Riverwalk Hotel to discuss the 2013-2014 Texas High School *Mariachi* Area Contests and *Mariachi* Championship. A reception followed with music by *Mariachi Nuevo Royal*.

On September 27, 2013, President Gloria Casas convened a meeting of the **MASBA Board** at the Dallas Convention Center. Meeting materials totaled more than 114 pages. The agenda follows:

- Roll Call – Executive Director Joe Muñoz
- Introduction of Guest Ted Beard, Black Caucus President
- Treasurer's Report – Juan Rangel
  - Marty Reyes appointed Treasurer in June
- President's Update
  - MASBA Planning Budget Update
  - Regional Representation
  - Strategic Plan Update
  - Memoranda of Understanding
  - Update on Items Discussed at June 13 Meeting
- Committee Reports
  - Nominations – Gloria Casas
  - Legislative – Louis Reyes, Danny Bueno, Juan Cabrera
  - Scholarship – María Leal
    - If Titanium sponsorship is approved, $2,500 will be earmarked in name of Walsh Anderson Gallegos Green & Trevino
- Executive Director's Report – Joe Muñoz
  - Dr. Edelmiro Escamilla, Texas A&M University College Station
  - Dr. Jan P. Seiter, Huston-Tillotson University
  - Application for Reinstatement – Rudy Colmenero, CPA
    - IRS Discussions
  - 2013 SLI Activity Report: San Antonio & Fort Worth
    - Cost
    - Membership Recruited
    - Marcos Orozco will sing in San Antonio
  - TASA/TASB Convention

- o July 22 Meeting of TAME in San Antonio, during Texas Band Masters Convention
- o *Mariachi* Update
  - Mrs. & Mrs. González will provide $25,000 check by October 1
  - Area competitions are scheduled for Fort Worth ISD, San Antonio ISD & Edinburg CISD, with finals at Southwest ISD
- Website & PR Update – Kurt Hixson
- Items for Consideration
  - o Processes for Memoranda of Understanding & Interlocal Agreements
  - o Titanium MOUs
  - o MASBA/TAME *Mariachi* MOU
  - o Jesse Treviño Insurance
- 2014 Conference in McAllen
  - o Music by Jimmy González y Grupo Mazz
- Closed Session
  - o IRS Update – Rudy Colmenero, CPA
  - o Review & Possible Approval of Executive Director Contract
  - o Review & Possible Approval of Executive Director Job Description
  - o Legal Update – Juan Aguilera

If you would like to share any photos, meeting minutes, conference programs, mementos, etc. from the presidency of Gloria Santillán Casas, for inclusion in Volume II, please email them to info@masbatx.org or mail them to MASBA | P.O. Box 474 | Austin, TX 78767.

Thank you for helping us to reconstruct our history!

"Hope, Accomplishments & Good Times"

Sam Guzmán

Thank you for the opportunity to be part of this document which will engrave MASBA's story into the annals of history. I played but a small part compared to others who were the pillars and linchpins of this most important and historical organization, which is arguably to be considered an institution.

Upon being elected to the Austin ISD Board of Trustees in 2007, I attended TASB events for the purpose of learning how to become an effective board member. I attended my first TASB conference in Dallas, which is where I ran into numerous individuals I knew and respected, such as Louis Reyes of the Seguin ISD, who served his community on the school board for 25 years, and Mike García, a contributing partner and vendor of MASBA. I quickly decided to devote my time and efforts to MASBA.

In previous years, Austin ISD Board Members like Gus García, Lydia Pérez, and Diana Castañeda were extensively involved in MASBA. By the time of my election, MASBA was no longer a priority for our district—as I remember, we were no longer a MASBA member. Some fellow board members thought of MASBA as a "party group"! Such perceptions didn't dissuade me from following my strong feelings for participating in MASBA, and I resolved to join MASBA, even if my district didn't. Thereafter, it didn't take long before our board unanimously approved joining MASBA, and the Austin ISD has been a prominent member ever since.

I became a member of the MASBA Board and shortly thereafter was elected President Elect. In this position, I participated in all MASBA events, including its Board meetings.

After serving two terms on the Austin ISD Board, MASBA offered me a part-time consultant position, which turned out to be full-time in terms of the amount of time and effort needed to respond to the needs and issues of members. I could clearly see that the leadership had already made major strides, and there was no lack of enthusiasm and passion for continuing to move forward. Deeply committed to the mission and vision of the organization, I never regretted coming aboard as a consultant.

The next three years were a bit rough, but mostly full of hope, accomplishments, and good times. It was indeed a fun and rewarding job! Some of the major accomplishments during this time included the following:

1. We created structure in the organization by working on standard operating procedures, like a travel reimbursement policy

2. We awarded the *La Campana* Award to such notables as:

   - Senator Gonzalo Barrientos, for drop-out prevention legislation and the passage of legislation like the "Top 10% Rule," which significantly increased the enrollment of Hispanic students in our major universities;

   - Ernesto Nieto, Founder and President of the prestigious and successful National Hispanic Institute; and

   - Kevin O'Hanlon, for his role in the drafting of the "Robin Hood" school finance plan in an effort to equalize the financing of school districts throughout the state. He also provided very valuable *pro bono* legal advice to MASBA.

3. We developed strong and effective working relationships and strategic alliances with strong and influential organizations like IDRA, MALDEF, and other member organizations of the Texas *Latino* Education Coalition. We collectively monitored, supported and fought legislation that impacted Hispanic students and school districts with high Hispanic student demographics, and we spent an inordinate amount of time at the Texas Legislature and Capitol!

4. We developed a Hispanic Heritage program, which we implemented in tandem with National Hispanic Heritage Month.

5. We testified numerous times before the State Board of Education in support of Mexican American Studies in our public schools.

6. We significantly improved MASBA's annual conferences by providing notable speakers, content experts, and relevant and valuable workshop sessions. I knew our conferences were getting good and going in the right direction when Willie

Tenorio, MASBA's current President, came up to me and said, "This is one of the best conferences I have attended!"

7. With the expert assistance and support of Brian Godínez and his staff at ERO Architects, we created MASBA's current logo.

8. I developed two business programs—an energy program and an employee benefits program—which, if implemented, would have generated a significant amount of funds for MASBA. To my disappointment, the MASBA Board decided not to implement these programs.

Some of my fondest memories of working with MASBA are the camaraderie and *esprit de corps* with colleagues, board members, and district members. I also enjoyed the genuine feeling that we were a service-oriented organization serving our members and assisting the children they served.

My hope for the future of MASBA is that, as its leaders change and turn over through the years, they will never forget the purpose and essence of the organization, which can now be considered an institution. I also hope that we never forget the mission and vision of its founders.

In closing I leave you with a well-known lesson: "If you want to go quickly, go alone. If you want to go far, go with others." Let's pledge to go far together!

Sam Guzmán served on the Austin ISD Board of Trustees from 2007 to 2012. He became MASBA Secretary in 2010, Vice President in 2011, and President Elect in 2012. Sam then served as MASBA's Director of Operations & Development through 2017.

"We Developed Friendships Throughout the State"

Danny Bueno

José "Keno" Rodríguez served on our school board here in the Ben Bolt-Palito Blanco ISD. When he was elected justice of the peace, he wanted me to take over for him on the school board, and I did. I stayed for 24 and a half years.

I had graduated from the district, where my mother worked for many years. Being a public servant myself, as a law enforcement officer, I feel I've continued her service. I worked for the City of Alice for 37 years, and for 12 and a half years as police chief—the longest police chief in the history of the City of Alice—so many people call me "Chief." I like to tell the story of the time when I joined Joe Muñoz and others at a conference in Arizona: The elderly, Native-American women in a restaurant there wanted a photo with me, because they heard the others calling me "Chief" —and they thought I was the chief of a Native-American tribe there! I'm no longer "Chief"; I now serve as Sheriff of Jim Wells County.

When I served on the school board, we believed it important for us to join MASBA. Before I knew it, I became very involved in MASBA and shared presentations at its annual MASBA conference. MASBA allowed me to meet thousands and thousands of people from throughout the state. It gives me a lot of joy to know that we were able to keep MASBA going, and that, because of our hard work, all of us working together were able to bring MASBA to where it is today.

When I served on the MASBA Board, we were a very good team. We developed friendships throughout the state: from South Texas, all the way up to Dallas, and over to El Paso. We came together and celebrated with a dance and dinner at our conference, where we talked about our accomplishments. Everyone pulled together to make sure that our children received the best possible education. That was our number one priority.

When I served as President, MASBA continued to be very involved in *mariachi*. I love *mariachi* music, and I sing *mariachi* myself—I can't count the number of times I've sung "*Las mañanitas*" late at night or early in the morning! Enthused about MASBA's *mariachi* program, I attended several of its *mariachi* events and competitions. We worked to push for the credibility of *mariachi*—a big accomplishment for the organization. Not every student is a track runner or basketball player or football player; we have kids who are good at instruments, so *mariachi* is a plus for them. I'm a six-foot-three football and basketball player, but I really appreciate MASBA pushing *mariachi*, so that kids who can't play football or run track also have an opportunity to be recognized.

Everyone looked forward to attending our conferences due to the relationships formed there. We always had MASBA receptions at TASB trainings—and they were like family reunions! As school board members lost their local school board races, we'd lure in the new school board members. We emphasized the need for school board member training. We wanted to train new school board members on the issues affecting our schools. We talked about how to assess the needs of kids, and how to help our kids and their teachers.

MASBA also had great celebrations. Joe played an important part in that: He loves music and invited some of the best bands available.

We had a scholarship program that started under Joe Muñoz and Sam Guzmán. Before we knew it, we had 25 requests for scholarships.

Later on, we started seeing African Americans participating in MASBA, so we participated with them in their Black Caucus, and it was great. They had many of the same issues we did. We worked hand-in-hand with them. We went to some of their classes, and they came to ours—all with the same purpose: ensuring that our children have the same education as everyone else.

As MASBA celebrates its 50th anniversary, it's my hope that members might keep pushing for the most-qualified teachers and for the best possible salaries for them, so that we can continue to inspire young people to teach and to be educators. We need educators who give it all they have, in a professional, caring, honest, humble way. We need people who tell our kids, "I am so proud of you!" MASBA can play a key role in issues like this.

A school board member on the Ben Bolt-Palito Blanco ISD Board of Trustees for 24.5 years, Danny Bueno served on the MASBA Board for at least four years before becoming MASBA President in 2014. Affectionately known as "Chief," for his role in the City of Alice police department, he now serves as Sheriff of Jim Wells County.

The Presidency of Danny Bueno

Few written records have been found from the presidency of Danny Bueno, who served from February 1, 2014 to January 24, 2015.

On May 17, 2014, MASBA co-hosted with ERO Architects and the Region One School Boards Association the 7th Annual After Party at the Doubleday Bar of Champions in Port Isabel. According to the invite, the event included a barbeque, spirits, karaoke, dancing and games.

If you would like to share any photos, meeting minutes, conference programs, mementos, etc. from the presidency of Danny "Chief" Bueno, for inclusion in Volume II, please email them to info@masbatx.org or mail them to MASBA | P.O. Box 474 | Austin, TX 78767.

Thank you for helping us to reconstruct our history!

"I Wanted to Make a Difference"

Louis Q. Reyes, III

In 1991, I wasn't thinking of serving on our local school board; I wanted to serve on the Seguin City Council! But Superintendent Jim Barnes and several Hispanic community leaders visited me and asked me to run for the school board, so I did, with the intention of serving for only one year. Then I attended the Celebrating Educational Opportunities for Hispanic Students conference in 1992, and it made me realize the importance of school board members. Celebrating Educational Opportunities for Hispanic Students brought together school board members from California, Arizona, New Mexico and Texas. We met in San Antonio, Albuquerque, Phoenix and San Diego, to share ideas and best practices. I attended my first such conference in Albuquerque in 1992. There I met Dr. Trujillo of the Ysleta ISD and heard about his learning center, which we brought to the Seguin ISD. It gave kids an opportunity to learn at their own pace and to catch up with their peers. It kept kids in school.

At that Celebrating Educational Opportunities for Hispanic Students conference, I listened to the story of a young, *Latino* boy whose new district placed him in the gifted and talented and in advanced courses. He later graduated as valedictorian of his class. Some years later, he earned his doctorate in physics. He eventually discovered that the transcripts of a gifted and talented student with his same name were accidentally placed in his file and that he, though quite ordinary, rose to the expectations of those who saw him as gifted and talented. That story made me realize that "a mind is a terrible thing to waste." It moved me to stay on the school board. I served as president of our school board for 12 years. During that time, we started a *mariachi* program, launched a learning center, and brought the ROTC to the Seguin ISD. I wanted to make a difference.

In 1992, when I started the Hispanic Chamber of Commerce in Seguin, I met Jimmie Adame and Juan Aguilera, who later shared with me their interest in bringing Hispanic school board members together. In 1993, my cousin, Albert Martínez, joined the board in the San Diego ISD. I also became friends with Diana Castañeda of the Austin ISD.

In 1993, Juan hosted our first big shindig in Dallas. We had *mariachi*. The event drew many Hispanic trustees and administrators. Back then, there weren't a lot of Hispanic school board members.

In 1995, Juan, Albert, Diana and I started meeting in Austin to talk about what we could do to improve the situation for our kids and how we could bring together Hispanic trustees. Sonny, a school board member from Waco, also joined us. We held at least four meetings in Austin, often over dinner, and Lupe Zamarripa of Linebarger would invite us to places like Fonda San Miguel, a famous restaurant in Austin.

At that time, there was a Black Caucus, but no organization for Hispanic school board members—and the standards for Hispanic children were much lower than for other children. We wanted to make sure every child was college- and career-ready.

I've always said that regardless of race, color, creed, gender or socio-economic status, we just fought to be treated the same as others. We took on that battle because we weren't treated the same. Others didn't want to give us opportunities. We came together to be treated the same. It wasn't easy. Many times, people tried to discourage us, but we were convinced that our children deserved the same education as everybody else. After we formed MASBA, Albert played a special role in that battle, and Juan was our leader, helping to take us to a higher level.

We started MASBA with 18 or 20 school districts. Seguin ISD was always involved, with our *baile folklórico* and our *conjunto*, and with our children who played the accordion.

Diana lost her local election in 1996, so I took over as Acting or Interim President for three months and presided over our small meetings. Too busy to serve as President, I did it as a favor to Diana and Sonny. I advocated for Theresa to be elected President. Albert followed her as President in 1998.

I became Vice President in 2013 and President Elect in 2014. I then became MASBA's President in 2015.

In 2014, four months after I became President Elect, the MASBA Board named me Executive Director. Danny Bueno sought changes and asked me if I wanted to serve as Executive Director. He thought I possessed the necessary experience. I had served many non-profit organizations. By 2015, I worked with our CPA, we got everything straightened out, and we were again in compliance with the IRS. Sam,

Kurt and I led the organization through 2017. Then I told Armando that I planned to retire and sell my insurance agency. He asked if I would consider being MASBA's Ambassador. I'm proud to continue representing MASBA. I am gratified to see where we've taken MASBA ever since.

My dream for MASBA is that we might one day have our own five acres of land, with a building that's paid for, in which to serve. I dream of the day when we will have enough resources to work for equitable education for our minority students. We have an opportunity to make a difference. I would love to see MASBA in every school district in Texas and in the nation!

Louis Q. Reyes, III served as President of the Seguin ISD for 12 years. He attended organizational meetings for MASBA in 1995 to 1996, served as Interim President for three months in 1996, then as Executive Director from 2014 to 2017. Louis was elected Vice President of MASBA in 2013 and President Elect in 2014. He assumed the presidency of MASBA in 2015 and served as Immediate Past President in 2016. "The Godfather" continues to serve the organization as MASBA Ambassador.

The Presidency of Louis Q. Reyes, III

Louis Q. Reyes, III of Seguin ISD became President of MASBA at the annual Member Assembly in 2015.

On March 28, 2015, President Louis Q. Reyes, III convened a **MASBA Board** strategic planning retreat. Brian Godínez of ERO Architects facilitated the encounter. Meeting notes share the following:

- MASBA is the leading Hispanic voice advocating premier public education for all and community leadership to create catalysts for their communities
- How unique are we?
  - We understand & share Hispanic board members' needs
  - We provide Hispanic-centric programs for board leadership and education
  - We understand the needs of Texas Hispanic students
  - We advocate for Hispanic causes
  - MASBA is the sole source of advocacy for and transformation of a bi-cultural public education system
  - We are a family of Hispanic board members who share information, resources, and practices
- Core Values
  - Unity: Working together as one family/community
  - Service: Taking care of our members and ourselves
  - Passion: for the cause, for change, positive, teaching/learning
  - Other Values mentioned: belief/faith, hard work, integrity, family, trust, accountability, community
- Strengths: values, Hispanic culture, 74 members, positive growth, history, *mariachi* program, conference, understanding Hispanic culture, education leadership
- Weaknesses: no follow-up, identity/image, bylaws, message, marketing/PR, membership recruitment, sponsor recruitment
- Opportunities
  - MASBA is in state of transformation
  - Growing Hispanic state leadership
  - Sponsors want to be part of Hispanic causes
  - Young leaders are hungry for mentors

- <u>Threats</u>
  - o Public education is under siege
  - o Texas public education system
  - o Private education system
  - o Lethargy/apathy
  - o Competing conferences
  - o Legal status
  - o Political environment: politicians not friendly to public education
- <u>Strategies to Increase Membership</u>
  - o Disseminate Hispanic public education news (Mando, Sam, Kurt)
    - Create digital platform with identity & message
    - Develop distribution list & content
    - Establish cost & resources
    - Establish launch date
  - o Create aggressive revenue-generating campaign (Lupe, Louis, Treasurer, Kurt)
    - Identify donors with similar vision
    - Create marketing plan & materials
    - Develop membership drive
    - Create measurable goals
    - Create annual budget
    - Create value-added revenue sources
  - o Build mission-driven organization structure (Louis, Sam)
    - Create a new identity system for MASBA
    - Create a new website & marketing materials
    - More MASBA & social networks
    - Create staffing plan
    - Develop effective communication system
  - o Change bylaws to reflect mission (Manuel, Viola)
    - Utilize legal support to review & modify bylaws
    - Model TASB & TAMACC bylaws
    - Define & communicate board member role
    - Define role of executive board members
  - o Prepare and empower board members to advocate and promote MASBA vision & mission (Willie, Lupe)
    - Create & promote strategic plan
    - Create focus groups for review & feedback
    - Embrace vision & mission of MASBA

- o Expand and enhance board training & mentoring (Manuel, Gloria)
  - Develop board mentor program
  - Enhance conference, so best event/training for Hispanic education leaders
  - Develop MASBA leadership program
  - Expand SLI business meeting time for more MASBA business
- o Close Hispanic achievement gap
- o Increase number of Hispanic graduates who are college- and career-ready

On May 16, 2015, MASBA co-hosted the eighth annual **ERO-ROSBA-MASBA Spring Conference Beach Party** at the Hilton Garden Inn South Padre Island Beachfront Hotel. According to a flyer, the event included food, spirits and dancing.

On June 11, 2015, President Louis Q. Reyes, III convened a meeting of the **MASBA Board** at SLI South in San Antonio. No agenda or minutes have been found for this meeting.

On October 2, 2015, President Louis Q. Reyes, III convened a meeting of the **MASBA Board** at the Austin Convention Center. Meeting minutes record the following:

- Treasurer Rudy Orona resigned; Louis will assume his duties.
- Louis supplied a financial report from Garza | González & Associates.
- Manuel Rodríguez reported on the 2016 MASBA conference.
- Kurt Hixson shared a membership report.
- Brian Godínez of ERO Architects has created a new MASBA logo, which will be introduced at the MASBA/ERO Hispanic Heritage Month Reception later this evening.
- First Financial Group presented a proposed interlocal agreement with MASBA for insurance and supplemental employee benefits. Directors expressed concerns that they did not have enough time to review the proposal, and they asked Legal Counsel to review it.

- The Board reviewed a proposal to create the MASBA Energy School Consortium, a cooperative to provide lower electric rates to districts. Directors asked Legal Counsel to review this.
- MASBA Golden *Molcajete* recipient State Representative Richard Raymond and Jesse Treviño suggested a proposal to create the Leadership Research Initiative, which would raise the necessary funds to provide a training session for Mexican American school board members.
- "The NEEAD Initiative presentation/concept was regarding the structuring of the MASBA training process and sessions, in order to ensure that they continued to be relevant and valuable to members. This concept, including the use of the NEEAD acronym, was not well received in the meeting; therefore, it was immediately dropped."

On February 18, 2016, President Louis Q. Reyes, III convened a meeting of the **MASBA Board** at the Hilton San Antonio Airport Hotel. Attendees included President Reyes, President Elect Irene Galán-Rodríguez, Vice President, Armando Rodríguez, Secretary Lupe Ruiz, Past President Viola García, Past President Manuel Rodríguez, Kurt Hixson and Greg Garza, CPA. Immediate Past President Danny Bueno was absent. Meeting minutes share the following:

- Greg presented a financial report for 2015.
- Kurt presented a draft budget.
- Louis reported that TASB has offered MASBA $75,000. The Board approved discussing a future partnership with TASB.
- At Danny's request, Kurt and Sam will oversee Officer/Director elections.

On February 18-21, 2016, MASBA hosted its **eighteenth annual conference & expo** at the Hilton San Antonio Airport Hotel. A conference flyer shares the following information.

General Sessions

"The White House Initiative"

"Update on the Mexican American Studies Initiative," Tony Díaz

Keynote Luncheon by Rubén Pérez

Superintendents Panel

ERO Architects Keynote Luncheon

Closing Session by TASB Affiliates

Breakout Sessions

"To Reform or Deform? Federal & State Policymaking and Its Impact on Local Board Governance"
David Hinojosa, IDRA

"Technology 101 for Trustees"
O'Hanlon Rodríguez Betancourt & Demerath

"Optimum Use of Educational Facilities & Planning"
Eli Ochoa, Robert Sands & Brian Godínez, ERO Architects

"Employee Benefits"
First Financial Group of America

"Investing in Youth Leadership Development"
Julio Cotto & Nicole Sada, National Hispanic Institute

"Superintendent Evaluations:
How to Let the Superintendent Know What You Want"
Katie Payne, Walsh Gallegos Treviño Russo & Kyle

"The Perfect Formula: Creating a Successful STEM Student"
Shane Haggerty & Liza Montelongo, El Paso STEM Foundation

"*Tejanos* Rising or Mexican Uprising:
How Historians Got It All Wrong"
Dr. Manuel Flores, Texas A&M University Kingsville

"Oh, the Places You'll Go!
A Success Story on Parent & Community Engagement"
Marta Salazar & Dr. Grace Everett, Alice ISD

"MASBA 101: Building Capacity & Increasing Engagement:
Reflections on the *Latino/a* Education Task Force"
Sam Guzmán, MASBA
Dr. Patricia D. López, San José State University
Celina Moreno, MALDEF

"College Orientation for Parents"
Luciano "Lucky" Salinas, Houston Community College

"How a STEM-focused Education
Can Help Fill the National Skills Gap"
Jesús Miranda, Universal Technical Institute, Dallas

"School Community Leader & School Board Policy Decisions
that Support English Language Learner Best Practices
Serving Students from Multiple Continents"
Jesse Jai McNeil, Jr.,
21st-century Leadership Principals Preparation Program
Marie Moreno, Houston ISD

"Coping with Change & Building a Leadership Team of Excellence
through Ongoing Systemic Planning & Decision-making"
Dr. Rubén Olivarez, The University of Texas at Austin

Student Performance

Seguin ISD

On February 20, 2016, President Louis Q. Reyes, III presided over the annual **MASBA Member Assembly** at the Hilton San Antonio Airport Hotel. Meeting minutes relay the following:
- Louis shared a financial report and budget.
- MASBA currently has 81 members, short of its goal of 103 districts.
- Sam Guzmán presented a report on operations and strategic planning.
- Sam Guzmán presided over Officer/Director elections:
  o MASBA Region 2: Willie Tenorio, Jr. (Hays CISD) was re-elected, and Ana Cortez (Manor ISD) was elected.
  o MASBA Region 4: David Espinosa (Grand Prairie ISD) and Larry Pérez (Waco ISD) were elected.

- o MASBA Region 5: Mario Ybarra (Lubbock ISD) was re-elected, and Homero García (South Texas ISD) was elected.
- o MASBA Region 6: Shane Haggerty (Ysleta ISD) is not up for re-election, and Orlando Flores (Fabens ISD) was elected).
- o Armando Rodríguez (Canutillo ISD) was elected President Elect, Mario Ybarra (Lubbock ISD) was elected Vice President, Servando Garza (Alice ISD) was elected Treasurer, and Shane Haggerty (Ysleta ISD) was elected Secretary.

At the conclusion of the Member Assembly, Irene Galán-Rodríguez (Big Spring ISD) assumed presidency of MASBA.

If you would like to share any photos, meeting minutes, conference programs, mementos, etc. from the presidency of Louis Q. Reyes, III, for inclusion in Volume II, please email them to info@masbatx.org or mail them to MASBA | P.O. Box 474 | Austin, TX 78767.

Thank you for helping us to reconstruct our history!

"MASBA Wanted to Make a Difference for All Kids"

Irene Galán-Rodríguez

My Service to My Local Board

When I joined the school board, my son had just graduated from high school the year before. There were things that had happened here in Big Spring, so they were looking for people to run for office. I actively participated in my kids' schools, and I knew our school board members. My kids were in band, baseball and football. I was a room mother and in the PTA and in all the booster clubs. I knew a lot of people in Big Spring, and I thought, "I don't have kids in school anymore, so that won't cloud my mind, and I'll be able to serve all kids. I served on my local school board through 2017.

A Little Card

It all started with a little card.

I was elected to the Big Spring Board of Trustees in May 1994, and I was the only woman on my board. The next month, I flew to San Antonio for my first TASB Summer Leadership Institute. There were some people there who were giving out little cards that talked about a MASBA event. I didn't attend the event that year.

When I returned to San Antonio the next year, I received another card with an invitation to another MASBA event. MASBA planned a get-together at a local pub. That time, I went—just to meet people, to listen to the conversation, and to learn about MASBA. Everyone else in the room was from South Texas and East Texas and other places; I was the only one there from West Texas, outside of El Paso, so I felt that my presence was important. Five hours away, El Paso is a combination of Mexicans and Hispanics, but West Texas is country western. We don't have *mariachi* or the culture of South Texas. We even speak Spanish differently. People say we have a hick, country sound in the way we speak!

I went back to the Summer Leadership Institute the following year and recognized familiar faces. We started talking, they encouraged me to keep coming, and so I did.

My Involvement in MASBA

I attended an organizational meeting of MASBA in June 2000. I graduated from Leadership TASB that year and joined in the meetings of both organizations.

When we first started gathering, it was difficult to recognize MASBA as a strong organization. We started to do things to let people know MASBA is serious. We did things not only the children of Texas, but also for our board members. We provided a lot of the same training as TASB, but with more cultural awareness: that we live along the border and among English Language Learners, that we have migrants in our community and in our schools, and even before we educate them, the state is making them take tests!

MASBA wanted to make a difference for all kids, including our English Language Learners. It was personal: We understood our kids' challenges. We understood how hard it is to learn English. Imagine if the shoe were on the other foot for Anglos, and they had to speak Spanish in school from day one. That's the situation in which our English Language Learners find themselves.

The Challenges Faced by English Language Learners

My maternal grandmother isn't from Mexico, so my mother spoke to us in English, and we were more prepared for school. I grew up speaking Tex-Mex — half English, half Spanish — and we could switch from one language to the other and keep talking. My daughter, who grew up speaking English, says, "Mom, I don't know how y'all do it: You're on the phone, speaking in English, and then you switch to Spanish without even taking a breath!" And my son is Hispanic, too, but he grew up speaking English. He would tell me, "Mom, I'm going over to the Guzmáns' home," but he pronounced their name like they did: "Gooseman"! They spoke Spanglish! My son once told me that I speak English with an accent, and I said, "I do have an accent, and I don't mind my accent: People know I'm not White. I'm Hispanic!" My kids spoke English before they went to school, but I often think how hard it would have been for them if they hadn't known English.

Serving on the MASBA Board

I joined the MASBA Board in 2006. I later ran for Secretary and served for one year, until another woman wanted to serve as Secretary. Shortly after that, some MASBA Board members asked me if I would run for Secretary again. I admit I did write some good meeting minutes! They named me Secretary for a second time in 2013. By that time, I knew a lot more people in MASBA.

I became Vice President in 2014, then President Elect in 2015. I served as President in 2016, then as Immediate Past President in 2017. We worked together and accomplished so many things. There were rough times, but we all worked together to make things better.

MASBA's Partnership with TASB

While I served as President of MASBA, we signed a partnership agreement with TASB. I'm very proud of that. Presidents before me had talked about this possibility but were never able to come to an agreement. I joined the TASB Board in 2001, and I "termed out" of that Board after 15 years of service, so I knew TASB's Executive Director, James Crow, very well. When we put our proposal for TASB on paper, in black and white, it began to feel real. I made an appointment to meet with Jim, and I brought along our Executive Director and Immediate Past President, Louis Reyes; our President Elect, Armando Rodríguez; our Vice President, Mario Ybarra; and Kurt Hixson from our MASBA staff. I remember asking Jim, "Would you like TASB to be as important as MASBA? Would you like to be our partner?" He just smiled. We were the little people, and they were the big people, but we were being proactive and positive. That was a lucky day for MASBA: We left with a signed three-year partnership agreement with TASB, which just renewed last year!

Our MASBA Staff

When I served as President, I often met with our Immediate Past President and Executive Director, Louis Reyes. We would often include MASBA Staff—Sam Guzmán and Kurt Hixson—in our conversations. They were very respectful and hardworking. When I said, "We would like to do this. What do you think?", they gave us feedback, and they would execute whatever we decided. We worked hand-in-hand with them, and I would see they were doing a good job. They made it easy for me to be President. It was the same with Louis. We all worked together, and those were great years for me. Louis has a way with people, and he has a lot of friends. He did a very good job at what he did. Joe Muñoz, our previous Executive Director, did an excellent job as well.

My Dream for MASBA

As MASBA prepares to celebrate 50 years, I hope that our scholarship program continues to grow, because there are so many kids out there who need those scholarships. They need our help to get ahead. MASBA has always been about the students, and that's my dream for MASBA!

Irene Galán-Rodríguez served on the Big Spring ISD Board of Trustees for 23 years and was involved in early organizational meetings of MASBA. Beginning in 2006, Irene represented West Texas on the MASBA Board. After serving two terms as Secretary, she became MASBA Vice President in 2014 and President Elect in 2015. Irene served as President of MASBA in 2016 and as Immediate Past President in 2017.

The Presidency of Irene Galán-Rodríguez

No extant records have been found from the presidency of Irene Galán-Rodríguez, who served from February 20, 2016 to February 25, 2017.

If you would like to share any photos, meeting minutes, conference programs, mementos, etc. from the presidency of Irene Galán-Rodríguez, for inclusion in Volume II, please email them to info@masbatx.org or mail them to MASBA | P.O. Box 474 | Austin, TX 78767.

Thank you for helping us to reconstruct our history!

"I Always Wanted MASBA To Be Bigger and Better"

Armando "Mando" Rodríguez

In 2005, at age 21, I was elected to the Canutillo ISD Board of Trustees. I had attended school board meetings even in middle school and high school and noted there was little talk of closing the achievement gap and providing opportunities for kids. I remember a conversation back then about a neighboring, more-affluent school district's high school, where graduating seniors received more than $3 million in scholarships, while Canutillo graduates earned only $500,000. Even the top ten percent of graduates in Canutillo had shockingly-low grade-point averages.

I wondered, "How can kids enjoy the opportunities that I had, and the ability to study at institutions like UTEP and others across the country? How can we get scholarships and financial aid for these kids, most of whom are socio-economically disadvantaged?"

Once elected, I set my focus on making significant changes to academic rigor and accountability. It's difficult to create change in large systems, and some people thought we were moving too fast. But for two years in a row now, Canutillo ISD has been an A-rated district, we have our first Blue Ribbon School, and we were recognized with an Excellence in Education Award from H-E-B!

I came to know MASBA by accident. During a reception at the TASA/TASB conference, some colleagues and I heard the distant but familiar sound of a *mariachi*. We knew we'd feel at home in that room, and we discovered that MASBA was having a big party next door, with only keg beer!

I went to the 2007 MASBA conference in Corpus Christi with fellow trustees Sergio Coronado and Mago Arellano, and that's when we started talking about equity and educational opportunity for our students back home. I remember flying into the small airport there, and we met Manuel Rodríguez in the hotel lobby. We came back from that conference, and our local board passed resolutions on including Mexican-American history in our textbooks and making *mariachi* a UIL-sanctioned event.

Our attendance at MASBA events wasn't consistent after that, but we'd go to their events here and there to learn about statewide and federal issues, like No Child Left Behind and high-stakes testing. With the TEA cheating scandal in El Paso, I knew that, if we were going to change those systems, we had to get involved at the state and federal level.

I joined the MASBA Board at the conference in McAllen. I became Vice President at the 2015 conference in Austin and President Elect in 2016. I became MASBA President in 2017. During those years, I joined the TASB Board of Directors, the NALEO Board, and I chaired the NSBA's National Hispanic Council.

As I learned more about MASBA, I realized all the labor that different people put into this organization in the past. I also understood that we had a lot of work to do, and that we had a huge opportunity in front of us.

As President, I had three goals: organizational growth, enhanced internal and external communication, and improved systems and structures that might help MASBA to organically grow.

I set high expectations for our MASBA staff and asked them for monthly reports. I wanted to ensure that MASBA provided a real value to its members and a track record of accomplishments. I began to wonder how MASBA might have a real impact for its member districts. Former MASBA President Juan Rangel helped us with a study of MASBA's value-add. Our MASBA Board met for a retreat in San Antonio to discuss this.

By June 2017, the "Godfather," Louis Q. Reyes, wanted to transition from his service as our MASBA Executive Director. He played a critical role in our organization. On a personal level, he mentored me, always emphasizing that we have to make decisions that are in the best interest of the organization. To recognize the tremendous groundwork that Louis had laid for MASBA, we named him our MASBA Ambassador in June 2017.

James Guerra assisted us with our search for a new executive director, guiding our MASBA Board through two rounds of interviews, first in San Antonio during September, then in Dallas in October. The process culminated in the October hiring of Dr. Jayme Mathias of the Austin ISD Board of Trustees as our new Executive Director.

Jayme formulated and implemented a schedule of monthly meetings, both for our Executive Committee and for our MASBA

Board. Previously, the MASBA Board met four times each year, with little communication or direction to staff between those meetings.

In December 2017, Louis and Jayme led us through the first-ever financial audit of our organization. We put policies and procedures in place. We brought our Executive Committee to Austin to work through the bylaws amendments that we proposed to our 2018 Member Assembly.

Change is difficult. Jayme and I were holding staff accountable. We endured an "anonymous" smear campaign against him and against me in our regions and in our districts. Those nasty politics consumed a lot of our time until we were able to make a necessary staff change. Despite that, we produced toolkits as a value-add for members, and we drew over 300 people to our annual conference.

I'm proud that we hired a dedicated Executive Director who continues the good work of "the Godfather" and who has put in place the necessary structures and systems to take MASBA to the next level.

I always wanted MASBA to be bigger and better than any individual, so that it can have a true impact within our community and help change the way public education serves all kids. As MASBA celebrates its 50th anniversary, I feel confident that this organization is poised for continued growth and success. I'm proud to have played a small role in helping MASBA to arrive at the place it is today!

Armando "Mando" Rodríguez was elected to the Board of Trustees of the Canutillo ISD on May 7, 2005, at the age of 21. He became MASBA Vice President in 2015 and President Elect in 2016. Armando served as MASBA President in 2017, and as Immediate Past President in 2018. He currently serves on the TASB Board of Directors, the NALEO Board of Directors, and as Chair of the NSBA's National Hispanic Council.

The Presidency of Armando Rodríguez

On February 25, 2017, Armando "Mando" Rodríguez became President of MASBA at the conclusion of the **annual Member Assembly**. No minutes have been found for this meeting.

On February 26, 2017, President Armando Rodríguez convened a meeting of the **MASBA Board** at the La Quinta San Antonio Riverwalk Hotel. The following members were present: President Rodríguez (Canutillo ISD), President Elect Homero García (South Texas ISD), Immediate Past President Irene Galán-Rodríguez (Big Spring ISD), Vice President David Espinosa (Grand Prairie ISD), Secretary Willie Tenorio, Jr. (Hays CISD), Treasurer Servando Garza (Alice ISD), Jessica Cantú (Raymondville ISD), Ana Cortez (Manor ISD), Ricardo Gutiérrez (Region 1 ESC) and Xavier Herrera (Stafford MSD). Orlando Flores (Fabens ISD), Larry Pérez (Waco ISD), Mike Rosales (Ysleta ISD) and Michael Vargas (San Benito CISD) were absent. Staff present included Director of Operations & Development Sam Guzmán and Marketing & Communications Kurt Hixson. Executive Director Louis Q. Reyes, III was absent. The minutes of the meeting report the following:

- Armando discussed plans for Board committees and named Willie chair of the Conference Committee.
- The Board reviewed and approved the budget.
- The Board approved payment of NALEO membership for all Officers and Directors.
- Kurt will post new bylaws & Board composition to the website and will produce three hardcopy newsletters for distribution to membership this year.
- The Board approved creation of the MASBA Language Acquisition Initiative.
- The Board discussed and approved a branding campaign for its 20th annual conference in 2018.
- The Board approved moving forward with a financial audit of the organization.
- The Board debriefed its 2017 conference. The conference for 128 attendees cost $60,000.

- MASBA Past President Juan Rangel provided suggestions to the Board.
- TASB has offered MASBA a breakout session at SLI South in San Antonio in June.
- The Board met in closed session to discuss personnel.

On April 13, 2017, President Armando Rodríguez hosted a meeting of the **MASBA Board** by conference call. No agenda or minutes have been found for this meeting.

On June 16, 2017, President Armando Rodríguez hosted a **MASBA Board** meeting at the Menger Hotel in San Antonio. The minutes report the following:

- The positions previously held by Servando Garza and Jessica Cantú were now listed as vacant, since they were not re-elected to their local boards. Diana Dávila of Houston ISD is listed as a Director. Staff included Louis Q. Reyes, Sam Guzmán and Kurt Hixson. Legal Counsel included Juan F. Aguilera of Escamilla & Poneck and Kevin O'Hanlon of O'Hanlon Rodríguez Betancourt & Demerath.
- Louis reported on his activities and presented a MASBA Travel Reimbursement Policy & Procedures Manual. The Board adopted only the mileage reimbursement rate contained therein.
- Kurt Hixson described his activities.
- The decision of whether MASBA will host a reception at TASA/TASB will be deferred until July.
- Kurt and Sam will solicit nominees by email for MASBA's Hispanic Heritage Award and *La Campana* Award.
- Sam reported on his activities.
- MASBA awarded $17,000 in scholarships this year to graduating high school seniors.
- The selection of an audit firm is pending.
- Armando selected the facilitator for the Board's July retreat.
- Sam reviewed the details for this evening's reception. Rosie, Julián and Joaquín Castro will be present.
- Willie presented a Conference Committee report.

- The Board agreed to hold a monthly conference call on the second Wednesday of the month, at 10:00 a.m., beginning on July 12.
- The Board discussed a Standard Operating Procedures Manual and a Code of Ethics & Conduct.
- After convening in closed session, the Board appointed Ricardo Gutiérrez as Treasurer and Jacinto Ramos, Jr. of Fort Worth ISD to fill Jessica's seat.

On July 8-9, 2017, President Armando Rodríguez convened a planning session of the **MASBA Board** at the Hilton San Antonio Airport Hotel. Items on the agenda included:

- Planning session I & II
- MASBA Board meeting & after-action review

During its planning session, the Board formulated the following draft vision and mission for the organization:

MASBA Vision

EDUCATE ALL stakeholders, regardless of race, on the specific needs of Hispanic communities in Texas,

INSPIRE a movement inclusive of all student voices, and

ACT to ensure that opportunity and access in education are created, with the belief that all students can succeed at the highest levels.

MASBA Mission

The mission of the Mexican American School Board Members Association, a representation of the fastest-growing population in the state of Texas, is to be a voice for Hispanic students, building a strong future through equity, education and advocacy. That is done by:

- Empowering school board members to promote relevant and coherent curriculum for their districts
- Providing specialized training and support for school board members who represent districts with Hispanic students
- Developing and advocating for legislative proposals and relevant polities that reflect student enrollment demographics at the local, state and national level

- Creating opportunities that maximize educational attainment that get students to and through college, workforce ready, and productive members of their communities
- Increasing parental involvement in schools and community participation in governance

The Board meeting minutes reflect the following:

- The Board approved awarding the Hispanic Heritage Award to Dr. Cayetano Barrera (President of *Tejano* Monument, Inc.), Renato Ramírez (principal fundraiser) and Armando Hinojosa (artist), for their work on the *Tejano* Monument on the Texas State Capitol grounds.
- The Board discussed a possible partnership with TALAS.
- Willie presented a Conference Committee report. The Board agreed to donate $5,000 to a charity specified by Eva Longoria, if she agrees to speak at MASBA's 2018 conference, and discussed opening her keynote to the public for a fee and decided not to pursue this.
- The Board discussed Board positions vacated by those missing two consecutive meetings (per newly-approved bylaws), including Diana Dávila, Orlando Flores and Larry Pérez. The Board moved to accept their "resignations."
- Two differing sets of bylaws are posted on the MASBA website.
- The Board approved moving Michael Vargas and Jacinto Ramos, Jr., who filled vacant seats in MASBA Region 5 (West Texas), to the vacant seats of their respective MASBA regions. The Board elected Sylvester Vásquez, Jr. of Southwest ISD to a vacant Region 5 seat through the conclusion of the 2018 Member Assembly.
- Louis Q. Reyes, III noted that he will serve as Executive Director only until a new Executive Director is hired; after that, he will accept a stipend to recruit member districts. The Board took no action on this.
- The Board approved an Executive Director job description, authorized Armando to contract with James Guerra of JG Consulting to assistant the Board's executive search, and met in executive session to discuss applicants for the Executive Director position.

On July 12, 2017, President Armando Rodríguez convened a **MASBA Board** meeting by conference call. The meeting minutes share the following:

- Sylvester Vásquez, Jr. (Southwest ISD) and Holly María Flynn Vilaseca (Houston ISD) are now listed as MASBA Directors.
- The Board approved paying James Guerra of JG Consulting $1,500 for his assistance with the Executive Director search.
- The Board agreed to meet at the July 27 TASB Board meeting, which will be attended by Armando, Irene and Michael.
- The Executive Committee will screen Executive Director candidates on August 11. Interview questions should be submitted by August 27.
- The Board will convene again by conference call on August 9.

On August 11, 2017, President Armando Rodríguez convened a **MASBA Board** meeting by conference call. Though no minutes have been found for this meeting, the agenda consisted of the following:

- New Executive Director update
- Update on replacement of new Board members
- Update on consultant and staff contracts
- Committee updates
- TASA/TASB conference update
- Future Executive Committee meetings: September 9 in Austin and September 23 in San Antonio

On September 9, 2017, President Armando Rodríguez convened a **MASBA Executive Committee** meeting by conference call. Though no minutes have been found for this meeting, the agenda consisted of the following:

- Bylaws
- Screening process for new Executive Director
- Interview process for new Executive Director

On September 23, 2017, President Armando Rodríguez convened a **MASBA Executive Committee** meeting at the Hilton San Antonio Airport Hotel. The Executive Committee interviewed seven candidates for Executive Director.

On October 6, 2017, President Armando Rodríguez convened a meeting of the **MASBA Board** at the Hilton Dallas Hotel. Items on the agenda included:

- Appointment of new directors
- Discussion & possible action on 2018 MASBA budget
- Discussion & possible action on bylaws
- Discussion & possible action on hire of new Executive Director
- Update on TASB conference
- Update on annual MASBA conference
- Update on external audit
- Staff & consultant reports
- Committee reports
- Old business
- New business

No minutes have been found for this meeting.

On October 11, 2017, President Armando Rodríguez formally hired **MASBA Executive Director Dr. Jayme Mathias** of the Austin ISD Board of Trustees.

On November 27, 2017, President Armando Rodríguez convened a meeting of the **MASBA Executive Committee**. The agenda included the following:

- Executive Director's update. Jayme is communicating regular updates to Officers and Directors through Basecamp, an online sharing platform
- MASBA contractors. Jayme shared an update on MASBA Staff Sam Guzmán and Kurt Hixson, who now prefer to be called contractors. The Executive Committee approved allowing him to work with Legal Counsel to resolve issues with contractors.
- Staff augmentation. As soon as the ambiguity with present MASBA contractors is resolved, Jayme proposed moving forward with augmented staff (1) to enhance MASBA's online and social media presence, (2) to reach out to all 1,020 school districts in Texas, and (3) to reach out to potential sponsors for their support of the "biggest and best MASBA conference ever" — even without the assistance of staff who pulled off this

event in the past. The Executive Committee approved $1,000 for website development and $1,000 for membership recruitment.

- <u>Advocacy assistance</u>. Escamilla & Poneck offered its advocacy services for $2,500 per month.
- <u>Bylaws</u>. Armando and Jayme are refining recommendations for possible bylaws amendments.
- <u>2018 Member Assembly</u>. Various details remain unresolved.
- <u>NSBA Conference in San Antonio</u>. Kurt Hixson suggested that our participation in this event may cost $7,500.
- <u>TASB Summer Leadership Institute</u>. TASB is asking what MASBA will present for its breakout session at SLI.

On November 27, 2017, Immediate Past President Irene Galán-Rodríguez convened a meeting of the **MASBA Nominations Committee**. The committee reviewed the 16 applications received for four available Officer positions and eight available Director positions.

On November 29, 2017, President Armando Rodríguez convened a meeting of the **MASBA Board** by conference call. The minutes include the following:

- Johnny "John" Betancourt (Amarillo ISD) and Alfonso "Al" Velarde (El Paso ISD) are now listed as MASBA Directors.
- Jayme is establishing an online archive of past MASBA meeting agendas and minutes.
- The Board approved allowing Jayme to work with Legal Counsel to resolve any issues with contractors.
- Jayme will bring to the Board three bids from firms willing to perform MASBA's financial audit for FY16/17.
- Armando sought input on a draft Advocacy Agenda. The Board tabled the idea of contracting with Escamilla & Poneck for its advocacy services.
- The Board approved the slate of Officer and Director nominations, as presented by the Nominations Committee.
- The Board discussed the April 2018 NASBA Conference and the concurrent *Latinx* 2020 conference, both in San Antonio.
- The Board agreed that MASBA's breakout session at SLI should focus on dual language programs.

On December 20, 2017, President Armando Rodríguez convened a meeting of the **MASBA Board** by conference call. The minutes include the following:

- Armando, Ricardo, Louis and Jayme met with our accountants at Garza | González & Associates. Unfortunately, MASBA's first-ever financial audit was performed for FY15/16 and not FY16/17 finances, the year immediately preceding Jayme's hire. Jayme has formulated financial roles and responsibilities and has implemented internal controls. A forensic audit of Dobermann Marcomm was suggested.
- The Board voted to sever ties with LASSO, since all MASBA golf tournament checks are written to Dobermann Marcomm and not to MASBA.
- The Board approved an amended budget.
- At Armando's request, Jayme presented scenarios for dividing the MASBA region that contains San Antonio and the *Río Grande* Valley.
- A new website (masbatx.org) has been created, as well as a new Facebook page and Twitter handle.
- 350 school districts have been called regarding possible MASBA membership.
- Event planner Yeraldín Yordi has been contracted to assist with the details of our 2018 conference. A conference budget is being prepared.
- Director of Operations & Development Sam Guzmán has requested an amicable separation from MASBA. Jayme reported, "He exemplifies the heights of professionalism." Legal Counsel is assisting with other contractor issues.
- Jayme has drafted a MASBA Advocacy Agenda and is working with Armando and Legal Counsel to clarify which of the two sets of bylaws from the old MASBA website are currently in effect.

On January 17, 2018, President Armando Rodríguez convened a meeting of the **MASBA Board** by conference call. Meeting minutes note the following:

- Staff and Contractors. Sam Guzmán amicably separated from MASBA on December 29. Legal Counsel is working to resolve remaining contractor issues. Vincent Tovar assists with membership, and Rocío Villalobos assists with social media and cleaning up & expanding MASBA's email list.
- Finances. Jayme shared detailed financial reports for November and December.
- Financial Audit. Jayme is still waiting for a bid from Bill C. Rocha, CPA to audit our FY16/17 finances.
- TASB Partnership. Jayme met with TASB representatives: Executive Director James Crow, CFO Steven McArthur, Governance Service Director Robert Durón, Leadership Team Services Director Phil Gore, Communications Director Karen Strong, and Information Technology Director Kathy Wetzel.
    - TASB will assist with graphic design and a photographer for our 2018 conference.
    - TASB will provide MASBA a Boardbook account.
    - TASB will share a list of email addresses from the TEA website, as well as TEA data on Hispanic students and English Language Learners.
    - TASB's current partnership agreement will automatically renew in April 2019.
- Social Media. MASBA's new Facebook page has three times more "likes" than MASBA's old Facebook page, which has been taken down, and MASBA's new Twitter account has four times more "followers" than MASBA's old Twitter account, which has been taken down.
- Eblast List. MASBA's email list has grown from 540 good email addresses, to over 5,900.
- Membership Drive. Jayme reported on our current membership drive.
- Conference. TASB designed and mailed a save-the-date card. Conference planning is in full swing. Conference Committee Co-chairs met on January 3, and the Conference Committee met on January 5.

- <u>Nominations Committee Update</u>. Liz Gutiérrez (West Oso ISD) has decided not to run for the 5B Seat on the MASBA Board. Three races are contested: for President Elect, Treasurer, and for Region 2B.
- <u>Sponsorship Solicitations</u>. Jayme reported on sponsorship solicitation.
- <u>LASSO Golf Tournament</u>. LASSO will host its golf tournament in April, rather than in connection with our 2018 conference. The MASBA logo remains on their website, despite the fact that all checks go to Dobermann Marcomm.
- <u>Voter Registration Project</u>. MASBA, TALAS and MALDEF have partnered on a project to encourage voter registration at Texas high schools.
- <u>MASBA Travel Policy</u>. The Board approved a travel policy for Officers, Directors and Staff.

On January 28, 2018, President Armando Rodríguez convened a five-hour meeting of the **MASBA Executive Committee** at the office of O'Hanlon Demerath & Castillo in Austin. Meeting minutes note the following:

- <u>Personnel</u>. The Executive Committee met in executive session to discuss an issue with a former MASBA contractor. Members reconvened in open session to approve next steps regarding the matter.
- <u>Redistricting of MASBA Regions</u>. As requested by Armando, Jayme presented possible scenarios for redistricting MASBA, so that San Antonio is separated from the *Río Grande* Valley. No action was taken on this.
- <u>Bylaws</u>. The Executive Committee reviewed proposed bylaws changes. Legal Counsel clarified that, in order to avoid controversy regarding which bylaws are in force, the 2018 Member Assembly will be asked to re-adopt an entire new set of bylaws. Three information sessions will be presented at the MASBA conference on proposed MASBA bylaws.
- <u>Advocacy Agenda</u>. The Executive Committee approved a draft advocacy agenda, for recommendation by the MASBA Board to the annual Member Assembly.
- <u>Member Assembly Details</u>. Executive Committee members reviewed the script for the 2018 Member Assembly.

On February 12, 2018, President Armando Rodríguez convened a meeting of the **MASBA Executive Committee** by conference call. Meeting records note the following:

- <u>Contractor Issue</u>. Jayme reported issues related to an unresolved contractor issue.
- <u>MASBA Contractors</u>. The Board authorized Jayme to contract with hourly contract workers for specific MASBA projects (e.g., membership, social media).
- <u>Finances</u>. The Board will revisit budget amendments after it receives a report on conference income and expenses.
- <u>Social Media</u>. Directors spread word of our Facebook page, increasing its "likes" to 340.
- <u>Eblasts</u>. Jayme provided an update on recent eblasts.
- <u>Membership</u>. Jayme provided a membership drive update.
- <u>TASA Midwinter</u>. Jayme reported on our presence at TASA Midwinter.
- <u>Equity Symposium</u>. Jayme reported on his attendance at the 2018 CUBE Equity Symposium. Armando expressed his desire for MASBA to co-host a statewide equity symposium with the Texas Caucus of Black School Board Members.
- <u>Conference Update</u>. Jayme presented a conference update.
- <u>Texas Caucus of Black School Board Members</u>. Jayme said that TCBSBM representatives have yet to respond to MASBA's invitation to collaborate in the future. Representatives of MASBA will attend the TCBSBM annual education summit.
- <u>MASBA Scholarships</u>. The question arose: How much money is owed MASBA from LASSO's golf tournaments? Homero, who will become MASBA President in less than two weeks, will assume responsibility for that relationship.
- <u>"Anonymous" Letters</u>. Officers discussed the libelous "anonymous" letters circulated about our MASBA President and Executive Director. They trace back to a former MASBA contractor.

On February 22, 2018, MASBA hosted its first-ever **Tour of Best Practices**, which replaced the MASBA golf tournament hosted in previous years. Site visits included the Harlandale ISD STEM Early College High School, Holmes High School of Northside ISD, and Southwest Legacy High School in the Southwest ISD. The latter provided transportation, lunch, and entertainment by the high school's *mariachi*.

On February 22, 2018, President Armando Rodríguez convened a meeting of the **MASBA Board** at the Hilton San Antonio Airport Hotel. Meeting minutes note the following:

- LASSO. The MASBA Board directed Staff to meet with LASSO representatives, to resolve perceived issues.
- Social Media. Jayme presented data on MASBA's growing social media presence.
- Membership Drive. Jayme reconstructed MASBA's membership history since SY13/14, based on financial records. MASBA currently has 70 member districts and 16 individual members, up from 56 districts and 7 individuals in SY16/17. He noted that, despite contrary claims, there is no evidence that MASBA membership ever exceeded 70 member districts.
- Conference Details. Jayme reviewed details for the annual MASBA conference.
- Gifts. Armando shared new MASBA lapel pins with all Officers and Directors, and Irene shared new MASBA T-shirts.

On February 22, 2018, President Armando Rodríguez opened the 20th **Annual MASBA Conference**, *¡MASBÁmonos!* at the Hilton San Antonio Airport Hotel. The program for the conference, hosted in memory of Manuel "Manny" Rodríguez, Jr. of the Houston ISD, contains the following:

Conference Co-chairs
Willie Tenorio, Jr., Hays CISD & Jacinto Ramos, Jr., Fort Worth ISD

General Sessions
"The Impact of Changing Demographics on Texas Education!"
Arturo Vargas, NALEO

"Governance That Improves Student Outcomes!"
A.J. Crabill, TEA Deputy Commissioner for Governance

"Impacting Our Economy
through Improved Student Learning & Graduation Rates!"
Former West Virginia Governor Bob Wise,
Alliance for Excellent Education

¡MASBÁmonos! Advocacy Update
Marty DeLeón & Ricco García, Escamilla & Poneck

¡Presente! General Session
Former State Representative Dr. Michael Villarreal

La Campana Luncheon Keynote
Henry Cisneros, Former San Antonio Mayor & U.S. HUD Secretary

"Educational Equity is a Function of Power!"
Dr. Robert Durón, TASB

Panel

Los Superintendentes Superintendents Panel
Dr. Xavier De La Torre, Ysleta ISD; Michael Cardona, San Marcos
CISD; Dr. Jeanette Ball, Uvalde CISD; Moderator Dr. Lucio
Calzada, TALAS

Breakout Sessions

"Racial Consciousness as an Educational Leader!"
Jacinto "Cinto" Ramos, Jr., Fort Worth ISD

"Defending Title IX Litigation: Lessons Learned!"
Marcy Barker, TASB Risk Management Fund
Craig Wood, Walsh Gallegos Treviño Russo & Kyle

"Are You a 10? The Ten Characteristics of a Servant Leader!"
Dr. Barbara Baggerly-Hinojosa, Leadership Empowerment Group

"Learning & Achieving Begins with Nutrition!"
Shauna Strub, Southwest Foodservice Excellence

"Solving the Challenge of Providing Our Students
Integrated Care!"
Daniel Barrett, Barrett Insurance Services
Shana Robinson, Baptist Health System
Scott Gibbs, McGriff Seibels & Williams

"Are Your District's Facilities
Helping to Close the Achievement Gap?"
Dr. Emilio Castro & Hestroverto Martínez, Edgewood ISD
Jeff Clemmons, TASB Facility Services

"Investing in Student Leadership Development!"
Kathryn Nicole Nieto de Sada & Julio Cotto,
National Hispanic Institute

"Support At-risk *Latina* Youth in Pursuit of Higher Education!"
Dr. Teresa Granillo, *Con Mi MADRE*

"Closing the Opportunity Gap in the San Marcos CISD!"
Michael Cardona & Clementina Cantú, San Marcos CISD

"Mexican American Studies: A New Era in Education!"
Tony Díaz, *Nuestra Palabra*

"Attract & Retain the Best of the Best!"
Eddie Contreras, TASB First Public

"Two is Better Than One: Double the Language, Double the Fun!"
Thomasina Montana, Freedom Elementary, Southside ISD
Theresa Sands, UT Austin Institute for Public School Initiatives

"Creating the Brown Space within the Black/White Binary!"
Jacinto "Cinto" Ramos, Jr., Fort Worth ISD

"Building Opportunities for All through District Equity Plans!"
David Hinojosa, IDRA

"Lead Your Board to Peak Performance!"
Gary Inmon, Good Governance Consulting Group
Sylvester Vásquez, Southwest ISD

"The MASBA Language Acquisition Initiative!"
Dr. Jesse Jai McNeil, Jr.,
McNeil Educational Leadership Foundation
Marie Moreno, *Las Américas* Newcomers School, Houston ISD

"Defending *Latino* Rights at the Capitol and in the Courtroom!"
Fátima Menéndez, MALDEF

"How Optimal Learning Environments Close Gaps!"
Thursten Simonsen & Tim "Boo" Podanoffsky,
Performance Services

"Naming & Shaming the Leaks
in a *Chicano/Latino* District of Innovation!"
Dr. Royce Avery & Ana Cortez, Manor ISD; Isaac Treviño, myON

"A Primer on Special Ed Services for Underserved Populations!"
Dr. Karlyn Keller, TASB Special Education Solutions

Student Entertainment
Southside High School Jazz Ensemble, Southside ISD
Gallardo Elementary *Baile Folklórico*, Southside ISD
Medio Creek Elementary *Baile Folklórico*, Southwest ISD
Mariachi Los Dragones, Southwest High School, Southwest ISD
Mariachis of Memorial High School & John F. Kennedy High
School, Edgewood ISD

Hispanic Heritage Award
Dr. Cayetano Barrera, Renato Ramírez & Armando Hinojosa
Texas State Capitol *Tejano* Monument

Entertainment   Roger Velásquez & the Latin Legendz

On February 24, 2018, President Armando Rodríguez presided over
the annual **MASBA Member Assembly**. The agenda consisted of the
following:

- Adoption of Credentials Committee Report
- Adoption of 2018 Member Assembly Rules
- Adoption of Agenda
- Executive Director's Report
- Treasurer's Report
- Nominations Committee Report
  - Election of Officers
  - Election of Directors
- Adoption of MASBA Bylaws
- Adoption of 2018 MASBA Advocacy Agenda

The following Officers were elected:

- President Elect Willie Tenorio, Jr. (Hays CISD)
- Vice President Jacinto Ramos, Jr. (Fort Worth ISD)
- Secretary Michael Vargas (San Benito CISD)
- Treasurer Xavier Herrera (Stafford MSD)

The following Directors were re-elected:

- 1A Director Michael Vargas (San Benito CISD)
- 2A Director Ana Cortez (Manor ISD)
- 2B Director Marco R. Ortiz (Taylor ISD)
- 3A Director Holly María Flynn Vilaseca (Houston ISD)
- 4A Director Jacinto Ramos, Jr. (Fort Worth ISD)
- 5A Director Johnny "John" Betancourt (Amarillo ISD)
- 5B Director Sylvester Vásquez, Jr. (Southwest ISD)
- 6A Director Alfonso "Al" Velarde (El Paso ISD)

The following Directors were re-elected:

- 2B Director Marco R. Ortiz (Taylor ISD)

MASBA's bylaws and advocacy agenda were unanimously adopted. At the conclusion of the meeting, President Elect Homero García assumed the presidency of MASBA.

If you would like to share any photos, meeting minutes, conference programs, mementos, etc. from the presidency of Armando Rodríguez, for inclusion in Volume II, please email them to info@masbatx.org or mail them to MASBA | P.O. Box 474 | Austin, TX 78767.

Thank you for helping us to reconstruct our history!

"We Get Together for a Purpose"

Homero García

I was elected to the South Texas ISD Board of Trustees in 1996 and have served ever since. As a superintendent and now as a trustee, I remain pro-education: I've always believed in education for all students and in helping the future leaders of our state.

Here in the South Texas ISD, we don't fund athletics, so we concentrate mostly on academics. Our graduates include doctors, lawyers, architects, you name it. They're motivated to continue their studies. I'm always so proud when I meet alumni from our high school. I'm happy that we're helping them advance, and that other districts see us as a model in STEM education.

I first learned about MASBA when I served as superintendent of Valley View ISD in Hidalgo County. Some board members were interested in being part of MASBA and attended the annual MASBA conference. So I went with them, and we learned a lot about the challenges facing Mexican American students.

After I joined the South Texas ISD Board, Tony González, a former board member there who was very active in MASBA, championed the organization. He inspired me to get more involved in MASBA. I joined the MASBA Board in 2016. I became President Elect the following year and served as President beginning in 2018.

In response to some events at the beginning of my presidency, we formulated the MASBA Standard. Our new Executive Director, Dr. Jayme Mathias, helped create that and get us through some rocky months of criticism. Some members saw MASBA as a social club, so our MASBA Standard helped us set expectations for actions at MASBA events going forward. We get together for a purpose, and that purpose is to help students and encourage them to continue their education.

We also took stands on several issues, including the incarceration of children along the U.S./Mexico border. Because I live so close to the border, those issues impact our community. More recently, we took a stand in support of the Houston ISD Board of Trustees. I'm proud that MASBA has taken stands on issues like that.

When I served as MASBA President, we partnered with the Texas Caucus of Black School Board Members, and we co-hosted an Advocacy Day reception at the Capitol during the legislative session and our first-ever Texas Public Schools Equity Symposium in February 2019. I hope we continue to work together for the benefit of our minority students.

I'm proud of the way that MASBA became better known over the years. MASBA has grown more respected throughout the state. MASBA remains involved in advocacy for education at the state and federal levels. That's very important to me.

We've come a long way as an organization. Sometimes we disagree, but we always work together as a team, doing what's best for students.

I served as President of MASBA when we had 104 member districts and over $260,000 in sponsorships. That growth made a difference for us. We also made a commitment to award a MASBA scholarship to a graduating senior in every MASBA member district — which is what we did in 2019.

As we celebrate MASBA's 50th anniversary, I hope MASBA will continue to grow — in terms of members and sponsors. I look forward to seeing all that MASBA will accomplish in the future!

Homero García has served on the South Texas ISD Board of Trustees since 1996. A middle school principal, then a superintendent for 15 years, Homero joined the MASBA Board in 2016 and became President Elect in 2017. He served as MASBA President in 2018 and continues to support MASBA as its Immediate Past President.

The Presidency of Homero García

On February 24, 2018, at the conclusion of the annual MASBA Member Assembly at the Hilton San Antonio Airport Hotel, Homero García of South Texas ISD assumed the presidency of MASBA.

On February 25, 2018, President Homero García convened a meeting of the **MASBA Board** at the Hilton San Antonio Airport Hotel. The MASBA Board now included the following Officers and Directors:

- President Homero García (South Texas ISD)
- President Elect Guillermo "Willie" Tenorio, Jr. (Hays CISD)
- Immediate Past President Armando Rodríguez (Canutillo ISD)
- Secretary & Region 1A Director Michael Vargas (San Benito CISD)
- Region 1B Director Ricardo Gutiérrez (Region 1 ESC)
- Region 2A Director Ana Cortez (Manor ISD)
- Region 2B Director Marco R. Ortiz (Taylor ISD)
- Region 3A Director Holly María Flynn Vilaseca (Houston ISD)
- Treasurer & Region 3B Director Xavier Herrera (Stafford MSD)
- Vice President & Region 4A Director Jacinto "Cinto" Ramos, Jr. (Fort Worth ISD)
- Region 4B Director David Espinosa (Grand Prairie ISD)
- Region 5A Director Johnny "John" Betancourt (Amarillo ISD)
- Region 5B Director Sylvester Vásquez, Jr. (Southwest ISD)
- Region 6A Director Alfonso "Al" Velarde (El Paso ISD)
- Region 6B Director Miguel "Mike" Rosales (Ysleta ISD)
- Executive Director Jayme Mathias, *ex officio*

Also present for the meeting were:

- MASBA Ambassador Louis Q. Reyes, III
- Legal Counsel Kevin O'Hanlon, O'Hanlon Demerath & Castillo
- Legal Counsel Juan Aguilera, Escamilla & Poneck
- Legal Counsel Nick Maddox, O'Hanlon Demerath & Castillo

Meeting minutes note the following:

- Conference Debrief. Jayme called for feedback on the annual MASBA conference.
- Member Assembly Debrief. Jayme asked for feedback on the 2018 Member Assembly.
- 2019 Conference Preview. Jayme suggested possible theme for the 2019 annual MASBA conference, which will be preceded by an Advocacy Day.
- Relationship with LASSO. Homero, Armando, Jayme and Louis reported on their meeting during the conference with Mike Bailey, Joel López and Gil González of LASSO.
- Strategic Planning. Homero suggested that the Board defer the idea of a strategic planning retreat in April, to save the organization this expense.
- 2018 MASBA Scholarships. Homero named Michael, Xavier, Ricardo, Al & Mike to the Board's Scholarship Committee.
- Possible Partnerships. MASBA will send representatives to the TCBSBM annual education summit.
- MASBA/TALAS/MALDEF Voter Registration Effort. The Board discussed this effort, suggesting that we might create a MASBA toolkit on this in the future.
- Purported Incident during the MASBA Conference. The Board discussed an incident that purportedly took place during our conference.
- The MASBA Standard. In the same way that NALEO has the "NALEO Standard," it was suggested that MASBA creates its own "MASBA Standard." This will be placed on a future agenda.

On March 12, 2018, President Homero García convened a meeting of the **MASBA Executive Committee** by conference call. Meeting minutes record the following:

- The Executive Committee is forwarding to the MASBA Board draft resolutions on TEKS for Mexican American Studies and on Addressing Gun Violence in Our Public Schools. The Executive Committee is also interested in approving a resolution on the extension of DACA.

- The Executive Committee convened in executive session to discuss pending litigation by MASBA and the incident that purportedly took place during our conference.
- The Executive Committee approved a draft "MASBA Standard" that it will recommend for Board approval.
- Jayme distributed an income/expense report from our 2018 conference.
- Jayme provided an abbreviated timeline for the determination and awarding of MASBA scholarships in 2018.
- Jayme updated the MASBA Board directory and organizational chart. He will print MASBA business cards for all Officers.
- MASBA will plan receptions at the Region 1 conference in May and at SLI South.

On March 21, 2018, President Homero García convened a meeting of the **MASBA Board** by conference call. Meeting minutes record the following:
- Jayme reported on his testimony on behalf of MASBA before the Texas School Finance Commission.
- The Board approved resolutions in support of TEKS (Texas Essential Knowledge & Skills) for Mexican American Studies and on the need to address gun violence in our Texas public schools.
- Officers discussed hosting a MASBA Advocacy Day on February 27, 2019, the day following TASB's planned Advocacy Day.
- The Board approved the "MASBA Standard," as amended.
- Jayme presented a financial report, noting that MASBA now pays for the use of a storage facility for its materials.
- Jayme provided an abbreviated timeline for the determination and awarding of MASBA scholarships in 2018.
- Jayme relayed an updated MASBA Board directory and organizational chart.
- Jayme reviewed upcoming events, including the March 29-31 TCBSBM annual education summit, the April 6-9 NSBA conference in San Antonio, the April 8-9 *Latinx* 2020

conference in San Antonio, the May 18-19 conference for Region 1 on South Padre Island, SLI South on June 14-16.

- Clarification is needed on whether the Board's policy of three consecutive absences leading to dismissal from the Board applies to conference call meetings as well.

On April 10, 2018, President Homero García convened a meeting of the **MASBA Executive Committee** by conference call. Meeting minutes note the following:

- The Executive Committee agreed to accept a settlement from a former contractor and dismiss the lawsuit against him.
- The Executive Committee discussed the possible need to create a public statement to respond to mistruths being spread by a conference attendee concerning a purported event at our annual conference.
- Now that MASBA has a record-keeping system, the Executive Committee will forward to the MASBA Board Jayme's proposal for allowing the dues year for any member to begin on the date on which payment is received, rather than on September 1.
- Director Mike Rosales was suggested for Board Secretary.
- Officers tabled the discussion of filling the 1A Seat recently vacated by Michael Vargas.
- The Executive Committee will forward to the MASBA Board a draft resolution on the 2020 U.S. Census.
- Jayme reported that our 14 MASBA Directors represent only eight of 20 ESC regions in Texas. He proposed a shift from a 15-member Board, to a 23-member Board, with a representative of each ESC in Texas. He will work with Legal Counsel to draft the necessary change in bylaws.
- MASBA and LASSO have experienced what might be characterized as a "happy divorce."
- Cinto told us that the Fort Worth ISD Board of Trustees is poised to make history this evening by being the first school district in Texas to declare a student holiday and day of service in honor of César Chávez and Dolores Huerta. He hopes that MASBA might encourage this in other districts.

On April 18, 2018, President Homero García convened a meeting of the **MASBA Board** by conference call. Meeting minutes note the following:

- Jayme noted that this was MASBA's first meeting utilizing TASB's Boardbook tool.
- Homero appointed Eva Castillo Watts of the Donna ISD to the MASBA Board. Confusion over how Directors are "elected or appointed" will result in a Board work session on our MASBA bylaws.
- Director Mike Rosales was elected MASBA Board Secretary.
- Jayme reported on the Texas *Latino* Education Coalition, A-F rulemaking by the TEA, and an update on movement by the State Board of Education to approve TEKS for "Ethnic Studies: An Overview of Americans of Mexican Descent."
- The Board approved a resolution on the 2020 U.S. Census.
- The Board discussed supporting TASB's 2019 Advocacy Day by co-hosting an advocacy event with the TCBSBM on the same day.
- Jayme presented financial reports for January through March, noting all deviations in income/expenses from the Board-approved budget.
- Jayme shared an initial summary of 2018 conference income and expenses.
- Changes to the MASBA membership year were discussed, and Staff will create a proposal on this.
- The Board approved budget amendments, as presented.
- MASBA will award 20 scholarships this year, up from ten scholarships last year.
- Staff will work with Legal Counsel to draft the necessary bylaws changes to transition to a 23-member Board, with representatives from all 20 ESC regions.
- After meeting in executive session, the Board approved accepting the settlement of a former contractor and dismissing the lawsuit against him, as well as ratifying that all conversations that occur in executive session are to remain confidential.

On May 14, 2018, President Homero García convened a meeting of the **MASBA Executive Committee** by conference call. Meeting minutes provide the following information:

- The Executive Committee reviewed a draft resolution in support of the extension and expansion of the Deferred Action for Childhood Arrivals (DACA) program.
- The Executive Committee reviewed a draft resolution in support of a student holiday and day of community service in Texas public schools, in honor of César Chávez and Dolores Huerta.
- A reception is being planned at the Capitol for MASBA's 2019 Advocacy Day.
- Jayme shared an income/expense report for our 2018 conference. Income totaled $108,890, and expenses totaled $104,184.
- The Executive Committee reviewed Articles I-III of our bylaws and discussed possible amendments to them for our 2019 Member Assembly.
- Officers suggested that MASBA not host a reception at SLI North this year.
- The Executive Committee will serve as our 2019 Conference Committee.

On May 23, 2018, President Homero García convened a meeting of the **MASBA Board** by conference call. Meeting minutes note the following:

- Jayme presented a report on recent advocacy efforts, including efforts on Career & Technical Education weights, tech app courses, elimination of the Student Success Initiative, an expansion of the bilingual education allotment, and TEKS for Mexican American Studies.
- Jayme gave an update on A-F rulemaking by the TEA.
- The Board voted to oppose any effort by the State Board of Education to require validation of credit-by-exam by third-party vendors.
- The Board approved a resolution in support of the extension and expansion of the Deferred Action for Childhood Arrivals (DACA) program.

- The Board approved a resolution in support of a student holiday and day of community service in honor of César Chávez and Dolores Huerta in Texas public schools.
- Jayme reported on 2018 conference income and expenses.
- The Board discussed possible amendments for Articles I-III of our bylaws.
- Jayme reported that some 100-170 people attended our reception at the Region 1 conference on South Padre Island. He thanked Louis for his leadership of and presence at the event.
- The Board approved a conflict of interest disclosure policy, a whistleblower policy, and a document retention policy.
- Jayme thanked Legal Counsel O'Hanlon for settling MASBA v. Kurt Hixson DBA Dobermann Marcomm.

On June 13, 2018, President Homero García convened a two-hour planning retreat by the **MASBA Executive Committee** at the San Antonio Marriott Rivercenter Hotel. Meeting minutes note the following:

- The Executive Committee engaged in a time of strategic planning, focused on what's working well and what's working less well within MASBA. It formulated five "buckets" of MASBA goals for SY18/19: advocacy, growth & membership, finances & sponsorships, member benefits, and structures & systems.

On June 14, 2018, President Homero García convened a meeting of the **MASBA Board** at the San Antonio Marriott Rivercenter Hotel. At Cinto's suggestion, the MASBA Board began its tradition of a "one-sentence check-in" and a "one-sentence check out." Meeting minutes contain the following:

- Directors spent 12 minutes sharing stories and better getting to know one another.
- Jayme presented a summary of the Executive Committee's planning retreat on June 13, and he led Officers and Directors in formulating goals for each of the five "buckets" identified at the planning retreat.

- The Board brainstormed possible Executive Director performance targets for possible approval at its meeting during TASA/TASB.
- Jayme said that, in light of recent Board conversations, MASBA's June 15 reception would be the first MASBA event in recent memory that would not provide free alcohol—except for the sharing of a free drink ticket with MASBA members and top sponsors.

On July 9, 2018, President Homero García convened a planning meeting of the **MASBA Executive Committee** by conference call. Meeting minutes note the following:

- Officers shared feedback on the face-to-face MASBA meetings held in San Antonio in June.
- A former trustee approached Jayme at SLI North with an idea for forming an energy cooperative for MASBA. Officers discussed the idea, which will not be brought to the MASBA Board at this time.
- Officers approved changes to the 2019 MASBA Scholarship selection process.
- Jayme reported on Staff's difficulty in finding a conference hotel in Austin during the legislative session. He also shared a list of possible keynote speakers.
- A conservative think tank in Texas might be pressuring a district to cancel its MASBA membership.
- Jayme will travel to the U.S./Mexico border, to represent MASBA on the issue of detained children and separated families there.

On July 18, 2018, President Homero García convened a meeting of the **MASBA Board** by conference call. Meeting minutes note the following:

- Jayme presented an update on Mexican American Studies, families separated at the U.S./Mexico border, the inclusion of a question on citizenship in the 2020 U.S. Census, and the July 18 Select Senate Committee on Violence in Schools & School Security.

- Jayme presented financial reports for April, May and June; the Board approved budget amendments, as presented.
- MASBA has purchased its first-ever Customer Relationship Management (CRM) platform, to track membership, sponsorships, and the contact information for all MASBA sponsors and all 1,020 school districts and 20 ESCs in Texas.
- Jayme shared a vision for MASBA webinars in the future.
- Jayme reported on the costs of room rates in Austin during the legislative session, which might dampen MASBA conference attendance. Staff continues to work on the issue.

On August 13, 2018, President Homero García convened a meeting of the **MASBA Executive Committee** by conference call. Meeting minutes note the following:

- Jayme drew attention to a draft summary of his activity for MASBA since his hire last year, in preparation for the Board's evaluation of his performance.
- Officers discussed possible amendments for Articles IV & V of our bylaws.
- MASBA will host its first-ever Texas Public Schools Equity Symposium on February 27, in partnership with the Texas Caucus of Black School Board Members.
- Homero suggested that MASBA donate to assist the students and families who have been separated at the U.S./Mexico border. MASBA will make five donations to organizations chosen by Officers, which assist such persons in El Paso, Austin, Dallas, Houston, and the *Río Grande* Valley.
- Jayme spoke of the interest of Katy ISD Trustee George Scott, who wishes to speak with our Board on possible statewide impact litigation. Jayme will coordinate a time and place for this conversation.

On August 22, 2018, President Homero García convened a meeting of the **MASBA Board** by conference call. Meeting minutes note the following:

- Al asked whether MASBA might take a stand on mandated health insurance, which eliminates the possibility of districts seeking competitive insurance providers at lower rates. Kevin expressed his willingness to work with the El Paso ISD and any other District of Innovation that seeks to eliminate the statutory requirement of investing in the Teacher Retirement System (TRS).
- Kevin suggested that MASBA consider supporting full-day Pre-K as a legislative priority, since the possibility exists of seeing action on this issue during the next legislative session.
- The Board discussed possible amendments for Articles IV & V of our bylaws.
- Jayme shared a draft summary of his activity for MASBA since his hire last year, and he suggested an annual rhythm of evaluating the Executive Director's performance, setting his/her performance targets, and establishing his/her salary and benefits.
- MASBA received its third $75,000 check from TASB. The partnership will automatically renew in 2019 for another three years, unless canceled by either party.
- The application for our 2019 MASBA scholarships is now available online.
- Jayme and Louis have signed a contract for our 2019 MASBA conference to be held at the Renaissance Austin Hotel.
- Al asked whether MASBA might send a letter of condolence to the community of Tippin Elementary in the El Paso ISD, where a mother was killed and three students injured on the first day of classes. Jayme will write a letter on MASBA's behalf.
- John asked whether MASBA might consider a resolution in support of diversity and persons of color on local school boards. Directors shared mixed responses, with some cautioning MASBA against getting involved in local politics in this way, and with others suggesting that inaction is unacceptable.

On September 10, 2018, President Homero García convened a meeting of the **MASBA Executive Committee** by conference call. Meeting minutes note the following:

- Officers agreed to hear Trustee George Scott's presentation on the possibility of statewide impact litigation re. school finance, accountability, and the closing of equity gaps, on September 27, in connection with TASA/TASB.
- Jayme reported on July and August income/expense and shared a balance sheet, profit/loss statement, general ledger and income/expense reports for FY17/18. He also presented a list of accounts receivable.

On September 28, 2018, President Homero García convened a meeting of the **MASBA Board** at the Hilton Austin Hotel. Meeting minutes contain the following:

- Jayme distributed maps and scatterplots for the 2018 state accountability data of MASBA member districts.
- Jayme shared a balance sheet, profit/loss statement and general ledger for FY17/18, and the Board approved the FY18/19 budget.
- The Board dialogued about 2019 MASBA Scholarship procedures.
- The Board convened in executive session to discuss possible statewide impact litigation, concluding in open session that the filing of a case may be premature in the absence of expert witnesses. We will refer the possible case to MALDEF and IDRA.
- The Board convened in executive session to evaluate our Executive Director and to discuss his compensation for FY18/19. Jayme will formulate three to five FY18/19 performance goals, for approval by the Board in October.

On October 8, 2018, President Homero García convened a meeting of the **MASBA Executive Committee** by conference call. Meeting minutes note the following:

- Jayme solicited feedback on the reception that MASBA co-hosted with TALAS at TASA/TASB.
- Officers discussed and approved Executive Director performance targets for FY18/19.
- Officers discussed staff recommendations for possible revisions to Articles VI & VII of our bylaws.
- Officers discussed preliminary ideas for our 2019 conference.

On October 17, 2018, President Homero García convened a meeting of the **MASBA Board** by conference call. Meeting minutes record the following:

- Jayme is in conversation with a firm interested in offering *pro bono* advocacy counsel for our organization.
- Mike offered an update on children separated from their families at the U.S./Mexico border.
- Jayme presented a schedule for our 2019 Advocacy Day.
- Jayme offered a staff review of our TALAS/MASBA reception at TASA/TASB.
- Jayme reported that all Officers and Directors have now signed the MASBA Standard.
- The Board discussed possible amendments to Articles VI & VII of our bylaws.
- Jayme presented a schedule for Officer and Director nominations leading up to our 2019 Member Assembly.
- The Board agreed to host a face-to-face meeting in San Antonio on January 18-19, to discuss possible bylaws changes.
- Gold sponsor Performance Services has expressed a willingness to host a golf tournament benefiting MASBA, to be held in conjunction with SLI South.
- The Board met in executive session to finalize the remuneration of our Executive Director for FY18/19.

On November 12, 2018, President Homero García convened a meeting of the **MASBA Executive Committee** by conference call. Meeting minutes record the following:

- Officers considered possible revisions to Articles VIII to XIV of our bylaws.
- Officers discussed whether to appoint a Vice Chair for the Nominations Committee and opted not to do so.
- Jayme raised three possibly-controversial legislative issues for discussion:
  - Whether MASBA should advocate for the graduation requirement of a year of fine arts *or* a year of career & technical education (CTE) (rather than the present requirement of a year of fine arts). Officers hesitated to support this.
  - Whether MASBA should advocate for flexibility in the use of the bilingual education allotment. Officers are interested in the stands of other organizations on this issue.
  - Whether MASBA should take a stand for or against SB 1882 partnership, since this allows for partnerships between districts and for-profit charter schools. Officers will refrain from taking a stand on this at present.
- Jayme distributed an updated workflow of 2019 MASBA conference details. All speakers and MASBA Directors will be caricatured as MASBA *"Superhéroes* for Kids."

On November 21, 2018, President Homero García convened a meeting of the **MASBA Board** by conference call. Meeting minutes record the following:

- Jayme presented an advocacy update, noting that State Representative Dennis Bonnen (R-Angleton) has stated that he has the necessary votes to be elected Speaker of the House.
- Jayme distributed a list of all possible bylaws revisions suggested since the 2018 Member Assembly. These will be discussed at the Board's face-to-face meeting in San Antonio.
- Applications for Officer and Director positions are due December 31.
- Al will share Kevin's communication on the possibility of Districts of Innovation opting out of the Teacher Retirement System.

- MASBA has spread word that Past President Viola García has been honored with a middle school in her name.
- Immediate Past President Armando Rodríguez asked that Directors consider district membership in the National School Board Association's National Hispanic Council.

On December 10, 2018, President Homero García convened a meeting of the **MASBA Executive Committee** by conference call. Meeting minutes note the following:

- Jayme presented an update on Officer and Director applications received to date.
- Officers discussed the services of our Advocacy Counsel.
- Jayme updated the Board on planning efforts for our February 26 Advocacy Day, our February 27 Equity Symposium, and our annual MASBA conference on February 28 to March 3.
- Jayme presented a quarterly update on the progress toward his annual performance targets.

On December 19, 2018, President Homero García convened a meeting of the **MASBA Board** by conference call. Meeting minutes note the following:

- The Board received a financial report for the first quarter of FY18/19.
- Our accountants at Garza | González & Associates suggested that MASBA's finances are so clear, straightforward and simple that the $12,000 for a financial audit might be directed to other mission-related organizational needs, like scholarships, and that the Board might consider a biannual financial review coupled with a biannual financial audit. The Board was split, with some insisting on an annual financial audit and others preferring to direct monies to scholarships and other needs.
- Jayme presented an update on details for our January face-to-face meeting, and our February events in Austin.
- Jayme presented a quarterly update on the progress toward his annual performance targets.

On January 14, 2019, President Homero García convened a meeting of the **MASBA Executive Committee** by conference call. Meeting minutes record the following:

- MASBA Past President Gustavo "Gus" García, the first *Latino* to be elected to the Austin ISD Board of Trustees in 1972, has passed away. He incorporated MASBA on December 6, 1973.
- Jayme presented ideas for a "sponsorship concierge" for our Diamond sponsors.
- Jayme shared a draft joint resolution between MASBA and the Texas Talent Musicians Association (TTMA), the producers of the annual *Tejano* Music Awards.
- Jayme gave an overview of the Advocacy Day and Equity Symposium that MASBA will co-host with the Texas Caucus of Black School Board Members on February 26-27. He also shared details on our February 28 Tour of Best Practices and our March 1-3 MASBA conference.
- Jayme listed Officer/Director applications received. There are no contested faces for these positions this year.

On January 19, 2019, President Homero García convened a meeting of the **MASBA Board** at the Embassy Suite San Antonio Airport Hotel. Meeting minutes note the following:

- The Board discussed a possible resolution in support of diversity in hiring and purchasing practices in our Texas public schools.
- Jayme distributed a copy of our recently-filed IRS Form 990 for FY17/18.
- The Board asked Jayme to draft a policy to implement a biannual financial audit coupled with a biannual financial review with our accountant.
- The Board approved a joint resolution, as amended, with the Texas Talent Musicians Association (TTMA), the producers of the annual *Tejano* Music Awards.
- Jayme discussed several details on MASBA's February and March events in Austin.
- The Board expressed support for the 2020 MASBA conference theme of *¡MASBAilemos!*

- The Board discussed possible bylaws revisions, agreeing to forward 17 possible amendments to our annual Member Assembly. There was no consensus regarding a possible dues increase, or the creation of an "*Amigo*" membership category for non-trustees.

On February 11, 2019, President Homero García convened a meeting of the **MASBA Executive Committee** by conference call. Meeting minutes note that Jayme spoke through details of MASBA's February 26 Advocacy Day, February 27 Equity Symposium, February 28 Tour of Best Practices, and March 1-3 MASBA Conference.

On February 28, 2019, President Homero García convened a meeting of the **MASBA Board** at the Renaissance Austin Hotel. Board members discussed their responsibilities for "*¡Superhéroes* for Kids!", the MASBA annual conference that would begin with a reception later that evening.

On February 28, 2019, President Homero García opened the 21st Annual MASBA Conference, *¡Superhéroes* for Kids! at the Renaissance Austin Hotel. The conference program records the following:

Keynotes

"From Surviving to Thriving:
How *Superhéroes* Bring SEL & Equity into Practice!"
Roberto Rivera, 7 Mindsets

"*Nuestros Superhéroes:* Why Our Stories Matter!"
Héctor Rodríguez, Comic Book Artist & McKinney ISD Teacher

¡Dale! Luncheon Keynote
Texas Education Agency Commissioner Mike Morath

"Being a Superhero & Living a Legacy!"
Consuelo Castillo Kickbusch, Educational Achievement Services

"Show Me the Money: Per-pupil, Per-school Reporting!"
Katie Hagan, Georgetown University

"How Superheroes Harness Family & Community Strengths
to Advance Equity!"
Dr. Charles R. Martínez, UT Austin

<u>Panels</u>
Los Superintendentes Superintendents Panel
Juan Cabrera, El Paso ISD
Dr. Paul Cruz, Austin ISD
Dr. Matthew Gutiérrez, Seguin ISD
Joe López, Taft ISD
Moderator Dr. José Leyba,
Association of *Latino* Administrators & Superintendents

Los Graduados Graduates Panel
Sandra Chávez, Dallas ISD
Irene Gómez, Wimberley ISD
Antonio "Tony" Hernández, Pharr-San Juan-Alamo ISD
Moderator Dr. Celina Estrada Thomas, Hutto ISD

¡Adelante! Luncheon Panel
MASBA President Homero García, South Texas ISD
MASBA President Elect Willie Tenorio, Jr., Hays CISD
MASBA Past President Armando Rodríguez, Canutillo ISD
MASBA Vice President Jacinto Ramos, Jr., Fort Worth ISD
MASBA Executive Director Dr. Jayme Mathias, Austin ISD

<u>Breakout Sessions</u>

"Uvalde CISD's Partnership Approach to Child Nutrition!"
Aurora A. Barrera, Uvalde CISD;
Richard Mallard, Southwest Foodservice Excellence

"Our Elementary Can Code! Can Yours?"
Joe López, Freddy Ramos & Joshua Rombs, Taft ISD

"The Impact of School Buildings
on Student Health & Performance!"
Jonathan Blackwell, Performance Services

"MH-U: Mental Health & You!"
Dan Barrett, Center for Healthcare Services

"Has Texas Abandoned At-risk Minority Students in Texas? Yes!"
George Scott, Katy ISD

"English Language Learners Score BIG with GOAL!"
Chris Ice & Adriana Cavazos, Denton ISD

"The ABC's of IEP's!"
Christina García, Walsh Gallegos Treviño Russo & Kyle

"Destination Manor: Diverse Pathways to Success!"
Dr. Royce Avery, Dr. Brian Yearwood, Dr. Creslond Fannin,
Dr. Scott Moger & Ana Cortez, Manor ISD

"School Facilities Impact Student Achievement!"
Jeff Clemmons, TASB Facility Services

"Racial Consciousness as an Educational Leader!"
Jacinto Ramos, Jr., Fort Worth ISD

"Old-school Department Head
vs. New-school Instructional Coach!"
Dr. Creslond Fannin, Manor ISD

"Effective K-12 Pre-bond Planning!"
Brian Godínez, Eli Ochoa & Robert Sands, ERO Architects

"*Pláticas*: How San Marcos CISD
Increases Community Support for At-risk Populations!"
James Barton & Benjamín Grijalva, San Marcos CISD

"Promoting Race-conscious Practice in Education
is Everyone's Job!"
Dr. Karlyn Keller & Jennifer Charles,
TASB Special Education Solutions

"Leaders Speak Out: Why Dual Language Education!"
Juan Cabrera, Al Velarde & Laila Ferris, El Paso ISD

"Stop the DRIP: Create Opportunities for All Students!"
Dr. Nathan Balasubramanian, Ana Cortez & Shouneille Moore,
Manor ISD

"Effective English Learner Program Implementation Rubrics"
Barbara Kennedy, Texas Education Agency

"The Missing Link:
What Does 21st-century Learning Mean to You?"
Mario Bracamontes & David Rocha, Pharr-San Juan-Alamo ISD

"Show Me the Money: Per-pupil, Per-school Reporting, Part II!"
Katie Hagan, Georgetown University

"The Naked Truth: School Districts & Social Media"
Kevin O'Hanlon, O'Hanlon Demerath & Castillo

"Our Path to Systemic Equity Transformation!"
Sherry Breed & Joseph Niedziela, Fort Worth ISD

"Be a Superhero — and Don't Let Your Staff Be a Statistic!"
Matt Escalante, TCG Advisors

Student Entertainment

Lanier High School Jazz Combo,
Lanier High School, Austin ISD

Mariachi Nuevo Cascabel
San Marcos High School, San Marcos CISD

Mariachi de Oro
Crockett High School, Austin ISD

Entertainment

Roger Velásquez & the Latin Legendz

On March 2, 2019, President Homero García presided over the annual **MASBA Member Assembly**. Meeting minutes contain the following:

- The Member Assembly adopted the Credentials Committee Report, Member Assembly rules, and the meeting agenda.
- Jayme presented the Executive Director's report.
- Xavier offered the Treasurer's report.
- Immediate Past President Armando Rodríguez presented the Nominations Committee report, and all proposed Officers and Directors were elected.
- The Member Assembly approved bylaws amendments. Most notably,
  o The membership year for a MASBA member will now be one year from the date on which membership dues are received.
  o Effective at the conclusion of the 2021 Member Assembly, MASBA will have a 23-member Board of Directors, with one director from each of the 20 education service center (ESC) regions in Texas.
  o The MASBA President nominates individuals to fill vacant Board positions, but the MASBA Board elects them to their positions.
  o Directors will no longer be automatically dismissed from the Board for missing three consecutive meetings; instead, the Board will review the service of Directors who are absent.

- o Officers will be contacted by phone and/or text if an emergency meeting of the Executive Committee is called.
- o The Executive Director hires all MASBA Staff, within the parameters of the Board-approved budget.
- No amendments were made to MASBA's advocacy agenda.

At the conclusion of the meeting, Homero García ended his term as MASBA President, and President Elect Guillermo "Willie" Tenorio, Jr. of Hays CISD assumed the presidency of MASBA.

If you would like to share any photos, meeting minutes, conference programs, mementos, etc. from the presidency of Homero García, for inclusion in Volume II, please email them to info@masbatx.org or mail them to MASBA | P.O. Box 474 | Austin, TX 78767.

Thank you for helping us to reconstruct our history!

"It's Powerful"

Willie Tenorio, Jr.

I started m service on the Hays CISD school board in December 2009—so I just celebrated my tenth anniversary on the school board. Several years before, I joked that I suffered an early midlife crisis and asked myself, "Why am I here? And what will be my legacy? What will I do to make this world a better place?" I made a list, and realized I wanted to make a bigger impact on society through education. I stuck that list in my drawer and didn't look at it for years, but then a trustee resigned, and my school board appointed me to serve until the special election. With the urging of my wife, Daphne, and community members, I decided to run for that school board position, and here I am!

Memories of my high school experience inspired me to serve on the school board: When I graduated, many *Latino* students didn't go to college, even though we had the same capabilities and received the same grades as the Anglo students who were going to college at higher rates. I saw the disparity. Those going to college were of comparable academic success—but they happened to be Anglo.

My parents also played a huge role in my desire to help public education. Education was a big deal in my family. My mother, Adelfa, never went to college, but she had always wanted to be a teacher, so I became her student at an early age. She spent a lot of time with me, teaching me how to read. She practically set up a little classroom in our house! I could read, write and count by age three. By kindergarten, I could read at the first- or second-grade level.

Later in life, I googled myself. My dad and I share the same name, so I came across a dissertation that mentioned my dad, Willie Sr., written by a student at Southwest Texas State University—today's Texas State University. I learned that my father worked to integrate the school system in Kyle, Texas. I had no idea he had done that! My dad told me that my grandfather, Roberto Tenorio, had attempted to integrate the Kyle public school system back in the 1930s, but didn't succeed. My dad, grandfather and another gentleman led the petition to integrate the Kyle public school system. Because of them, Kyle integrated before the federal government required public schools to integrate. So, advocating for our public schools runs in our family. In addition, two of my cousins, Sandra Tenorio and Abel Tenorio, served on the Hays CISD Board before me.

After I was elected to our local school board, two of my fellow trustees, Bert Bronaugh and Ralph Pfluger, encouraged me to attend the 2010 MASBA conference. They were impressed with MASBA's conferences. My local board appointed me to fill a seat previously held by Joe Muñoz, who then served as MASBA's Executive Director. Joe helped me fall in love with MASBA, and María Leal, the President of MASBA, and Manuel Rodríguez, the President Elect, warmly welcomed me. MASBA felt like a family right from the beginning.

At my first MASBA Conference, I attended MASBA's *mariachi* competition. Many MASBA members were unhappy that the University Interscholastic League didn't recognize *mariachi*. Though often not recognized as such, *mariachi* is a powerful, complicated musical art form. So MASBA set up a system where students could compete, just like band and choir. This allowed the various *mariachi* programs to measure themselves against others, and it created a system where high school *mariachis* could set goals and improve. MASBA's goal to gain recognition of the music validated the work of the students and cultivated broader acceptance of our culture. It gave MASBA a higher purpose, it became the focus of our organization, and we were all very proud of it.

MASBA's continuing education opportunities—on topics you could not find anywhere else—also helped to draw me and many others into the organization. IDRA, MALDEF and the Texas Freedom Network hosted sessions on Mexican American Studies, equity, and textbooks more representative of our community. At one MASBA conference, Harlandale ISD taught trustees about a response-to-intervention program that produced better, more-equitable outcomes for its students. MASBA members hungered for such topics, which you couldn't find at other conferences.

MASBA provided tremendous opportunities for networking and trustee-to-trustee mentoring and friendships. Charles Stafford coached me on preparing for our bond election. I also remember a conversation with Sylvester Vásquez on leadership, when I first became involved with MASBA. His philosophy on common purpose and how we need to work with people with whom we disagree made a big impact on me. I doubt Sylvester remembers that conversation, but I certainly do. Those interactions with more-experienced trustees were always helpful for me.

MASBA has evolved greatly since I joined the Board. We set up strong bookkeeping systems and regular financial audits. We accomplished our goal of UIL recognition of *mariachi*. The monthly conference calls, started by President Armando Rodríguez beginning in 2017, in addition to the three in person meetings a year, ensure we regularly monitor our progress. The hiring of Dr. Jayme Mathias as our Executive Director moved us even more forward.

My hope is that MASBA will continue to be an organization where people can learn about strategies for closing gaps. I'd also like to see MASBA get to the point that it is top-of-mind when people think about issues affecting *Latino* students and English Language Learners. MASBA participated in a press conference at the beginning of this last Legislative Session, and it was obvious that we weren't as well-known as other organizations at that press conference. We've started the process to change that. I'd like to see us become the ones the media comes to hear!

My dream is that MASBA might also one day have a publishing arm, creating articles, audio programs and videos on equity and closing achievement gaps. That's been one of my goals for the *¡MASBÁmonos!* show that I share on Facebook Live: giving people a voice and highlighting what they're doing with respect to equity issues. I recently highlighted Dr. José Arturo Puga and Soor-el Puga, who wrote and illustrated the book, *The Blue Horse That Wanted to Go to College*. It's the story of an English Language Learner who dreamed of going to college. When I was in the sixth grade, our teacher asked us what college we wanted to go to, and I had never thought about that. When the teacher came to me, I copied the answer of another student, saying, "I want to go there, too!" Frankly, though, I had never thought about college before then. I want those conversations to be happening earlier for *Latinx* kids.

The *¡MASBÁmonos!* show is designed to provide value for the entire community on topics important to us. We have covered the story of Fort Worth ISD's Dolores Huerta/César Chávez Day of Service with President Elect Jacinto Ramos, Jr. and the importance of *Latinx* representation in comic books with Héctor Rodríguez. The show also spreads awareness of our organization and our mission.

MASBA is a home for many of us. We can find others who care about closing achievement gaps and creating opportunity for all students. This common purpose unites us. Trustees have many options to fulfill educational requirements, but MASBA allows us to fulfill our shared visions of equity and fairness.

When you get together a bunch of people who have a common purpose and who really care about a mission, like closing gaps, it's powerful. That's what's happening with MASBA: We now have a system in place that will grow stronger over time. The MASBA that we'll have in ten years will be very different from the MASBA of today. It will be stronger, more powerful, and more effective. I'm proud that MASBA is now headed in that direction!

I conclude with a story.

When I was young, my politically-involved father gave me a book, *A Gringo Manual on How to Handle Mexicans*, written by José Ángel Gutiérrez, a *Chicano* activist and co-founder of MASBA. The work exposed tactics and strategies used to disenfranchise Mexican Americans in Texas. The lessons from that book helped me realize everything our community has suffered, but more importantly how to break through those barriers. So it has come full-circle: One of the founders of MASBA has greatly influenced and also motivated the current President of MASBA! My hope is that this book on MASBA history might also influence young people to commit to serve our community!

Guillermo "Willie" Tenorio, Jr. began his service on the Board of Trustees of the Hays Consolidated Independent School District in 2009. An alumnus of Leadership TASB, he joined the MASBA Board in 2013. After serving as Secretary, then as President Elect, he became MASBA President in March 2019.

The Presidency of Willie Tenorio, Jr.

On March 2, 2019, at the conclusion of the annual MASBA Member Assembly, President Elect Guillermo "Willie" Tenorio, Jr. of Hays CISD assumed leadership of MASBA. In a ceremony later that evening, Immediate Past President Homero García of South Texas ISD ceremoniously handed the gavel to President Tenorio.

The MASBA Board of Directors then consisted of the following Officers and Directors:
- President Guillermo "Willie" Tenorio, Jr., Hays CISD
- President Elect Jacinto "Cinto" Ramos, Jr., Fort Worth ISD
- Immediate Past President Homero García, South Texas ISD
- Vice President & Region 2A Director Ana Cortez, Manor ISD
- Secretary & Region 6B Director Miguel "Mike" Rosales, Ysleta ISD
- Treasurer & Region 3B Director Xavier Herrera, Stafford MSD
- Region 1A Director Eva C. Watts, Donna ISD
- Region 1B Director Ricardo Gutiérrez, Region 1 ESC
- Region 2B Director Marco R. Ortiz, Taylor ISD
- Region 3A Director Holly María Flynn Vilaseca, Houston ISD
- Region 5A Director Johnny "John" Betancourt, Amarillo ISD
- Region 5B Director Sylvester Vásquez, Jr., Southwest ISD
- Region 6A Director Alfonso "Al" Velarde, El Paso ISD

On March 3, 2019, President Willie Tenorio, Jr. convened a meeting of the **MASBA Board** at the Renaissance Austin Hotel. Directors debriefed the annual MASBA conference, signed thank you notes for sponsors, and approved a schedule of meetings for the year.

On March 27, 2019, President Willie Tenorio, Jr. convened a meeting of the **MASBA Board** by conference call. The meeting agenda and minutes report the following:

- Jayme presented an advocacy update on the House Public Education Committee and the House Appropriations Committee. He recently submitted testimony on behalf of MASBA in support of Individual Graduation Committees.
- MASBA members visited the offices of 187 legislators during our Advocacy Day on February 26. The evening reception that we co-hosted with the Texas Caucus of Black School Board Members at the Texas State Capitol was a success.
- Our first-ever Texas Public Schools Equity Symposium on February 27 drew 68 attendees. Event evaluations have been compiled.
- 15 superintendents & trustees took part in our February 28 Tour of Best Practices, which visited six school sites in the Manor ISD, Austin ISD and Del Valle ISD.
- 233 persons attended our March 1-3 annual MASBA conference, "*Superhéroes* for Kids!" Discussion ensued on the reasons for lighter attendance this year, which likely included the higher room rate of conferences in Austin, the greater distance from South Texas, and the longer week of activity by MASBA (with our Advocacy Day on Tuesday and our Equity Symposium on Wednesday).
- Jayme and Event Planner Yeraldín Yordi are working to plan a June 12 Topgolf night with Performance Services in San Antonio and a June 14 MASBA reception at SLI South.
- Jayme presented a balance sheet, profit/loss statement and general ledger for the second quarter, which concluded on February 28.
- Our revised bylaws, with all amendments passed by our March 2 Member Assembly, are now posted online.
- Jayme presented a quarterly report on his progress toward performance targets.
- The Texas Talent Musicians Association agrees in substance with the joint resolution proposed by our Board; the partnership was announced at our Saturday evening dance on March 2.

- Regina Cantú has said that her family will not need MASBA's assistance with the Manuel Rodríguez, Jr. STEAM on to Lead Scholarship this year.

On April 8, 2019, President Willie Tenorio, Jr. convened a meeting of the **MASBA Executive Committee** by conference call. The meeting agenda and minutes report the following:

- Jayme presented an extended advocacy update, detailing the present contents of House Bill 3, which will overhaul school finance. He will testify against charter schools tomorrow.
- MASBA was represented at the annual NSBA conference in Philadelphia on March 30 to April 1 by Cinto, Ana, Ricardo, Holly María, Sylvester, Jayme, and MASBA Membership Director Vincent Tovar. At the event, Cinto was elected Chair of the NSBA Council of Urban Boards of Education.
- For the first time ever, MASBA now has over 100 members!
- 1,656 applications were received for our 94 MASBA scholarships. Jayme has divided the applications among trustees willing to assist with scoring.
- Our MASBA brochure has been redesigned to reflect the changes on our Board since our March 2 Member Assembly.

On April 17, 2019, President Willie Tenorio, Jr. convened a meeting of the **MASBA Board** by conference call. The meeting agenda and minutes report the following:

- The Board reviewed all items from the April 8 meeting.
- Jayme presented an extended advocacy update. He will testify this week with the Texas *Latino* Education Coalition in support of House Bill 3893, for an exemption from college tuition for those who are preparing to teach high-need areas like special education, math, and bilingual education.
- All 94 MASBA scholarships have been awarded. Jayme thanked all who assisted with the selection of winners: Viola García (Aldine ISD), John Betancourt (Amarillo ISD), Cindy Anderson, LaTisha Anderson & Ann Teich (Austin ISD), Al Velarde (El Paso ISD), Willie Tenorio & Teresa Tobías (Hays CISD), Holly María Flynn Vilaseca (Houston ISD), George Scott (Katy ISD), Ana Cortez (Manor ISD), Ricardo Gutiérrez

(Region 1 ESC), Miguel Arredondo (San Marcos CISD), María Leal (South Texas ISD), Sylvester Vásquez (Southwest ISD), Xavier Herrera (Stafford MSD), Marco R. Ortiz (Taylor ISD), Mike Rosales (Ysleta ISD), Juan Aguilera (MASBA Legal Counsel), & Vincent Tovar (MASBA Staff).

- To better serve the large number of students applying for our MASBA scholarships, the Board agreed to increase our scholarship program from 94 scholarships this year, to 220+ scholarships in 2020. One scholarship will be awarded to each district with less than 1,000 students, two scholarships will be awarded to each district with 1,000 to 9,999 students, and three scholarships will be awarded to each district with 10,000 students or more.

On May 6, 2019, President Willie Tenorio, Jr. convened a meeting of the **MASBA Executive Committee** by conference call. The meeting agenda and minutes report the following:

- Jayme presented an advocacy update on the "fast-and-furious" legislative session, which will end on May 27. House Bill 3 (school finance reform) is now in conference committee.
- Jayme presented financial reports for our February 26 Advocacy Day, February 27 Equity Symposium, and March 1-3 annual conference. He also shared lessons learned from each event. He presented proposed budget amendments, for approval by the Board.

On May 15, 2019, President Willie Tenorio, Jr. convened a meeting of the **MASBA Board** by conference call. The meeting agenda and minutes report the following:

- The Board reviewed all items from the May 6 Executive Committee meeting.
- Our annual MASBA conference will be hosted at the Wyndham San Antonio Riverwalk Hotel on February 20-23, 2020 and February 18-21, 2021.
- The Board received second quarter financial reports and approved budget amendments.
- John Betancourt was not re-elected to his local board, so our 5A seat is now open. Applications are available for trustees interested in filling our 4A, 4B or 5A seats.

On June 10, 2019, President Willie Tenorio, Jr. convened a meeting of the **MASBA Executive Committee** by conference call. The meeting agenda and minutes report the following:

- Jayme summarized MASBA's advocacy during the 86th Legislative Session, which concluded on May 27.
- Jayme presented a summary of our May 18 MASBA reception at the Region 1 conference on South Padre Island. Louis Reyes led the planning of the event. , Homero, Eva, Ricardo, and Holly María attended the event.
- Jayme presented a list of the sponsors for our June 12 Topgolf night and the details for our June 14 *¡MASBA Cumbia! cumbia/merengue* reception with *Orquesta Mi Rumba* at SLI South. Kevin O'Hanlon of O'Hanlon Demerath & Castillo will receive our Golden *Molcajete* Award.
- Jayme shared a copy of the contract for our annual conference at the Wyndham San Antonio Riverwalk in 2020 and 2021.
- Jayme presented financial reports for the third quarter, which concluded on May 31, as well as proposed budget amendments.
- The Executive Committee reviewed draft questions proposed for reflection during our June 14 MASBA Board Retreat.
- Jayme shared a proposal from a consultant proposing a MASBA energy partnership opportunity. The Executive

Committee discussed this at length and asked Jayme to gather more information.

On June 14, 2019, President Willie Tenorio, Jr. convened a meeting of the **MASBA Board** at the San Antonio Marriott Rivercenter Hotel. The meeting agenda and minutes report the following:

- Attendees debriefed the May 18 MASBA reception at the Region 1 conference on South Padre Island.
- The Board debriefed its June 12 Topgolf Night, attended by 156 people, and spoke through details of its June 14 *¡MASBA Cumbia!* reception.
- Jayme distributed draft ideas for a MASBA Superintendent of the Year Award.
- Jayme presented a financial report for the third quarter, and the Board approved budget amendments.
- Jayme said that for the first time in years, MASBA has a directory of all known Past Presidents.
- Willie led the Board in a time of strategic planning. Possible future initiatives include MASBA webinars, a mini TedTalk series, a MASBA dual language education program, a MASBA governance initiative, Leadership MASBA (modeled on Leadership TASB), a new board member training, a partnership for insurance benefits, a MASBA podcast, a MASBA training with a focus on policy & closing gaps, a MASBA YouTube channel, a MASBA magazine, and a MASBA energy cooperative.

On July 8, 2019, President Willie Tenorio, Jr. convened a meeting of the **MASBA Executive Committee** by conference call. The meeting agenda and minutes report the following:

- The Executive Committee debriefed MASBA's June 14 *¡MASBA Cumbia!* reception, attended by at least 310 people.
- Jayme proposed a MASBA "affiliate" status for school districts outside Texas to enjoy the benefits of MASBA membership, including a scholarship for a graduate in each district.
- Willie has now recorded two Facebook Live conversation on his recently-debuted *¡MASBÁmonos!* show.

- Willie has researched possible platforms for MASBA webinars.

On July 17, 2019, President Willie Tenorio, Jr. convened a meeting of the **MASBA Board** by conference call. The meeting agenda and minutes report the following:

- The Board reviewed all items from the July 8 Executive Committee meeting.
- The Board approved moving forward with the idea of MASBA webinars, surfaced during the Board's June 14 strategic planning retreat.
- The Board approved a MASBA "affiliate" status for school districts outside Texas.

On August 12, 2019, President Willie Tenorio, Jr. convened a meeting of the **MASBA Executive Committee** by conference call. The meeting agenda and minutes report the following:

- Cinto represented MASBA at the August 2-4 *UnidosUS* annual conference in San Diego.
- Staff is gathering contact information for all school districts in Colorado, Florida, Illinois, New Jersey, New Mexico, and Nevada. The MASBA Affiliate program will not launch in Arizona or California until we've had conversations with the *Latino* School Boards Associations of those states.
- VLK Architects has offered to produce two videos to promote MASBA and its scholarship program.
- Two applications were received for the 4A & 5A seats and will be forwarded to our MASBA Board.

On August 21, 2019, President Willie Tenorio, Jr. convened a meeting of the **MASBA Board** by conference call. The meeting agenda and minutes report the following:

- The Board reviewed all items from the August 12 Executive Committee meeting.
- Jayme shared a copy of the letter that will be mailed to school districts outside of Texas.
- Jayme shared a plan for MASBA webinar implementation.
- Jayme spoke through details of the MASBA Board's meeting on September 20 in Dallas.
- The Board elected Charles Stafford of Denton ISD to the 4A seat and Adam Soto of Plainview ISD to the 5A seat, through the conclusion of our 2020 Member Assembly.

On September 9, 2019, President Willie Tenorio, Jr. convened a meeting of the **MASBA Executive Committee** by conference call. The meeting agenda and minutes report the following:

- Jayme presented a financial summary of FY18/19, which concluded on August 31.
- Jayme distributed an evaluation of his performance during the past year.
- Officers discussed possible domains for Executive Director performance targets for FY19/20.
- Officers discussed ideas for Executive Director compensation in FY19/20.

On September 20, 2019, President Willie Tenorio, Jr. convened a meeting of the **MASBA Board** at the Dallas Omni Hotel. The meeting agenda and minutes report the following:

- The Board welcomed Charles Stafford of Denton ISD and Adam Soto of Plainview ISD.
- Al and Mike spoke of the effect on their communities of the racially-motivated August 3 mass shooting in El Paso.
- The Board previewed MASBA's new online toolkits on closing gaps, equity, dual language, Mexican American Studies, celebrating *Latinx* leaders, DACA, charter schools, racial violence, and *Latinx* resources.

- Jayme discussed details on the evening's TALAS/MASBA *Latinx* Legacy Month reception. Student entertainment will be provided by *Mariachi Sol Azteca* of Grand Prairie ISD and *Mariachi Espuelas de Plata* from Fort Worth ISD.
- Jayme shared a balance sheet, income/expense report and general ledger for FY18/19. The organization ended the fiscal year with a profit of $6,335 and has $103,814 in the bank. Jayme also presented a budget-to-actual comparison.
- The Board approved a budget for FY19/20.
- Jayme presented a report on recent sponsorships.
- The Board evaluated the performance of its Executive Director in closed session. The Board also discussed possible Executive Director performance targets & compensation for FY19/20.

On October 7, President Willie Tenorio, Jr. convened a meeting of the **MASBA Executive Committee** by conference call. The meeting agenda and minutes report the following:

- Officers debriefed the September 20 Board meeting in Dallas and the TALAS/MASBA *Latinx* Legacy Month reception.
- Officers reviewed Jayme's strategic plan for expanding MASBA outside of Texas.
- Jayme offered an update on details for MASBA's 2020 conference.

On October 16, 2019, President Willie Tenorio, Jr. convened a meeting of the **MASBA Board** by conference call. The meeting agenda and minutes report the following:

- The Board reviewed all items from the October 7 Executive Committee meeting.
- Cinto and Jayme reported on their participation in the CUBE annual conference in Miami. Cinto chairs the organization's steering committee, on which Jayme also serves.
- Subsequent to an inquiry from a member district, Jayme is preparing a draft resolution on alternative celebrations to Columbus Day.
- Mike and Juan are researching the possibility of establishing a MASBA scholarship endowment.

- The Board approved Executive Director performance targets and compensation for FY19/20.

On November 4, 2019, President Willie Tenorio, Jr. convened a meeting of the **MASBA Executive Committee** by conference call. The meeting agenda and minutes report the following:

- Jayme presented a draft resolution for Board consideration "in Support of Alternative Celebrations to Columbus Day in Our Texas Public Schools."
- On October 22, Jayme and Louis Reyes met with Josie Smith Wright, presumed Executive Director of the Texas Caucus of Black School Board Members.
- Officers chose Montemayor Britton Bender to perform our FY18/19 financial audit.
- Jayme distributed a list of Tier 1 and Tier 2 interview prospects for our upcoming promotional videos for MASBA.
- Officers discussed the possibility of a resolution in support of the Houston ISD Board of Trustees, which faces possible takeover by the Texas Education Agency.

On November 13, 2019, President Willie Tenorio, Jr. convened a meeting of the **MASBA Board** by conference call. The meeting agenda and minutes report the following:

- The Board reviewed all items from the November 4 Executive Committee meeting.
- The Board approved a resolution in support of alternative celebrations to Columbus Day in our Texas Public Schools.
- Jayme executed the contract for our FY18/19 financial audit.
- Jayme reviewed a draft schedule of webinars to launch in January.
- Staff has moved MASBA to a larger storage space in Austin.
- Willie has now recorded six episodes of the *¡MASBÁmonos!* show on Facebook Live.

On December 9, 2019, President Willie Tenorio, Jr. convened a meeting of the **MASBA Executive Committee** by conference call. The meeting agenda and minutes report the following:

- Jayme presented a first-quarter update on Executive Director performance targets for FY19/20.
- Officers decided to forego the possibility of a 2020 equity symposium in February, opting instead to support the Texas Caucus of Black School Board Members if it decides to go forward with an equity symposium in connection with its annual summit.
- Our 2020 conference registration site is up; sponsorships for the event are coming in.
- Officers agreed that the Board will not meet at TASA Midwinter in Austin, as previously suggested, for the purpose of capturing B-roll for videos to promote MASBA.
- Eleven seats on our Board will expire at the conclusion of our 2020 Member Assembly. Officer & Director applications are now online.
- Mike and Juan distributed an initial draft policy for a MASBA scholarship endowment.

On December 18, 2019, President Willie Tenorio, Jr. convened a meeting of the **MASBA Board** by conference call. The meeting agenda and minutes report the following:

- The Board reviewed all items from the December 9 Executive Committee meeting.
- Jayme piloted a webinar on closing gaps on December 10.

On January 13, 2020, President Willie Tenorio, Jr. convened a meeting of the **MASBA Executive Committee** by conference call. The meeting agenda and minutes report the following:

- Jayme presented a balance sheet, income/expense report and general ledger for the first quarter of FY19/20. Officers reviewed proposed budget amendments.
- Jayme reviewed details for our February MASBA events in San Antonio.
- No bylaws amendments are recommended by Staff for the 2020 Member Assembly.

- We received 15 applications for the 11 available seats that will be filled at our 2020 Member Assembly.
- Jayme presented ideas for two subsequent book projects by MASBA.

On January 22, 2020, President Willie Tenorio, Jr. convened a meeting of the **MASBA Board** by conference call. The meeting agenda and minutes report the following:

- The Board reviewed all items from the January 13 Executive Committee meeting.
- MASBA webinars will launch on February 6.

If you would like to share any photos, meeting minutes, conference programs, mementos, etc. from the presidency of Willie Tenorio, Jr., for inclusion in Volume II, please email them to info@masbatx.org or mail them to MASBA | P.O. Box 474 | Austin, TX 78767.

Thank you for helping us to reconstruct our history!

"MASBA Has Only Gotten Better"

Charles Stafford

I first learned about MASBA through Dr. Rudy Rodríguez of the Denton ISD Board of Trustees. We were the two members of our local board who pushed things for *Latino* kids. We were also the two people on our board who spoke Spanish: Rudy was a native speaker, and I picked up Spanish in school.

Rudy told me about MASBA. He thought it would be a great idea for our district to join. It was absolutely an "easy sale" for our board: About 30 or 35% of our kids in the Denton ISD were *Latino* — and the number was climbing.

MASBA leadership immediately recruited Rudy to be Treasurer. He got on the officer track and was "cooking right along." At that time, I started attending MASBA's annual conferences, probably 12 years ago. Even after Rudy stopped serving as MASBA's Treasurer, I continued to go to MASBA's conferences. I made friends and became more familiar with the statewide issues that concerned MASBA.

I can't remember missing a MASBA conference during those years. Attending that annual conference was high on my list of things I should be doing, and my district has maintained MASBA membership for years.

I remember MASBA President Dr. Manuel Flores of the Corpus Christi ISD Board of Trustees. An earnest and dedicated man, he took MASBA really seriously.

I remember when María Leal became president of MASBA in 2009. A longtime, tireless laborer in the vineyard of public education, she expended a lot of effort to make things better. She was over-the-top dedicated to schools in the Valley, and to the *Latino* children of the state. You could count on her for sure.

Manuel Rodríguez of the Houston ISD became MASBA's president in 2010. He led from the front and from the rear. He took over the conference — and you can't be the President of the Houston ISD Board of Trustees and not have a few ideas! Under Manuel's leadership, the quality of the conference really improved. A very strong leader, he did a great job — both out front, greeting people and being nice, and just sitting in the audience, raising his hand and asking questions.

Wise, likeable and extremely well-respected, Many was one of my favorite people to hang out with after dinner and run up a tab with. He could see ways to make things better, before others saw them. He took over the planning of the MASBA conference, and he improved the presentations.

Sylvester Vásquez of the Southwest ISD had a meteoric rise within TASB, which benefited MASBA. Sylvester joined the TASB Board, rocketed to the top, and became President of the TASB Board in 2010. A fun guy with a magnetic personality, Sylvester worked hard, and he played hard. He "burned the candle at both ends": He stayed up late and got up early. When he moved over from TASB to MASBA, he opened people's eyes to MASBA. Respect followed him in both organizations, and his celebrity in one pond fell on the other.

In 2012, MASBA President Juan Rangel, a very capable administrator, did an incredible job of keeping the organization going. He was very skilled at talking to people and making people feel good, and you couldn't question his devotion to the cause.

Time moved on. There were not any real red flags to the rank-and-file members of MASBA. Management issues arose at times: When you're operating on a shoestring budget — and in those days MASBA truly operated on a shoestring budget — you have one person wearing six hats. Understandably, it's difficult to divvy up all the responsibilities. They all tended to fall on one or two people.

Along came Gloria Casas in 2013. She and I flew together from the Valley to D.C., and she told me a lot about MASBA management. The executive director didn't have a job description. As a result, the tail wagged the dog. Frustrated, she assembled a group that I called the wise women of TASB: Marty Reyes from Ysleta ISD, Gloria Peña from Arlington ISD, and María Leal from South Texas ISD. They were all TASB directors, and Gloria got them to join the MASBA Board. This group of high-performing women plowed into MASBA's management issues.

The scariest discovery they made indicated that MASBA hadn't filed its IRS Form 990 for some five years. That could have been a horrible disaster. Some Republicans at the national level would have loved nothing more than to drop a stink bomb on an organization like MASBA. Gloria spent her year as president working on a list of reforms and things that needed to happen.

The next MASBA Member Assembly, though, was a palace coup, ousting the wise women of TASB. They were strong women and strong leaders. As president of MASBA, Gloria tried her very best to make a whole lot of change in a hurry. A true and courageous changemaker, she persisted in doing the right thing. She's a great model for any young person in life. She never gives up, never quits.

An astute politician, Louis Reyes played a role in TASB reevaluating its financial relationship with MASBA — the betrothal of MASBA and the Black Caucus and TASB. Louis played a nice, behind-the-scenes role in moving things forward for MASBA. Every organization needs a Louis Reyes.

After a few more years, MASBA had an incredibly courageous leader in Armando Rodríguez of the Canutillo ISD. He took on the task of cleaning up MASBA. He was the Lyndon Baines Johnson of MASBA. Kennedy had "Great Society" ambitions, but he didn't know how to get his initiatives passed through Congress. His death took the handcuffs off of LBJ, who railroaded Kennedy's programs through Congress. Armando recruited directors to the MASBA Board and lined up a succession of officers. He knew he'd be President for only a year, so, to make lasting change, he thought of the long-term game. The MASBA Board got its books cleaned up, wrote job descriptions, and hired stellar staff members. With Armando, the quality of MASBA conferences took a quantum leap, and MASBA is now doing some really cool stuff. It was a breath of fresh air for MASBA, and that kind of thing feeds on itself: When people go to a conference and see great stuff, they hunger for more, they come to the next conference, and they bring their friends. As a result, MASBA has a really healthy growth outlook.

Armando and more recent presidents have seen the value of enhancing and improving MASBA's reputation and MASBA's performance levels. They've pulled MASBA up and have helped us to be better poised for the future — mainly because they have a really smart executive director.

Change is never easy. The changes in staff resulted in personal attacks on Armando and the new staff. I was extremely proud of the 2017 MASBA Board for not falling prey to the bigotry play being made: A lot of Roman Catholics bit their tongue and endorsed an Independent Catholic priest with an alternative lifestyle as their new executive director. I wouldn't have bet a whole lot of my retirement money on that one coming out well! But it did, and it made me so proud of all those MASBA directors. It was a huge, huge decision, and MASBA has only gotten better.

I'm happy to now be serving on the MASBA Board. After I had attended the MASBA conference for four years, Manny Rodríguez approached me about serving on the MASBA Board. We had a long talk about it. I was really flattered. As we ate lunch, he said, "I can tell you're one of the good guys. You come to our conferences. You ask questions. Your mind works in great ways. But I really just want to ask you, 'What the hell are you doing here?'"

I told him, "I started learning Spanish at age 13, I'm in a district that has a growing *Latino* population, and the problems faced by MASBA and by the *Latino* population will be the problems of Texas in ten years. I would just like to get an inside look at what's coming!"

Then he asked me to consider joining the MASBA Board. I said, "As much as I'd love to, I don't want to do it if there's going to be anybody who feels like I took a seat that belonged to them." I told him, "You tell me when the time is right, and I'll be ready."

He said, "You have a great point. I don't know when that will be."

I am extremely humbled that the MASBA Board saw me as someone who supported the cause and would be cheerfully willing to do the work. The demographics of many of our districts are changing. It isn't really about what your percentage of a particular group of people is: All students deserve and have a right to a first-class education, and the fastest-growing demographic in our state and in our country is poverty. We're fools if we don't take every opportunity to formulate solutions for children in poverty.

I'm most proud of MASBA's ability in recent years to improve the level of participation of *Latino* board members. Even to this day, our State Board of Education steadfastly refuses to allow the true history of the Mexican American community to be taught. People like Cinto Ramos are aware of this history. He's part of a new generation of leaders who will be more vocal and effective in getting justice for those who are now the majority of the population of Texas.

Those conservative, old, White men who've tried to keep the *Latinos* and African Americans down: they're going to change, adapt and grow—or they're going to be swept out. Nothing good happens fast, but I see a tipping point coming, and I see a whole bunch of leaders in MASBA coming together to increase awareness—and that's where the power is. We have the numbers—and, in this sense, I count myself as a *Latino* — to start jerking this whole thing around. I hope we're smart. I hope we don't burn ourselves down. We need to be building an identity and a sense of pride in a bunch of kids, and, if we do that, they're smart enough: They'll figure the rest of it out. They just don't need to be made to feel marginalized and minimized. They don't need people telling them, "You can't vote because you're not the right color, or you don't have the right ID."

There are so many people who've done so much great work in property-poor districts — in South Texas and in other parts of Texas. Their story is largely untold. I would just like to see a level playing field. House Bill 3 makes a definite difference in that direction, but the Texas Legislature has never really embraced equal educational opportunity. Every time the Supreme Court says the system is inequitable and inadequate, the resistors have a special session and throw money at it. They make it better, but they don't really fix it. The scary part is: What are they going to do the next time oil prices go flat, and we come into the Legislative Session with a $20 billion deficit? I have this terrible feeling that, unless we really expand our influence and get the right folks elected — people who say that rainy days call for use of the Rainy Day Fund — they'll cut five billion dollars from public education. We can't stand that kind of abuse again.

I hope MASBA continues to see accelerated development of the organization, like the improvement in outreach that is really starting to roll. I want to see community involvement by people who are not typically involved, and I want to see it switch the levers of power. If we build it, and if we respect our folks at the grassroots level, and if we continue to pour adequate, equitable resources into public education, we'll achieve that. We can't fix all wrongs immediately. We can't automatically undo decades and decades of discrimination. Institutional racism still operates openly and successfully — just read any voter ID bill — but I'm an optimist. I believe that MASBA is in the best shape it's ever been in, and is poised to do even greater things!

Charles Ramsey Stafford was elected in 1998 to the Board of Trustees of the Denton Independent School District. From 2006 to 2018, he served on the Board of Directors of the Texas Association of School Boards, leading the organization as its President in 2017-2018. Charles joined the MASBA Board of Directors in August 2019.

"MASBA Hasn't Been Afraid to Step Up"

Ana Cortez

I owned the first-ever coffee shop in Manor, Texas. We brought the community together around comedy nights and open mic nights, which led to my becoming a founding member of the Manor Arts Council. We started bringing elected officials to speak at the coffee shop, and people began suggesting that I serve in public office myself. I was appointed to the Manor ISD Board of Trustees in June 2014, and was elected to the Board that November.

In 2015, I attended the annual TASA/TASB conference in Dallas. MASBA hosted a reception, so I went. They honored State Senator Eddie Lucio, so I met him and Rubén Cortez of the State Board of Education. I started meeting a lot of people. Everyone asked me, "Where's Manor?" I kept explaining that Manor is six miles east of Austin, but obviously no one had heard of Manor. No one.

After that reception, various MASBA directors encouraged me to apply for the MASBA Board. I joined the MASBA Board in 2016. I remember my excitement: Recently elected to our Manor ISD Board, I now served on a state board! After that, the Manor ISD became a MASBA member for the first time.

I fondly remember MASBA's advocacy for Mexican American Studies. I remember one press conference we held outside the State Board of Education, before one of its hearings on possible TEKS—Texas Essential Knowledge & Skills, or teaching standards—for Mexican American Studies. MASBA was well represented there by many people wearing MASBA buttons.

I'm a first-generation immigrant in the United States, so the battle for TEKS for Mexican American Studies motivated and inspired me. I strongly believe we need materials and curricula for Mexican American students. Growing up in La Joya, the daughter of migrant farmworkers, my first language was Spanish. We had nothing—we didn't even have hot water. We traveled every year to Nebraska and Colorado, leaving a month or so before the end of the school year and returning to Texas a month or two after the start of the new school year. At eight years old, I began working in the fields, among the beans and sugar beets—first by carrying water to my father and brothers. I killed my first rattlesnake in the fields at age ten! We traveled as migrant workers through half my high school years.

My dad used to tell me, "If you don't get an education, this is where you're going to end up working: here in the fields." Not wanting that future for myself, I decided to excel in school. I saw how hard my parents worked. I knew I needed to do something to get out of that situation!

Being an English Language Learner, I loved math but struggled in reading. I remember a teacher once giving me a book on Mexican Americans and saying, "Read this book." We didn't have a TV that summer, so I started reading that book. Its stories reminded me of my *abuelita* [grandmother], and my mom and dad. That book triggered me to read. I started talking about it. Then it inspired my mom to become a volunteer!

My parents are from a little town in Nuevo León, close to the mountains outside of Monterrey. My *abuelitos* [grandparents] lived there. When we started fighting for TEKS for Mexican American Studies, I thought, "I'm living proof of the value of Mexican American Studies! We need more materials that discuss our population. That connection is so important for our kids!"

I'm proud to have been part of the battle. Because Manor is so close to Austin, I could easily get to Austin to oppose the use of the racist book by Cynthia Dunbar, proposed for use in Mexican American Studies. People from across the whole state of Texas—university professors and legislators at all levels—came together around the issue of Mexican American Studies. In the end, the State Board of Education approved "Ethnic Studies: Americans of Mexican Descent." They couldn't even say it: "Mexican American Studies"!

Those battles fit within MASBA's mission of being a voice and serving underrepresented communities. We understood the importance of MASBA's mission, and we were willing to do what it took to make a difference—advocating for a day in honor of César Chávez and Dolores Huerta, or more recently standing in solidarity with the Houston ISD Board of Trustees against its takeover by the Texas Education Agency. MASBA hasn't been afraid to step up, and MASBA has been an example for other organizations.

My dream for MASBA, as we celebrate 50 years, is that we take MASBA nationwide. Imagine if we could take what we're doing in Texas and amplify that nationwide! Imagine the impact we could make for *Latino* students across the nation. Then we could inspire others to work toward closing the achievement gap. When I consider MASBA's future, I see MASBA becoming something really big!

Ana Cortez has served on the Board of Trustees of the Manor Independent School District since 2014. She joined the MASBA Board in 2016 and became MASBA Vice President in 2019.

"MASBA is on the Cusp of Making a Big Difference"

Mike Rosales

I come from Central El Paso, which is close to downtown. My dad worked for the railroad for about 45 years, and my mother worked as a retail clerk for J.C. Penney. A fireball and an exceptionally-bright woman, she won top salesperson in the nation for two years straight. If she had received an education, who knows how many millions she would have made!

We only spoke Spanish at home, so I was totally deficient in English. It was hard: We would get spanked or swatted every time we spoke Spanish at school. Looking back, I realize I was dyslexic. I had problems reading. I didn't realize it at the time.

In high school, I played the clarinet, then the alto saxophone. During my sophomore year, I gave up sports and started playing in bands. I could play Glenn Miller, and I could play rock-and-roll. The experience of playing in bands opened my eyes and my mind, and I met a lot of people.

Eventually, I graduated from high school, but I unfortunately found out how totally unprepared I was for college. My high school counselors never advised me. They looked at my skin color—like they did with a lot of my friends—and they put us "in a box." They assumed we'd all be truck drivers and factory workers. That's why I'm really sensitive to the work of college counselors today: I want every counselor to give every kid every opportunity. If my counselors had done that with me, my world would have been a little different.

In college, I needed to study remedial English and remedial math, and I ate a lot of "humble pie." But the more challenges I experienced, the more determined I was to get a degree. In 1966, I graduated from college, I married my wife, Cecilia, and she became pregnant the next month. By the end of that year, the Army drafted me and sent me to infantry school. I received $35 per month, and Cecilia received $95.50. I didn't have money for anything, so enrolling in Officer Candidate School—even though it would add another year to my service—made economic sense. I finished in 1967. Half my class went to Vietnam, and I went to Fort Sill, Oklahoma, where they assigned me to the Third Corps Artillery. In light of the anti-war riots in California, I created riot response maneuvers for Oklahoma City, Dallas, Fort Worth and San Antonio, should trouble break out in any of those cities. In an age before the internet, I had to use maps, and they would fly me over those cities, to see them from above. The draft, as ugly as it was, created an opportunity for guys like me to see the world outside our hometowns.

I was sent to Vietnam, where the Army stationed me at the command center. I'll never forget how a colonel there judged me by the color of my skin. I said to him, "I passed all the same tests, classes, and obstacle courses as all the blue-eyed, White guys of my rank. Judge me by what I can do!" He snarled, "You're going to work your ass off." And I did. But that was the least of my worries. I just wanted to get back to my family.

I never imagined that one day I'd serve on a school board. In 2015, a member of the Ysleta Teachers Association approached me with the idea. The association had previously endorsed my predecessor, who now suffered from brain cancer. I hesitated at first, because I didn't want to get into something that I couldn't correctly perform. I asked her, "What commitment are we talking about on a monthly basis?" She said, "It's only about four hours a month." I thought, "I can handle that." If only it *were* a commitment of four hours a month!

After joining the school board in the Ysleta ISD, I learned about MASBA through our Board President, Sean Haggerty. He invited me to a MASBA conference in San Antonio. I've always been pro-*Latino*, but many districts in Texas are still not sensitive to *Latino* kids. In many places, *Latino* children are being taken for granted in Texas. In some places, *Latino* students in special education aren't receiving the services they need. MASBA can make a difference on issues like that.

In order to make an organization strong, you need diversity and "new blood." That's what's happening in MASBA now. Armando Rodríguez took MASBA from where it used to be—somewhat disorganized—and he set up bylaws and structures. We now have a common goal: making things better for the children of Texas. In Texas, we have pockets that are well-integrated between *Latinos* and Whites and African Americans, but there are other places where we need to advocate for representation for our children. I believe that MASBA is on the cusp of making a big difference for children throughout the state of Texas.

If MASBA continues to have strong leadership, it will continue to impact legislation and be a catalyst for our schoolchildren. That's where we need to make a difference. We need to be unafraid to speak up, as MASBA recently did when it stood up for the Houston ISD Board of Trustees, which faced the threat of takeover by the Texas Education Agency.

Latinos remain underrepresented today. Look at the cable news shows: You see Blacks and Whites, but *Latinos* are hardly represented! MASBA can play a role in this by making sure that our kids enjoy the same opportunities as other kids, and that they are prepared for the world.

There's a false narrative that *Latinos* are "breaking" America. No. We are a part of America, and we are making America strong. I'm proud to be part of an organization like MASBA that's making a difference in changing that narrative!

Mike Rosales has served on the Ysleta ISD Board of Trustees since 2015. He joined the MASBA Board in 2017 and has served as MASBA Secretary since March 2018.

"MASBA Has Taken Strong Stands"

Al Velarde

I'm in my fifth year on the El Paso ISD Board of Trustees. The Texas Education Agency previously took over the district and installed a Board of Managers, and I was elected as part of the first Board of Trustees after that Board of Managers in 2015. Prior to that, people called me, saying, "We need good, credible people to be on the board, and we'll support you if you run for election!" I heeded that call.

Of the first seven board members who took their seats after the Board of Managers in 2015, I was the only *Latino* — in a city that's 80% *Latino*! So, I thought it was important that I get involved in MASBA and represent the *Latino* culture and show my support for the *Latino* community.

El Paso is the largest binational metropolitan area in the world, with 800,000 people in El Paso County and over 2,000,000 people in Juárez — and the only thing that divides us is a riverbend. People cross the border every day as part of their daily lives. That drives our culture. We have a proximity and direct connection to Mexico, and we're very much influenced by Mexican culture and traditions. Our people here have family in Mexico, so there's direct, personal connection to Mexico. We celebrate holidays like Mexico's Independence Day and *el día de los muertos* [the Day of the Dead]. Farther from the border, people are expected to adapt and assimilate to the American way; we don't have the same pressures here in El Paso to give up the language and culture of Mexico. To the contrary, we have a very close relationship with Mexico. We are one community here, with our sisters and brothers in Mexico. What happens across the border affects us. My CFO here lost two cousins to the violence of the cartels in Mexico, and the Walmart shooting in El Paso claimed the lives of at least six Mexican citizens.

I first came to know of MASBA through our El Paso ISD superintendent, Juan Cabrera. He had connections with MASBA, and he frequently discussed the Mexican American School Boards Association. I also had a conversation with MASBA President Armando Rodríguez of the Canutillo ISD. At Armando's invitation, I attended my first MASBA reception during a TASB event. He introduced me to some MASBA Board members. I thought, "What a great group of people!" I really enjoyed the camaraderie. These people advocated for Hispanic culture, but not to some radical degree where everyone is protesting and saying, "We're *la raza*!" These professionals advocated and moved forward an agenda inclusive of all *Latinos*.

In 2017, a vacancy on the MASBA Board led Armando to ask if I wanted to fill that seat. After my experience of getting to know people within MASBA, I thought, "Absolutely! This is a great idea!"

We are in a somewhat unique position here in El Paso, being on the border with Mexico. During these two years in which I've served on the Board, MASBA took strong stands against the incarceration of immigrant children at the border, and also against racial violence after the August 3, 2019 racially-motivated mass shooting here in El Paso. At the very next meeting of our MASBA Board, I suggested that MASBA take a stand against racially-motivated violence against people of Hispanic descent. And we did.

In El Paso, since we're 88% Hispanic, we're the vast majority here. So, we don't see a lot of racial discrimination. We're somewhat sheltered from that reality. But, with this one, violent act by a non-Hispanic individual against our community, the entire city became a victim. We always thought we were immune from things like this, then, all of a sudden, assault changed the environment. Fear spread into our schools. Students now live with that. I sometimes wonder whether the active shooter drills we now have aren't also traumatizing our kids.

At that MASBA Board meeting, I noted this shooting wasn't simply an El Paso issue: This attack happened in El Paso, but that individual could have emerged anywhere in the state. There are other likeminded individuals who might perpetrate similar acts against Hispanics in the future. Sadly, messages come from the top office in our government that *Latinos* are less than other people, particularly Whites. The rhetoric of a "border crisis" translates into sentiments against *Latinos*. I firmly believe MASBA can play a leading role in getting out the message that all our children have the right to be treated just like any other child. *Latinos* are Americans. We should be treated as such. There should be no different treatment of us just because of the color of our skin.

That single attack pulled us back decades. As a culture, we achieved for decades. Now our kids live with the fear that their ethnicity can make them a target of an attack. It's different from a random school shooting: Hispanics were targeted at a favorite family location, a Walmart in El Paso!

The message was loud and clear: There are individuals in our country who believe that we don't belong. Within this context, MASBA can play a strong role in countering that narrative and influencing educators and the students they educate. We possess the ability to demand that *Latino* children be treated just like any other child in their communities.

Our *Latino* population has always been the majority here in El Paso. Many of our elected officials are now *Latino*. Our U.S. Congresswoman is *Latina*. The majority of our county commissioners and city council members are *Latino*. But this phenomenon is new: 30 years ago, you didn't see *Latinos* in the mayor's office or on city council. In El Paso, *Latinos* began to step up and take on leadership roles, but the process is still too slow. I was the only *Latino* elected to our local school board in 2015, but only *Latinos* run for my single-member district. Two more *Latinos* were elected to our El Paso ISD Board during the last election cycle. In a city that's 88% Hispanic, only three of seven school board members are *Latino*!

We're coming into these leadership positions not through protest or violence, but because we're educating ourselves. That's a threat to people like the Walmart shooter, who wrote a manifesto against our community. We're smart. We're intelligent. We have the capacity to be leaders. We're learning and growing, and we're beginning to come into leadership positions.

I now serve on the Texas Medicaid Managed Care Committee. It's a 23-member committee, and I'm the only Hispanic on the committee! That's the extent of the representation of our community on that committee. That's one of the reason I applied to be part of the committee. As Hispanics, that's what we need to do: We need to step up to the plate! If we don't, someone else will. By stepping up, just as I have on our El Paso ISD Board and on our MASBA Board, we show our youngsters that they can achieve levels of leadership as well.

Our biggest problem in regard to this is that Hispanics still don't vote. We have larger numbers of White people voting than *Latinos* — in a city that's 80% Hispanic. The biggest challenge we have is getting the message out to vote. In MASBA, we must make that a priority. When they turn 18, we need to get our kids registered to vote. We need to teach them the importance of voting.

One of my proudest accomplishments while serving on the MASBA Board came from sharing with my district the connections I made at MASBA that enabled the El Paso ISD to be the first school district in the state of Texas to develop a new health insurance program for teachers and staff and to break away from the Teacher Retirement System. I'll always cherish the way we did that together, to provide better coverage and better rates for our district's employees. Our MASBA legal counsel delivered a huge victory for the El Paso ISD, providing our district the necessary legal support to do this.

I hope that, through MASBA, we might continue to strengthen our position as a *Latino* culture and expand our ability to have a direct impact on the lives of young Hispanic students in our schools, and that they might be inspired by our leadership and our advocacy,

We need to be advocates for that. Our message must go beyond Texas, to Washington D.C. I dream that MASBA might become a powerful, national force that advocates for our Hispanic kids and their heritage — our Mexican American children, but also all our students with Spanish-speaking ancestry. I dream that MASBA might be a strong force for equal education by eliminating the barriers.

Alfonso "Al" Velarde was elected in 2015 to the Board of Trustees of the El Paso Independent School District. He has served on the MASBA Board of Directors since 2017.

Working to Benefit Texas Schoolchildren

James B. Crow

We, at the Texas Association of School Boards, are proud to have been associated with MASBA throughout its fifty-year history. We join you in honoring the various individuals who worked hard to see that MASBA continued its dedicated efforts on behalf of Texas students. Indeed, the goals of MASBA and TASB are tightly aligned, so it is no surprise that our two organizations evidence a history of mutual support. Working to benefit Texas schoolchildren is fundamental to the future to which we all aspire.

As others note in this history, there exists significant overlap among the leaders of our two organizations, with many MASBA leaders serving on the TASB Board of Directors and in other leadership roles with TASB. That shared leadership helped our two organizations stay connected, and it facilitated common goals, initiatives, and programs. Both organizations owe much to the locally-elected board members who generously share their time and talents to see that MASBA and TASB stay focused on the most important goals.

In the early years, before MASBA hosted its own stand-alone conferences, TASB was pleased to provide meeting opportunities for MASBA members at a variety of TASB events. In some cases, TASB arranged for meeting spaces, and TASB very often helped share information with its board members about MASBA meetings. TASB's support of MASBA and its members fostered a history of close relationships.

Over the years, TASB provided a wide variety of in-kind supports to MASBA, including printing, complimentary lanyards, publicity, photography, and other assistance from TASB staff. Additionally, TASB's affiliated entities sponsored MASBA and its events. TASB also provided speakers for MASBA trainings on topics ranging from governance issues and legislative briefings, to legal and risk management topics. Through the years, TASB staff has enjoyed assisting MASBA when MASBA has requested help.

In 2016, the relationship between TASB and MASBA was formalized when MASBA endorsed the products and services of TASB and its related entities. That legal agreement resulted in an infusion of funds to MASBA to expand its activities. We, at TASB, are honored to see that formal relationship continue.

My favorite personal anecdote related to MASBA occurred in 2002, when I was honored to receive the organization's Golden *Molcajete* Award. During a MASBA reception, as then-MASBA Executive Director Tommy Molina presented the award, the very heavy *molcajete* fell off its wooden base. Miraculously, I was able to catch it before it hit the floor! Now securely attached to its base, the Golden *Molcajete* Award continues to be proudly displayed on my desk at TASB.

As MASBA grows stronger, both organizations find more and more opportunities to stand together, particularly in the advocacy to benefit the 5.4 million school children in Texas schools. Here at TASB, we look forward to a continued partnership and a future filled with joint efforts.

Congratulations to MASBA on its 50th anniversary!

James B. Crow has served Texas public schools as an employee of the Texas Association of School Boards since 1981, and as Executive Director of TASB since 1995.

"MASBA Is Not Confused"

Jacinto Ramos, Jr.

Why I Ran for School Board

I'll be honest: I didn't run for my local school board because I focused on student outcomes. I didn't. I ran because of the inequities I saw in our district. Our football team didn't have proper equipment—they practiced with volleyball pads, and they weren't winning any games. The second thing that caught my attention: Wearing old *mariachi* outfits at competitions, our phenomenal *mariachi* lost points at competitions because our students didn't have newer *mariachi* outfits. Third, I saw almost no parent engagement in my district. The traditional PTA system didn't seem to fit the needs of the parents in our neighborhood, and the idea of serving as PTA president or treasurer intimidated recent immigrants. Those three concerns got me elected to the Fort Worth ISD Board of Trustees in June 2013, over a *Latino* incumbent with a Ph.D., who ran on a political platform. He focused on school board dynamics, and I ran on issues that apparently resonated with the community.

Fort Worth ISD's Racial & Ethnic Equity Policy

During my service on the Fort Worth ISD Board, we passed a racial and ethnic equity policy. That served as the umbrella under which we did other things. It cleared the way for *Latinx* studies and African/Africana Studies. It opened the door to a student holiday and day of community service in honor of César Chávez and Dolores Huerta. It opened the door to welcoming *Con Mi MADRE* and My Brother's Keeper—programs focused on children of color. Last budget session, we increased the stipend for bilingual administrators, to promote the number of bilingual folks getting promoted. All of that flowed from our racial and ethnic equity policy. One of the most important pieces is that we formed a Racial and Ethnic Equity Committee composed of board members, administrators, staff, teachers, parents, students, and community leaders, and that became a driving force for a lot of the work we do.

How I Learned About MASBA

I learned about MASBA at the 2013 TASA/TASB conference. Manuel Rodríguez saw me walking in the hallway of the convention center, he rolled up to me on his scooter, and he handed me a MASBA flyer. That's how I first learned about MASBA. I wanted to be around likeminded people, so I attended MASBA's 2014 conference in McAllen. It felt like a homecoming: to walk in and see Brown people, to hear music that resonated with me, and to listen to people who felt like I felt.

MASBA is not confused about what point in history we're in right now. We acknowledge that policies and practices of racism—like SB4, the "show me your papers" law—target our population. This acknowledgement allows us to formulate the necessary strategies to counter the attacks on our communities. Our resolutions and proposals and policies are an avenue that we can utilize to push back.

Texas' First Student Holiday for César Chávez & Dolores Huerta

In the Fort Worth ISD, the genesis for a holiday in honor of César Chávez and Dolores Huerta came about as a result of the awareness that students in the Fort Worth ISD weren't familiar with those two individuals. 63% of our students in Fort Worth are Brown, and they could name heroes and sheroes of other ethnic backgrounds— especially White heroes and sheroes, and some Black heroes and sheroes—but they knew almost no Brown heroes and sheroes. I realized that even if these students could name them, they couldn't tell me what those people had done.

I struggled with the idea of what it meant for me to sit in a position of power, as a school board member, and to perpetuate that. I took the issue to our board, and we voted unanimously in favor of it. My colleagues on the board saw the vision. They understood how the social construct of race worked, and how we could counter it. It was a great day when we passed a student holiday in honor of César Chávez and Dolores Huerta. Our students would now learn about those two individuals and begin to ask themselves, "How many other Brown heroes and sheroes are out there?" In reality, there are so many! We wanted to jumpstart that train of thought in our district, which happened when Dolores Huerta came to our first-ever student holiday in her honor and spoke to our community, parents, faculty and staff. It became a very powerful day, especially knowing that we were the first in Texas to do so. We were embracing our power as trustees!

MASBA initiated that same conversation at a statewide level. After that, Grand Prairie ISD and Houston ISD followed suit. It sent a very powerful message to have people who are willing to utilize their positions to ensure that Brown children know that they are reflected in the history of this country, that we are not invisible, and that we will engage. I want our students to see people like us in positions of power utilizing it to move our systems and to force them to reflect on where they're failing Brown children.

One Hero: A Co-founder of MASBA

We have several heroes and sheroes here in Texas who have paved the way for us. One in particular stands out: Dr. José Ángel Gutiérrez, my professor at UT Arlington, who helped lead the Crystal City movement. I studied under one of the three founders of the *Raza Unida* political party! I reflect a lot on what he taught me about people like Joaquín Murrieta, a person I had never heard about prior to entering Dr. Gutiérrez's classroom. I also reflect on the methods he taught us for getting people elected, beginning with school board members. In fact, I modeled my campaign after Dr. Gutiérrez's autobiography, *The Making of a Chicano Militant*. We mobilized young people who couldn't vote, to knock on doors. We brought in senior citizens to be part of phone banking. We visited folks after church services, and we mobilized university students to help tailor our message. That's how we ran our campaign, to demonstrate that everybody has value.

Alternative Celebrations to Columbus Day

MASBA also engaged in a recent conversation on alternative celebrations to Columbus Day. In the Fort Worth ISD, we had implemented American Indian Day in place of Columbus Day, as advocated by the students of that population. Students educated me and parts of our community with their powerful perspective. Our students said they didn't want to be confused with other indigenous people in the world; for them, this was personal, local and immediate, and they wanted us to call it American Indian Day. The action showed our board's respect and its acknowledgment that the narrative historically associated with Christopher Columbus is not reflective of what truly happened. For MASBA to take a stance on this issue shows that MASBA is not confused about why and how these narratives were written. It's incomprehensible that we continue to teach in public schools that Christopher Columbus discovered a land that already had people on it! For me, MASBA's resolution on this issue acknowledges that we live on stolen land.

The Greatest Joys of Being Part of MASBA

One of the greatest joys of being part of MASBA has been feeling part of a team, being part of a family, where we work together to push for social change, where we balance the scales of justice, and where we won't let up on that mindset until we truly see progress. My frustration with history has been with seeing how people make advances, and how systems can very quickly and very easily undo them. I understand how systems operate, even with the killing and name-bashing of our heroes and sheroes—the demonizing of our people! Hopefully, the next generation will build upon our successes and minimize our mistakes. I'm an irrational idealist and optimist, and I believe that the greatest leaders never showed that they were losing hope. That's what we have in MASBA: We are irrationally hopeful people who aren't going to think themselves out of action!

In my current role as MASBA President Elect, I've enjoyed walking into spaces like the Region 1 conference, *UnidosUS*, and the National Black Caucus as a representative of MASBA. I've enjoyed some great and powerful memories as the representative of a Brown organization, sharing a real message with others, and pushing for solidarity and action with our friends. My involvement on the TASB Board and as Chair of the Council of Urban Boards of Education has also shown me that our message is resonating statewide and nationwide. Our perspective brings a lot of values into those spaces.

Looking Toward the Future

I look forward to working with trustees to strengthen their "muscle" on race. You don't have to be Brown to be part of MASBA, and, if we work together, we'll be impactful. Let's be an example and a voice for our children. My mentor, Rickie Clark, says, "You can't love the fruit, if you don't love the root." Let's teach our kids to love everything they see in the mirror: their skin color, their culture, and everything about their heritage!

Jacinto "Cinto" Ramos, Jr. has served on the Fort Worth ISD Board of Trustees since 2013. He joined the MASBA Board in 2017. Cinto became MASBA Vice President in 2018 and President Elect in 2019. He also serves on the Board of Directors of the Texas Association of School Boards and as Chair of the National School Boards Association Council of Urban Boards of Education.

MASBA Membership 2013-2019

Records note the following membership information for school year 2013-2014 to school year 2018-2019. Based on size, member districts paid $500, $750 , $1,000 or $1,500 per year.

Héroes de MASBA—districts recognized for MASBA membership during five of the previous six years—are marked with an asterisk.

Agua Dulce ISD	2016-2017
Aldine ISD*	2014-2019
Alice ISD	2013-2014, 2015-2017
Allen ISD	2017-2018
Arlington ISD	2018-2019
Austin ISD*	2013-2019
Bastrop ISD	2018-2019
Ben Bolt-Palito Blanco ISD	2013-2016, 2018-2019
Big Spring ISD	2014-2019
Brooks County ISD	2013-2014, 2015-2017, 2018-2019
Brownfield ISD	2018-2019
Brownsville ISD	2013-2015, 2018-2019
Buena Vista ISD	2018-2019
Canutillo ISD*	2014-2019
Carrizo Springs ISD	2017-2018
Cedar Hill ISD	2013-2014, 2018-2019
Corpus Christi ISD	2014-2018
Cotulla ISD*	2013-2019
Crowley ISD	2018-2019
Crystal City ISD	2014-2015
Culberson County-Allamoore ISD	2017-2019
Cypress-Fairbanks ISD	2018-2019
Del Valle ISD	2017-2019
Denton ISD	2014-2016, 2017-2019
DeSoto ISD	2015-2016, 2018-2019
Dilley ISD*	2013-2019
Donna ISD*	2013-2017, 2018-2019

Ector County ISD 2018-2019
Edcouch-Elsa ISD 2014-2017, 2018-2019
Edgewood ISD 2016-2019
Edinburg CISD* 2014-2019
El Paso ISD* 2013-2019
Region 1 Education Service Center* 2013-2019
Region 2 Education Service Center * 2014-2019
Region 8 Education Service Center 2014-2015, 2016-2018
Region 19 Education Service Center 2016-2019
Fabens ISD 2015-2019
Fort Bend ISD 2016-2019
Fort Worth ISD* 2013-2019
Galena Park ISD 2014-2017
Garland ISD* 2014-2019
Gonzales ISD* 2014-2019
Goose Creek CISD 2018-2019
Grand Prairie ISD* 2013-2014, 2015-2019
Grapevine-Colleyville ISD 2018-2019
Greenville ISD 2018-2019
Harlandale ISD* 2014-2019
Harlingen CISD 2013-2016, 2017-2018
Hays CISD* 2014-2019
Hidalgo ISD 2013-2018*
Houston ISD* 2013-2019
Hurst-Euless-Bedford ISD 2016-2017
Hutto ISD 2018-2019
Ingleside ISD 2018-2019
Iraan-Sheffield ISD 2014-2015
Jarrell ISD 2018-2019
Jasper ISD 2018-2019
Jim Hogg County ISD 2015-2019
Katy ISD 2018-2019
Kenedy ISD 2016-2019
Kermit ISD 2015-2016, 2018-2019
Kingsville ISD 2014-2016

La Feria ISD 2015-2016
La Gloria ISD* 2014-2019
La Joya ISD 2013-2016, 2017-2018
La Pryor ISD 2014-2015
Lake Worth ISD 2018-2019
Lasara ISD 2014-2015, 2018-2019
La Vega ISD 2018-2019
La Villa ISD 2014-2016, 2017-2019
Lockhart ISD 2017-2019
Longview ISD 2014-2016, 2018-2019
Los Fresnos CISD 2018-2019
Manor ISD 2015-2019
Mathis ISD 2013-2015, 2018-2019
McAllen ISD 2013-2014
Mercedes ISD* 2013-2019
Mesquite ISD 2014-2017
Mexia ISD 2014-2017
Mission CISD 2013-2016, 2017-2018
Monte Alto ISD 2013-2014, 2015-2018
Natalia ISD 2014-2015
Northside ISD 2018-2019
Olfen ISD 2017-2019
Palacios ISD 2018-2019
Pearsall ISD 2014-2015, 2017-2018
Pecos-Barstow-Toyah ISD 2014-2015, 2018-2019
Pflugerville ISD 2018-2019
Plainview ISD 2014-2015, 2018-2019
Point Isabel ISD 2014-2015
Poteet ISD 2014-2016, 2017-2018
Presidio ISD 2013-2014
Ramírez CSD 2018-2019
Raymondville ISD 2014-2016, 2017-2019
Ricardo ISD* 2013-2018
Richardson ISD 2018-2019
Río Grande ISD 2013-2014

Robstown ISD 2016-2017
Rocksprings ISD 2014-2016
Roma ISD 2015-2017, 2018-2019
Royal ISD 2017-2018
San Antonio ISD 2013-2017
San Benito CISD* 2013-2019
San Diego ISD 2014-2017
San Elizario ISD 2017-2019
San Felipe-Del Río CISD 2018-2019
San Marcos CISD* 2013-2019
San Perlita ISD 2013-2014, 2015-2016
Santa María ISD* 2013-2014, 2015-2019
Santa Rosa ISD 2014-2018
Schertz-Cibolo-Universal City ISD 2017-2019
Seguin ISD* 2014-2019
Sharyland ISD 2013-2014
Socorro ISD* 2013-2016, 2017-2019
Sonora ISD 2015-2016
South San Antonio ISD 2016-2017
South Texas ISD* 2013-2019
Southside ISD* 2014-2019
Southwest ISD* 2014-2019
Spring ISD 2018-2019
Stafford MSD* 2014-2019
Stanton ISD 2017-2018
Sterling City ISD 2016-2019
Taft ISD* 2014-2019
Taylor ISD 2017-2019
Texas City ISD 2013-2014, 2015-2016
Tuloso Midway ISD 2014-2016, 2018-2019
Tyler ISD 2017-2018
United ISD 2018-2019
Uvalde CISD 2017-2019
Valley View ISD (Hidalgo County) 2013-2014, 2015-2019

Individual members paid $300 each for dues. To date, individual members were tracked only for the 2018-2019 school year and included the following:

John Betancourt, Amarillo ISD
Aarón Montesnieto, Cleveland ISD
Carla Mills Windfont, Crosby ISD
Jaime Reséndez, Dallas ISD
Gloria Gonzales-Dholakia, Leander ISD
Lala Chávez, Lubbock ISD
Jimmie Alaniz, Sinton ISD
Larry Pérez, Waco ISD

MASBA Sponsorship 2013-2019

Records note the following sponsorship information for school year 2013-2014 to school year 2018-2019. MASBA remains grateful to all who continue to support its mission of closing gaps in our Texas public schools—and its scholarship program, which will award scholarships to 220+ graduates in 2020!

MASBA Partner
Texas Association of School Boards – 2015-2019

Titanium Sponsor
ERO Architects – 2014-2015

Diamond Sponsors
ERO Architects – 2013-2014
First Financial – 2014-2015
O'Hanlon Demerath & Castillo – 2013-2014, 2017-2019
Southwest Foodservice Excellence – 2018-2019
Walsh Gallegos Treviño Russo & Kyle – 2018-2019

Gold Sponsors
Barrett Insurance Services – 2017-2019
E3 Entegral Solutions – 2018-2019
ERO Architects – 2018-2019
Houston ISD Medicaid Finance & Consulting Services – 2018-2019
O'Hanlon Demerath & Castillo – 2014-2017
Performance Services – 2017-2019
Southwest Foodservice Excellence – 2017-2018
TCG Group Holdings – 2018-2019
Texas Association of School Boards – 2013-2015
Walsh Gallegos Treviño Russo & Kyle – 2017-2018

Silver Sponsors
AECOM – 2018-2019
Aramark – 2013-2014
Baltazar Salazar – 2014-2017
ERO Architects – 2015-2016
FBMC – 2016-2017
Financial Benefit Services – 2018-2019
Frost Bank – 2014-2015
Johnson Controls – 2013-2017
Linebarger Goggan Blair & Sampson – 2013-2019
Pearson – 2013-2015
Walsh Gallegos Treviño Russo & Kyle – 2014-2017

Bronze Sponsors
ADM Group – 2018-2019
Aramark – 2014-2016
Balfour Beatty – 2018-2019
Bartlett Cocke – 2014-2016, 2017-2018
Claycomb Associates Architects – 2018-2019
Dallas County Schools – 2014-2015
DK Haney Roofing – 2016-2017
El Paso STEM Foundation – 2016-2017
Estrada Hinojosa – 2017-2019
Excel Energy Group – 2017-2018
Forecast Five Analytics – 2018-2019
Frost Bank – 2015-2016, 2018-2019
FTN Financial – 2014-2016
Huckabee Architects – 2015-2017
Johnson Controls – 2018-2019
LASSO – 2015-2016
McCall Parkhurst & Horton – 2014-2015, 2017-2018
McGraw Hill Education – 2018-2019
NAH Sports Flooring – 2013-2014
Nerdvana – 2016-2017
Pearson – 2015-2016

Perdue Brandon Fielder Collins & Mott – 2018-2019
Pfluger Associates – 2015-2016, 2017-2019
Progressive Roofing – 2018-2019
Region 19 Education Service Center – 2016-2017
Southwest Foodservice Excellence – 2014-2015
Stantec – 2017-2019
TASB Energy Management Services – 2013-2014
TASB Risk Management – 2015-2016
TIPS – 2018-2019

Amigos
ABS Commercial Cleaning – 2018-2019
Achieve3000 – 2017-2018
AECOM – 2017-2018
Agora Benefits – 2015-2016
A.L. Berry Consulting – 2018-2019
American Constructors – 2017-2019
Austin ISD Trustee Cynthia Anderson – 2018-2019
Ascension Seton – 2018-2019
Autoarch Architects – 2016-2017
Balfour Beatty – 2017-2018
Bartlett Cocke – 2013-2014
Beldon Roofing & Remodeling – 2018-2019
BGK – 2017-2018
BLGY Architecture – 2017-2019
Braun & Butler Construction – 2018-2019
Center for Equity – 2014-2015
Chartwells K12 Student Nutrition – 2017-2019
CheckAccents.com – 2014-2015
Climatec, Austin – 2018-2019
Climatec, Houston – 2018-2019
Daikin – 2018-2019
DK Haney Roofing – 2015-2016, 2017-2018
E3 Entegral Solutions – 2017-2018
ECM Holding Group – 2018-2019

Eichelbaum Wardell – 2018-2019
Energy Systems Design – 2018-2019
Escamilla & Poneck – 2017-2018
ESS | Source4Teachers – 2017-2019
Estrada Hinojosa – 2016-2017
Excel Energy Group – 2018-2019
Fields & Associates – 2018-2019
Forecast Five Analytics – 2017-2018
Foster CM Group – 2017-2019
Frost Bank – 2016-2018
FTN Financial – 2017-2019
Gilbane – 2018-2019
Gignac – 2015-2016
Government Capital – 2018-2019
Hill Country Software – 2013-2014
Hilltop Securities – 2015-2017, 2018-2019
Huckabee Architects – 2013-2014
Imagine Learning – 2013-2014
J-III Concrete Company – 2018-2019
Jaco Roofing – 2013-2014
JG Consulting – 2017-2018
JGA Roofing System – 2017-2018
Lexia Learning – 2018-2019
Lockwood Andrews & Newnam – 2017-2019
McCarthy Construction – 2018-2019
McNeil Educational Leadership Foundation – 2014-2016
MNK Architects – 2018-2019
Mullen Pension – 2014-2016
myON – 2017-2018
NAH Sports Flooring – 2015-2016
NALEO – 2015-2019
O'Connell Robertson – 2017-2019
Page Southerland Page - 2017-2019
Parsons Roofing – 2013-2014
Pearson – 2016-2018

Pedal Valves – 2018-2019
Perdue Brandon Fielder Collins & Mott – 2013-2014, 2017-2018
Perkins+Will – 2017-2018
Ploy Printer – 2016-2017
Public Finance Management – 2015-2016
Reasoning Mind – 2014-2015
Siebert Brandford & Shank – 2016-2019
Sodexo – 2017-2019
Southwest Sports/Courts – 2014-2017
Stantec – 2014-2015
Texas Freedom Network – 2013-2014
TF Harper – 2013-2014
Think Through Learning – 2015-2016
Tim "Boo" Podanoffsky – 2018-2019
TIPS – 2017-2018
UT Austin *Lucha* – 2013-2014
Utility Metering Solutions – 2018-2019
Waypoint Lighting – 2018-2019

Appendix A

Events in MASBA History

1970   Dr. José A. Cárdenas, Superintendent of the Edgewood ISD, conceived of MASBA, according to *Tejana* historian Teresa Paloma Acosta

1973   The U.S. Supreme Court heard San Antonio Independent School District v. Rodríguez, which was brought by the parents of Dr. Cárdenas

c. 1973   School board members and superintendents in one corner of a hotel ballroom decided to form MASBA, while university professors in another corner of the room formed the Texas Association of *Chicanos* in Higher Education

December 6, 1973   Chris Escamilla of San Antonio, Rubén E. Hinojosa of Mercedes, and Gustavo L. García of Austin incorporated the Mexican American School Board Members Association; García purportedly served as MASBA's first President

February 8-9, 1975   MASBA reportedly hosted its first-ever conference, for which historical records have yet to be found

September 11, 1975   The Texas Comptroller of Public Accounts exempted MASBA from franchise tax effective December 6, 1973

Prior to 1986   Dr. Robert Sepúlveda of Weslaco ISD served as MASBA President

September 11, 1986   Lydia M. Pérez of the Austin ISD Board reported to the Texas Secretary of State that she, as MASBA President, was the registered agent of the organization

1987	MASBA hosted its last annual leadership program (for which historical records have yet to be found) before going dormant
October 26, 1987	Amancio J. Chapa, Jr. of the La Joya ISD Board reported to the Texas Secretary of State that he, as MASBA President, was the registered agent of the organization
1988 to 1989	Óscar G. Hernández of San Antonio ISD, a future TASB President, served as President of MASBA
1989	Santiago "Jimmie" Adame of Taft ISD was elected President of MASBA
October 11, 1993	The Texas Secretary of State issued a letter stating that MASBA had forfeited its right to conduct business in Texas, for failing to file necessary paperwork
c. September 1993	Trustee Juan Aguilera of the Round Rock ISD gathered Hispanic trustees during a reception during a TASA/TASB conference in Dallas
c. 1995	Diana Castañeda of the Austin ISD became the first President of MASBA after its resurgence
Summer 1996	Louis Q. Reyes, III of Seguin ISD served as Interim President of MASBA for approximately three months after Diana Castañeda lost her local election in May 1996
Fall 1996	Theresa Gutiérrez of Victoria ISD became MASBA President
1996	Juan Aguilera, formerly of the Round Rock ISD, began serving as Executive Director of MASBA, through 2004
1998	Albert Martínez of San Diego ISD became MASBA President and served through September 22, 2001

1999 MASBA hosted its first annual conference after its resurgence, at the University of Texas at San Antonio

September 22, 2001 Santiago "Jimmie" Adame of Taft ISD became MASBA President and served through January 19, 2003

January 19, 2003 Dr. Viola García of Aldine ISD became MASBA President and served through January 17, 2004

January 17, 2004 Óscar García of Ben Bolt-Palito Blanco ISD became MASBA President and served through March 4, 2005

January 2004 Tommy Molina became MASBA Executive Director and served through March 4, 2005

March 4, 2005 Dr. Manuel C. Flores of Corpus Christi ISD became MASBA President and served through circa May 2006; Mari Carmen Aguilera was named Interim Executive Director and served for an unknown length of time

c. February 2006 Juan Aguilera became MASBA Executive Director again, serving through June 2006

c. May 2006 Joe Muñoz of Hays CISD became MASBA President and served through circa January 2009

January 14, 2007 Santiago "Jimmie" Adame became MASBA Executive Director and served through c. February 2008

c. January 2009 María Leal of South Texas ISD became MASBA President and served through January 22, 2010

January 22, 2010 Manuel Rodríguez of Houston ISD became MASBA President and served through January 22, 2011

c. September 2010 Joe Muñoz became MASBA Executive Director and served through c. February 2014

January 22, 2011 Joshua Cerna of Harlandale ISD became MASBA President and served through January 21, 2012

January 21, 2012 Juan Rangel of Fort Worth ISD became MASBA President and served through January 19, 2013

January 19, 2013 Gloria Santillán Casas became MASBA President and served through February 1, 2014

February 1, 2014 Danny "Chief" Bueno of Ben Bolt-Palito Blanco ISD became MASBA President and served through January 24, 2015

c. June 2014 Louis Q. Reyes of Seguin ISD became MASBA Executive Director and served through July 2017

January 24 2015 Louis Q. Reyes of Seguin ISD became MASBA President and served through February 20, 2016

February 20, 2016 Irene Galán-Rodríguez of Big Spring ISD became MASBA President and served through February 25, 2017

February 25, 2017 Armando Rodríguez became MASBA President and served through February 24, 2018

October 11, 2017 Dr. Jayme Mathias of the Austin ISD became MASBA Executive Director

February 24, 2018 Homero García of South Texas ISD became MASBA President and served through March 2, 2019

March 2, 2019 Willie Tenorio, Jr. of Hays CISD became MASBA President

February 20-23, 2020 MASBA was scheduled to host its golden jubilee conference at the Wyndham San Antonio Riverwalk Hotel, with the Annual MASBA Member Assembly scheduled for February 22

Appendix B

Presidents of MASBA

Gustavo L. "Gus" García, Austin ISD
c. 1974

Rubén E. Hinojosa, Mercedes ISD
c. 1975

Dr. Robert Sepúlveda, Weslaco ISD
Prior to 1986

Lydia M. Pérez, Austin ISD
1986 – 1987

Amancio Chapa, La Joya ISD
1987 – 1988

Óscar G. Hernández, San Antonio ISD
1988 – 1989

Santiago "Jimmie" Adame, Taft ISD
1989

Diana Castañeda, Austin ISD
c. 1995 – May 1996

Louis Q. Reyes, III, Seguin ISD (Interim)
c. May 1996 to c. July 1996

Teresa "Theresa" Gutiérrez, Victoria ISD
c. 1996 – c. 1998

Alberto "Albert" Martínez, San Diego ISD
c. 1998 – September 22, 2001

Santiago "Jimmie" Adame, Taft ISD
September 22, 2001 – January 19, 2003

Dr. Viola García, Aldine ISD
January 19, 2003 – January 17, 2004

Óscar García, Ben Bolt-Palito Blanco ISD
January 17, 2004 – March 4, 2005

Dr. Manuel C. Flores, Corpus Christi ISD
March 4, 2005 – January 13, 2007

Joe Muñoz, Hays CISD
January 13, 2007 – 2009

María Leal, South Texas ISD
2009 – January 22, 2010

Manuel "Manny" Rodríguez, Jr., Houston ISD
January 22, 2010 – January 22, 2011

Joshua "Josh" Cerna, Harlandale ISD
January 22, 2011 – January 21, 2012

Juan Rangel, Fort Worth ISD
January 21, 2012 – January 19, 2013

Gloria Santillán Casas, La Feria ISD
January 19, 2013 – February 1, 2014

Danny "Chief" Bueno, Ben Bolt-Palito Blanco ISD
February 1, 2014 – January 24, 2015

Louis Q. Reyes, III, Seguin ISD
January 24, 2015 – February 20, 2016

Irene Galán-Rodríguez, Big Spring ISD
February 20, 2016 – February 25, 2017

Armando "Mando" Rodríguez, Canutillo ISD
February 25, 2017 – February 24, 2018

Homero García, South Texas ISD
February 24, 2018 – March 2, 2019

Guillermo "Willie" Tenorio, Jr., Hays CISD
March 2, 2019 to present

Appendix C

Executive Directors of MASBA

Chris Escamilla, Edgewood ISD
c. 1974 – [unknown date]

Juan F. Aguilera, Round Rock ISD
c. 1996 – January 2004*

Tomás F. "Tommy" Molina, San Diego ISD
before February 2003* – before March 4, 2005

Mari Carmen Aguilera (Interim)
March 4, 2005 – [unknown date]

Juan F. Aguilera, Round Rock ISD
c. February 2006 to June 2006

Santiago "Jimmie" Adame, Taft ISD
January 14, 2007 – c. February 2008

Joe Muñoz, Hays CISD
c. September 2010 – c. February 2014

Louis Q. Reyes, III, Seguin ISD
c. June 2014 – July 2017

Dr. Jayme Mathias, Austin ISD
October 11, 2017 to present

* It is unclear whether Juan Aguilera and Tommy Molina served as Executive Director at the same time: Juan is listed as Executive Director prior to 2003, Tommy is listed in meeting minutes as Executive Director on February 14, 2003, Juan is listed in meeting minutes as Executive Director on January 17, 2004, and Tommy resigned as Executive Director prior to the Board's meeting on March 4, 2005. Juan and Tommy worked closely together since

before 2000, when they were both listed as facilitators of an organizational meeting.

Appendix D

Glossary of MASBA Directors & Staff

Adame, Santiago "Jimmie" (Taft ISD). Jimmie was elected MASBA President circa September 1989, before MASBA fell into dormancy. He attended the 2000 MASBA conference and was elected MASBA President Elect in October 2000. Jimmie served as MASBA President from 2002 to 2003, then as Immediate Past President. He continued to be active in MASBA and was hired as Executive Director in January 2007, a position in which he served until circa February 2008.

Aguilera, Juan (Round Rock ISD). In the 1990s, Juan led efforts to bring MASBA back to life, beginning with a reception for Mexican Americans at the TASA/TASB conference in 1993. With Tommy Molina, he served as co-facilitator of an October 2000 organizational meeting. He served as Executive Director through 2003, as Assistant Executive Director through 2005, then as Interim Executive Director and as Executive Director in 2006. In 2007, he began serving as MASBA's Legal Counsel, a service he continues today.

Aguilera, Mari Carmen. Mari Carmen, the daughter of Juan F. Aguilera, was named Interim Executive Director on March 4, 2005. She succeeded Executive Director Tommy Molina. It is unclear how long she served in this capacity, though her service was likely no longer than ten months, since meeting minutes state that Juan Aguilera was Assistant Executive Director (perhaps assisting her) in June 2005 and that he was named Interim Executive Director in January 2006.

Alvarado, Juan (Southwest ISD). Juan attended the 2000 MASBA conference and was named an interim MASBA Director in June 2000. There is no record of him after being re-elected to the MASBA Board at the January 19, 2003 Member Assembly.

Anchía, Rafael (Dallas ISD). Rafael was elected to the MASBA Board at the January 19, 2003 Member Assembly. There is no record of him after the June 11, 2004 MASBA Board meeting. He was elected to the State House of Representatives in November 2004.

Bueno, Danny Joe "Chief" (Ben Bolt-Palito Blanco ISD). Known for his nickname as police chief of Alice for 12 years, "Chief" is listed in *mariachi* programs as a member of the MASBA Board in 2010 to 2012, as President Elect in 2013, as President in 2014, and as Immediate Past President in 2015. In 2016, he was elected sheriff of Jim Wells County.

Caballero, Carlos (ESC Region 19). Carlos was named an Interim MASBA Director in June 2000. He was elected to the MASBA Board at the January 19, 2003 Member Assembly and was named to the Board's Funding, Budget & Finance Committee. There is no record of him after a June 20, 2003 event program, where he is listed as a MASBA Director.

Cabrera, Juan. Juan is listed as Legal Counsel at MASBA Board meetings from January to September 2013, when he was named Superintendent of El Paso ISD. At that time, he was Of Counsel with O'Hanlon McCollum & Demerath.

Calvillo, Jesús (Edgewood ISD). Jesús was elected to the MASBA Board at the January 19, 2003 Member Assembly. The minutes of the MASBA Board's December 18, 2003 meeting state that he had resigned from the Edgewood ISD Board and was thus no longer eligible to serve on the MASBA Board.

Cantú, Jessica (Raymondville ISD). Jessica is listed as a MASBA Board member in February 2017 and April 2017 meeting minutes. June 16, 2017 minutes state that her seat was vacated.

Casas, Gloria Santillán (La Feria ISD). Gloria was present at the MASBA organizational meeting of June 16, 2000. She was elected to the MASBA Board at the January 13, 2006 Member Assembly and was named to the Board's Membership & Recruitment Committee. Gloria served as Secretary in 2011, as Vice President in 2012, as President beginning on January 19, 2013, and as Immediate Past President in 2014.

Castañeda, Diana (Austin ISD). Diana is remembered for her enthusiasm for bringing together Mexican American trustees in the mid-1990s. She is remembered as the first MASBA President after the organization's resurgence, likely named circa 1995 and serving through the end of her local board service in May 1996.

Cerna, Joshua "Josh" (Harlandale ISD). Josh was apparently appointed to the MASBA Board prior to January 2007, when he was named to the Board's Programs & Member Services Committee. *Mariachi* programs suggest he was elected President Elect at the 2010 Member Assembly. He became MASBA President on January 22, 2011, then served as Immediate Past President in 2012.

Chapa, Amancio J., Jr. (La Joya ISD). Amancio served as President of MASBA circa 1987 to circa 1988. He attended the 2000 MASBA conference and was listed as absent at a May 2000 organizational meeting.

Cortez, Ana (Manor ISD). Ana has served on the MASBA Board since 2016. She was elected Vice President at the March 2, 2019 Member Assembly, and she continues to serve in that capacity.

Dávila, Diana (Houston ISD). Diana is listed as a MASBA Board member in meeting minutes from April. Meeting minutes of July 8-9, 2017 state that she missed two consecutive Board meetings and had been dismissed from the Board.

DeLeón, Linda (Lubbock ISD). Linda was named an interim MASBA Director in June 2000. She was re-elected to the MASBA Board at the January 19, 2003 Member Assembly. There is no record of her after the June 11, 2004 MASBA Board meeting. Minutes from the March 4, 2005 MASBA Board meeting state that she resigned from the Board after winning a seat on her local city council.

Enríquez, Ann (San Elizario ISD). Amancio Chapa recalls Ann serving on the MASBA Board in the 1980s.

Escamilla, Chris (Edgewood ISD). Chris is listed as an incorporated of MASBA on December 6, 1973. He has been referred to as MASBA's first Executive Director.

Escobar, Daniel. It is unknown whether Daniel was considered a staff member of MASBA. Likely a student at San Antonio College, the MASBA Board recognized him for his role in organizing presentations and breakout sessions for the 2003 MASBA conference.

Espinosa, David (Grand Prairie ISD). David served on the MASBA Board in 2016. He was elected Vice President at the February 25, 2017 Member Assembly and served in that position for one year. He served through the end of his term at the conclusion of the March 2, 2019 Member Assembly.

Flores, Ishmael (Seguin ISD). Ishmael was appointed to the MASBA Board on February 22, 2003. He was elected Treasurer at the January 17, 2004 Member Assembly, a position in which he served through at least 2008.

Flores, Dr. Manuel (Corpus Christi ISD). Manuel attended the 2000 MASBA conference and joined the MASBA egroup in September 2000. He was elected to the MASBA Board at the January 19, 2003 Member Assembly. Manuel was elected Vice President at the January 17, 2004 Member Assembly and President Elect at the January 8, 2005 Member Assembly. He was named Acting President on March 5, 2005 and was elected to his own term as President at the January 13, 2006 Member Assembly. In May 2006, he lost his local election and ceased to serve on the MASBA Board.

Flores, Orlando (Fabens ISD). Orlando was elected to the MASBA Board on February 20, 2016 and served through circa July 2017.

Flores, Sally (Anthony ISD). Sally attended the 2000 MASBA conference and was elected to the MASBA Board at the January 19, 2003 Member Assembly, when she was named to the Board's Programs & Member Services Committee. She was re-elected to three-year term at the January 8, 2005 Member Assembly. In 2007, she was named to the Board's Funding, Budget & Finance Committee. There is no record of her after that.

Flynn Vilaseca, Holly María (Houston ISD). Holly María has served on the MASBA Board since August 2017. She continues her service to the MASBA Board.

Galán-Rodríguez, Irene Bustamente (Big Spring ISD). Irene was present at the MASBA organizational meeting of June 16, 2000. She was elected to the MASBA Board at the January 13, 2006 Member Assembly, when she was named to the Board's Membership & Recruitment Committee. She is listed in MASBA *mariachi* competition programs as Secretary in 2013, as Vice President in 2014, and President Elect in 2015. Irene became MASBA President at the

February 20, 2016 Member Assembly and Immediate Past President at the February 25, 2017 Member Assembly.

García, Homero (South Texas ISD). Homero has served on the MASBA Board since 2016. He was elected President Elect at the February 25, 2017 Member Assembly, and he began his service as President at the conclusion of the March 2, 2019 Member Assembly. He currently serves as Immediate Past President.

García, Gustavo L. "Gus" (Austin ISD). Gus is listed as an incorporated of MASBA on December 6, 1973. An accountant, he used the mailing address of his firm as the official address of MASBA through 1986. He is referred to as the first President of MASBA.

García, Lionel (Plainview ISD). Lionel was present at the MASBA organizational meeting of June 16, 2000 and was elected to the MASBA Board at the January 19, 2003 Member Assembly. There is no record of him after the June 11, 2004 MASBA Board meeting. Minutes from the March 4, 2005 MASBA Board meeting state that he lost his bid for reelection to his local board.

García, Óscar O. (Ben Bolt-Palito Blanco ISD). Óscar was present at the MASBA organizational meeting of June 16, 2000. After serving as President Elect in 2003, Óscar became MASBA President at the January 17, 2004 Member Assembly. After the January 8, 2005 Member Assembly, Óscar continued to lead MASBA through March 4, 2005, when Dr. Manuel Flores was elected President and Óscar became Immediate Past President.

García, Saúl (Edcouch-Elsa ISD). Saúl was elected to the MASBA Board at the January 12, 2008 Member Assembly. There is no record of him after February 2008.

García, Dr. Viola M. (Aldine ISD). Viola was named an interim MASBA Director in June 2000. She became MASBA President at the start of the January 19, 2003 Member Assembly. After serving as Immediate Past President, she continued to be active in MASBA and was present at several MASBA Board meetings from 2011 to 2016. She currently serves as Secretary-Treasurer of the National School Boards Association.

Garza, Corando (Kingsville ISD). Corando was elected to the MASBA Board on January 19, 2013. He listed in *mariachi* programs as a member of the MASBA Board in 2013 and 2015.

Garza, Jerome (Dallas ISD). Jerome was elected to the MASBA Board on January 8, 2005. He is noted as a Board member in the minutes of the June 9, 2006 MASBA Board meeting.

Garza, Juan (Kingsville ISD). Juan was elected to the MASBA Board at the January 13, 2006 Member Assembly. He is listed in meeting minutes and *mariachi* competition programs through January 2011.

Garza, Louis (Corpus Christi ISD). Louis was elected to the MASBA Board at the January 8, 2005 Member Assembly. By October 2006, he was no longer on the Board.

Garza, Richard A. Together with Juan Aguilera, Richard is listed as MASBA Executive Staff at the January 19, 2003 Member Assembly. He is listed as "MASBA Assistant" at the February 14, 2003 Executive Committee meeting.

Garza, Servando "Wolf" (Alice ISD). Wolf is listed in *mariachi* programs as a member of the MASBA Board in 2014 to 2015. Meeting minutes note that he was elected Treasurer on February 20, 2016 and that he served in this capacity in February 2017. The June 16, 2017 meeting minutes note that his seat was vacant.

González-Peterson, Ada (El Paso ISD). Ada was named an Interim MASBA Director in June 2000. She served on the Board's Funding Committee.

Govea, Andy (Lockhart ISD). Andy was appointed to the MASBA Board on June 11, 2004, and he was elected to his own term of board service at the January 8, 2005 Member Assembly. He lost reelection to his local board in May 2005.

Guajardo, Arturo (Pharr-San Juan-Alamo ISD). Arturo was elected to the MASBA Board on January 19, 2003, when he was named to the Board's Membership & Recruitment Committee. There is no record of him after the June 11, 2004 MASBA Board meeting

Guajardo, Manuel (Texas City ISD). Manuel was elected to the MASBA Board at the January 19, 2003 Member Assembly. The minutes of the June 11, 2004 MASBA Board meeting report that his successor was chosen "pending Mr. Guajardo's agreement to vacate his position."

Gutiérrez, Liz (West Oso ISD). Liz is listed in meeting minutes as MASBA Secretary in 2014.

Gutiérrez, Luis (Unknown). Jimmie Adame recalls a Dr. Luis Gutiérrez sitting among MASBA Officers at the meeting at which he was first elected MASBA President circa 1989. He recalls that Luis wore "two hats," as a superintendent of one district and a trustee of another.

Gutiérrez, Ricardo (ESC Region 1). Ricardo has served on the MASBA Board since 2017. He was appointed Treasurer in July 2017 and served in that capacity through the conclusion of the February 24, 2018 Member Assembly. He continues his service to the MASBA Board.

Gutiérrez, Teresa "Theresa" (Victoria ISD). Theresa served as MASBA President circa 1996 to 1997. She is remembered as MASBA's first Vice President after the organization's resurgence in the mid-1990s.

Guzmán, Sam (Austin ISD). Sam is listed in *mariachi* programs as MASBA Secretary in 2010 and 2011. He was elected Vice President in 2011 and as President Elect in 2012. He later served on MASBA Staff through 2017.

Haggerty, Shane (Ysleta ISD). Shane was elected to the MASBA Board at the January 24, 2015 Member Assembly. He served as MASBA Secretary in 2016.

Hernández, José "Joe" (unknown district). It is presumed that Joe was elected to the MASBA Board at the January 17, 2004 Member Assembly, for which minutes have not been found. Joe Muñoz reported at the Board's June 11, 2004 meeting that Joe "could no longer serve" on the MASBA Board.

294

Hernández, Óscar G. (San Antonio ISD). Óscar served on the San Antonio ISD Board of Trustees from 1973 to 1996. An article in Shirley Hall's 1989 40-year history of TASB (p. 78) says that Óscar "serves as president of the Texas chapter of the Mexican-American School Boards Association." He was the first *Latino* to serve as TASB President in 1985-1986. He also served on the Board of the National School Boards Association.

Hernández, Rebecca "Lisa" (El Campo ISD). Lisa was elected to the MASBA Board at the January 8, 2005 Member Assembly, and she was elected Secretary at the January 13, 2007 Member Assembly. She did not seek reelection to her local board in May 2007.

Herrera, Rosa "Rose" (Fort Worth ISD). Rose was named an Interim MASBA Director in June 2000. She was re-elected to the MASBA Board at the January 19, 2003 Member Assembly, when she was named to the Board's Programs & Member Services Committee. There is no record of her after the June 11, 2004 MASBA Board meeting.

Herrera, Xavier (Stafford MSD). Xavier has served on the MASBA Board since 2017. He was elected Treasurer at the February 24, 2018 Member Assembly, and he continues to serve in this capacity.

Hinojosa, Cruz (Galena Park ISD). Cruz was appointed to the MASBA Board on June 11, 2004. He was elected Vice President at the January 13, 2006 Member Assembly, and he was recommended for President Elect at the January 13, 2007 Member Assembly. He did not seek reelection to his local board in May 2007, leaving Joe Muñoz to serve a second full term as MASBA President in 2008.

Hinojosa, Rubén E. (Mercedes ISD). Rubén is listed as an incorporated of MASBA on December 6, 1973. Teresa Paloma Acosta suggests that he served as President of MASBA. He received MASBA's Golden *Molcajete* and *La Campana* Awards in 2016.

Hixson, Kurt. Kurt is listed as MASBA Staff and Marketing & Communications in meeting minutes from 2010 to 2017.

Leal, María (Mission CISD, South Texas ISD). María was elected MASBA Secretary at the January 13, 2006 Member Assembly, when she named Chair of the Board's Membership & Recruitment Committee. She was elected Vice President at the January 13, 2007 Member Assembly. Meeting minutes of June 15, 2007 note that María "stated that she would be willing to be named President Elect, but that she was not ready to take the Presidency in 2008." She became President at the 2009 Member Assembly and Immediate Past President at the 2010 Member Assembly. She continued to attend MASBA Board meetings through 2014, and she continues to attend MASBA conferences.

Leos, Kathleen (Dallas ISD). Kathleen was named an Interim MASBA Director in June 2000.

Longoria, Joe (Stafford MSD). Joe was named an Interim MASBA Director in June 2000.

López, Pedro "Pete" (Taft ISD). Pete attended the June 15, 2007 MASBA Board meeting as a guest. He was appointed at that meeting to the MASBA Board. *Mariachi* programs suggest he was on the MASBA Board through at least January 2011.

Maddox, Nicholas "Nick." An attorney for O'Hanlon Demerath & Castillo, Nick has served as MASBA Legal Counsel since at least 2017.

Maldonado, Diana M. (Round Rock ISD). Diana was elected to the MASBA Board at the January 13, 2006 Member Assembly. She served through at least June 2007. She was elected to the State House of Representatives in November 2008.

Martínez, Alberto "Albert" (San Diego ISD). Albert was involved in MASBA's resurgence in the early 1990s, meeting on the matter with Tommy Molina, Diana Castañeda, Theresa Gutiérrez, and Juan Aguilera. He was elected MASBA President circa 1998 and served in this capacity through September 22, 2001.

Martínez, Juan, Jr. (Southwest ISD). Juan attended the 2000 MASBA conference and was named an interim MASBA Director in June 2000. He was elected MASBA Treasurer at the January 19, 2003 Member Assembly, at which he was named a member of the Board's Funding, Budget & Finance Committee. He attended his last MASBA Board meeting on March 4, 2005.

Martínez, Raymundo (Hidalgo ISD). Raymundo served on the MASBA Board from January 2015 through at least November 2016.

Mathias, Dr. Jayme (Austin ISD). Jayme was hired as MASBA Executive Director in October 2017, a position in which he serves to the present day.

McVey, Ron (Mercedes ISD). Ron is listed in *mariachi* programs as a member of the MASBA Board in 2010 to 2012. He is listed in meeting minutes as MASBA Treasurer from February 2012 through January 2013.

Medrano, Adam (Dallas ISD). Adam was elected to the MASBA Board at the January 12, 2008 Member Assembly.

Mireles, Brígido "Brig" (Round Rock ISD). Brig attended the 2000 MASBA conference and was elected to the MASBA Board at the January 19, 2003 Member Assembly. Minutes of the Board's July 31, 2003 meeting state that he no longer served on the board at that time.

Molina, Tomás "Tommy" F. (San Diego ISD). Tommy served on the TASB Board and connected San Diego ISD Trustee Albert Martínez with other trustees hoping to bring together Mexican-American trustees. Tommy was present at the MASBA organizational meeting of June 16, 2000. He subsequently joined the MASBA egroup and was a co-facilitator with Juan Aguilera of an organizational meeting in October 2000, when the first President of MASBA was elected after MASBA's reorganization. Tommy is first mentioned as MASBA Executive Director in the minutes of a February 14, 2003 MASBA Board meeting. He resigned as Executive Director prior to the Board's March 4, 2005 meeting.

Montoya, Rudy (Austin ISD). Rudy attended the 2000 MASBA conference and was named an interim MASBA Director on May 17, 2000. He was listed as a Director in a June 20, 2003 event program. July 31, 2003 meeting minutes state that he no longer served on the Board.

Moreno, William "Bill" (Mathis ISD). Because he was elected Vice President at the January 8, 2005 Member Assembly, it is presumed that Bill was elected to the MASBA Board at the January 17, 2004 Member Assembly, for which minutes have not been found. On March 4, 2005, Bill was appointed President Elect. By January 2006, he was no longer on the MASBA Board, such that Dr. Manuel Flores continued to serve as MASBA President.

Moya, Lori (Austin ISD). Lori is listed in *mariachi* programs as a member of the MASBA Board in 2013 to 2014.

Muñoz, Joe F. (Hays CISD). Joe attended the June 11, 2004 MASBA Board meeting as a guest and reported that he was willing to assume the seat of Joe Hernández, who could no longer serve on the Board. He was elected to the MASBA Board at that meeting. Joe was appointed Acting President circa May 2006, after MASBA President Dr. Manuel Flores lost his local election. Joe was elected to his own term as President at the 2007 MASBA Member Assembly. After the resignation of President Elect Cruz Hinojosa just prior to the 2008 MASBA Member Assembly, Joe agreed to serve a second term as President, through 2009. After coordinating the first Texas High School *Mariachi* Competition in January 2010, he served as MASBA Executive Director from 2010 to 2014. He coordinated the *mariachi* competition through 2015, at which time *mariachi* was recognized as a sanctioned UIL event.

Navarro, Danny (*Aprende* Technology). Danny is listed as MASBA's webmaster in the minutes of the Member Assemblies of 2006 to 2008.

Navarro, Raúl "Roy" (Pharr-San Juan-Alamo ISD). Roy was elected MASBA Vice President at the January 19, 2003 Member Assembly and as President Elect at the January 17, 2004 Member Assembly. He failed to appear at the January 8, 2005 Member Assembly, where he was scheduled to become MASBA President.

Nieto, Carlos (Presidio ISD). Carlos was present at the MASBA organizational meeting of June 16, 2000 and was subsequently part of MASBA's egroup. He was elected an Interim MASBA Director in October 2000. Carlos is listed as being absent from the MASBA Board during its June 11, 2004 meeting. He served as TASB President in 2002, when MASBA honored him with a reception on June 14, 2002.

O'Hanlon, Kevin. For years, Kevin has provided *pro bono* legal services as MASBA Legal Counsel, presented at MASBA conferences, and supported MASBA as a gold and diamond sponsor.

Orona, Rudy (Waelder ISD). Rudy is listed in *mariachi* programs as a member of the MASBA Board at the beginning of 2014. He was elected MASBA Treasurer at the February 1, 2014 Member Assembly. Meeting minutes of October 2, 2015 announce his resignation.

Ortiz, Marco R. (Taylor ISD). Marco was elected to the MASBA Board at the March 2, 2019 Member Assembly. He continues his service to the MASBA Board.

Osuna, Norma (Slaton ISD). Norma was named an Interim MASBA Director in June 2000. She was elected MASBA Secretary at the January 19, 2003 Member Assembly, a position she held through the January 13, 2006 Member Assembly.

Peña, Aguie (unknown district). Aguie was MASBA Secretary for the January 12, 2002 meeting of the MASBA Board. She is listed in meeting minutes as the outgoing MASBA Secretary prior to the January 19, 2003 Member Assembly.

Peña, Gloria (Arlington ISD). Gloria is listed in *mariachi* programs as a member of the MASBA Board in 2010 and 2011, and as MASBA Secretary in 2013 and 2014.

Pérez, Larry (Waco ISD). Larry is listed in *mariachi* programs as a member of the MASBA Board in 2010 to 2014. Meeting minutes note that he was on the MASBA Board in 2016, through July 2017.

Pérez, Lydia M. (Austin ISD). Lydia served as MASBA President in 1986 to 1987. On September 11, 1986, she became MASBA's registered agent with the Secretary of State.

Ramos, Jacinto "Cinto," Jr. (Fort Worth ISD). Cinto was appointed to the MASBA Board in July 2017. He was elected Vice President at the February 24, 2018 Member Assembly, and as President Elect at the March 2, 2019 Member Assembly. He continues to serve in this capacity.

Rangel, Juan (Fort Worth ISD). Juan was present at the MASBA organizational meeting of June 16, 2000 and was subsequently part of MASBA's egroup. He was elected to the MASBA Board at the January 8, 2005 Member Assembly. He served as Vice President in 2010, and became President at the January 21, 2012 Member Assembly. He served as Immediate Past President the following year.

Reyes, Louis Q., III (Seguin ISD). Louis recalls serving as Interim President for some three months after MASBA President Diana Castañeda lost her local election in May, 2006. He attended the 2000 MASBA conference. He is listed in *mariachi* programs as a member of the MASBA Board in 2013. He was elected Vice President at the January 19, 2013 Member Assembly, and as President Elect at the February 1, 2014 Member Assembly. Louis served as MASBA President beginning at the January 24, 2015 Member Assembly, and as Immediate Past President in 2016. One source suggests he served as Executive Director from circa June 2014 to July 2017, when the MASBA Board named him Chief Ambassador. Louis continues to serve as MASBA Ambassador.

Reyes, Marty (Ysleta ISD). Marty is listed in *mariachi* programs as a member of the MASBA Board in 2010 to 2013. Meeting minutes state that she was elected (or perhaps re-elected) on January 19, 2013. She was appointed MASBA Treasurer on June 8, 2013.

Reyna, Art. Art is listed as MASBA Staff and Governmental Relations in *mariachi* programs from 2010 to 2013. Meeting minutes list his name from June 2010 through June 2013.

Rivera, Ram (Santa María ISD). Ram was elected to the MASBA Board at the January 13, 2006 Member Assembly, when he was named to the Board's Nominations Committee and Bylaws & Resolutions Committee. He was appointed to the Bylaws & Resolutions Committee again in 2007. He is listed in MASBA's 2010 *mariachi* competition program.

Rocha, Connie (San Antonio ISD). Connie attended the 2000 MASBA conference and was named an Interim MASBA Director in June 2000. She presented a breakout session on early childhood education at MASBA's 2003 conference.

Rodríguez, Armando "Mando" (Canutillo ISD). Mando is listed in *mariachi* programs as a member of the MASBA Board in 2014. He was elected Vice President at the January 24, 2015 Member Assembly and as President Elect at the 2016 Member Assembly. He became President at the February 25, 2017 Member Assembly, and Immediate Past President at the conclusion of the February 24, 2018 Member Assembly.

Rodríguez, Manuel "Manny," Jr. (Houston ISD). Manuel was elected to the MASBA Board at the January 13, 2006 Member Assembly. He was elected Vice President at the January 12, 2008 Member Assembly and President Elect at the 2009 Member Assembly. He became MASBA President on January 22, 2010, and Immediate Past President on January 22, 2011. Manuel continued to attend MASBA Board meetings and lead the planning of MASBA conferences. Before his death in 2017, he was looking forward to serving as 2018 MASBA Conference Chair.

Rodríguez, Rudy (Denton ISD). Rudy is listed in *mariachi* programs as MASBA Secretary and Treasurer in 2010 and 2011. Meeting minutes state that he was tasked with branding & marketing recommendations on June 11, 2010, and that he served as Treasurer, assisted with conference preparations and co-presented on MASBA membership on September 24, 2010. He presented breakout sessions on bilingual education at MASBA's 2010 and 2013 conferences.

Rosales, Miguel "Mike" (Ysleta ISD). Mike has served on the MASBA Board since 2017. He was elected Secretary at the February 24, 2018 Member Assembly, and he continues to serve in this capacity.

Rubio, Lucío "Lucy" (Corpus Christi ISD). Lucy was elected to the MASBA Board at the January 13, 2006 Member Assembly, where she was named to the Board's Funding, Budget & Finance Committee. She was appointed to the Committee again in 2007. Lucy was appointed Secretary on June 15, 2007 and was elected to that position by the January 12, 2008 Member Assembly.

Ruiz, Guadalupe "Lupe" (Raymondville ISD). Lupe was elected MASBA Secretary at the January 24, 2015 Member Assembly. He served in this capacity through at least February 28, 2016. During a March 28, 2015 planning retreat, he was tasked with assisting committees on revenue and advocacy.

___, Sonny (Waco ISD). Though Sonny's surname is not known at present, various persons remember his presence at organizing meetings in the mid-1990s. Albert Martínez recalls that Sonny was a MASBA Officer at that time.

Sublasky, David (ESC Region 19). David attended the 2000 MASBA conference and was appointed to the MASBA Board before the Board's June 11, 2004, at which he was absent. He served on the MASBA Board through 2007 and had vacated his seat before January 2008.

Saldívar, Óscar (Santa María ISD). Óscar is listed in *mariachi* programs as a member of the MASBA Board in 2011 and 2013.

Salinas, Héctor (Corpus Christi ISD). Héctor is listed in *mariachi* programs as a member of the MASBA Board in 2014 to 2015.

Sepúlveda, Roberto "Robert" (Weslaco ISD). Robert served as President of MASBA at some point prior to August 1986. He was present at the MASBA organizational meeting of June 16, 2000 and was subsequently part of MASBA's egroup.

Simms, Terry. Terry was also present at a June 11, 2010 MASBA meeting, presumably as Staff. He is listed as MASBA Staff at the February 1, 2014 Member Assembly.

Soto, Adam (Plainview ISD). Adam was appointed to the MASBA Board in August 2019. He continues his service to the MASBA Board.

Soto, Paul (Seguin ISD). Paul was named an Interim MASBA Director in June 2000. It seems he was still on the MASBA Board in September 2001.

Stafford, Charles (Denton ISD). A Past President of TASB, Charles was appointed to the MASBA Board in August 2019. He continues his service to the MASBA Board.

Tenorio, Guillermo "Willie," Jr. (Hays CISD). Willie is listed in *mariachi* programs as a member of the MASBA Board in 2013 to 2015. Meeting minutes note that he continued his service and was MASBA Secretary in 2017. He was elected President Elect at the February 24, 2018 Member Assembly, and he began his service as President at the conclusion of the March 2, 2019 Member Assembly. He currently serves as MASBA President.

Torres, Jesse (Lamar CISD). Jesse was elected to the MASBA Board at the January 19, 2003 Member Assembly. There is no record of him after the June 11, 2004 MASBA Board meeting.

Tovar, Vincent. Vincent has assisted MASBA since 2017. In October 2019, he was named Associate Executive Director.

Vargas, Michael Anthony (San Benito CISD). Presumably elected at the 2017 Member Assembly, Michael resigned shortly after being elected Secretary by the February 24, 2018 Member Assembly.

Vásquez, Sylvester, Jr. (Southwest ISD). A former TASB President, Sylvester has was elected to the MASBA Board during its meeting on July 8-9, 2017. He continues his service to the MASBA Board.

Velarde, Alfonso "Al" (El Paso ISD). Al has served on the MASBA Board since November 2017. He continues his service to the MASBA Board.

Villalobos, Rocío. Rocío is listed in January 2018 minutes, in a section labeled "MASBA Staff & Contractors." She assisted with social media and with the clean-up and expansion of MASBA's email list.

Watts, Eva Castillo (Donna ISD). Eva was appointed to the unexpired term of Michael Vargas in April 2018. She was elected to her own term as Director during the March 2, 2019 Member Assembly. She continues her service to the MASBA Board.

Ybarra, Mario (Lubbock ISD). Mario is listed in *mariachi* programs as a member of the MASBA Board in 2014 to 2015. He was re-elected to the MASBA Board on February 20, 2016.

Appendix E

A History of MASBA Awardees

MASBA has conferred a number of awards through the years. Written records note the following awards and awardees.

Texas Association of School Boards Executive Director
James B. Crow
2002 Golden *Molcajete* Award

State Representative Dora Olivo
2006 *La Campana* Award

Former Houston ISD Trustee
Olga Gallegos
2006 *La Campana* Award

University of Houston Professor
Dr. Guadalupe San Miguel
2006 *La Campana* Award

State Board of Education Member
Mary Helen Bonilla Berlanga
Golden *Molcajete* Award – January 2006

National Hispanic Institute Founder
Ernest Nieto
Golden *Molcajete* Award – January 2006

Kingsville ISD Trustee
Dr. Larry Garza
La Campana Award – June 2006

Weslaco ISD Trustee
Dr. Robert Sepúlveda
La Campana Award – June 2006

**Ben Bolt-Palito Blanco ISD Superintendent
Alberto Byington**
Golden *Molcajete* Award – January 13, 2007

Joel López
2008 Golden *Molcajete* Award

Mariachi Campanas de América **Director
Juan Ortiz**
La Campana Award – June 2008

Hidalgo ISD Board of Trustees
2009 Golden *Molcajete* Award

**National Hispanic Institute Founder
Ernest Nieto**
2009 *La Campana* Award

**State Board of Education Member
Mary Helen Bonilla Berlanga**
2010 *La Campana* Award

Mullen Pension & Benefits Group
2010 Golden *Molcajete* Award

**Southwest ISD Trustee
Sylvester Vásquez, Jr.**
2012 Golden *Molcajete* Award

**San Antonio ISD Interim Superintendent
Dr. Sylvester Pérez**
La Campana Award – January 19, 2013

Texas Association of School Boards Affiliates
Golden *Molcajete* Award – June 7, 2013

ERO Architects
Golden *Molcajete* Award – June 7, 2013

State Senator Gonzalo Barrientos
La Campana Award – January 24, 2015

Intercultural Development Research Association
Special Recognition Award for Outstanding Service & Commitment
in the Fight for Equitable School Financing
January 24, 2015

Mexican American Legal Defense & Educational Fund
Special Recognition Award for Outstanding Service & Commitment
in the Fight for Equitable School Financing
January 24, 2015

State Representative
Richard Peña Raymond
Golden *Molcajete* Award – June 2015

Senator Eddie Lucío, Jr.
ERO/MASBA Hispanic Heritage Award – October 2, 2015

Former MASBA President Manuel Rodríguez
ERO/MASBA Hispanic Heritage Award – October 2, 2015

Former MASBA President María G. Leal
ERO/MASBA Hispanic Heritage Award – October 2, 2015

U.S. Congressman Rubén Hinojosa
2016 *La Campana* Award

Kevin O'Hanlon
O'Hanlon Law Firm
2016 *La Campana* Award

U.S. Congressman Rubén Hinojosa
2016 Golden *Molcajete* Award

Julián & Joaquín Castro
Golden *Molcajete* Award – June 16, 2017

Former MASBA President Dr. Viola García
Award for Outstanding Service & Leadership – June 16, 2017

Former MASBA President Manuel Rodríguez
Award for Outstanding Service & Leadership – June 16, 2017

Former U.S. Secretary of Housing & Urban Development
Henry Cisneros
La Campana Award – February 24, 2018

Tejano **Monument, Inc. President**
Dr. Cayetano Barrera
Hispanic Heritage Award – February 24, 2018

Tejano **Monument Principal Fundraiser**
Renato Ramírez
Hispanic Heritage Award – February 24, 2018

Tejano **Monument Artist**
Armando Hinojosa
Hispanic Heritage Award – February 24, 2018

Kevin O'Hanlon
Golden *Molcajete* Award – June 20, 2019

Appendix F

A History of MASBA Conferences

According to Teresa Paloma Acosta, "on February 8-9, 1975, MASBMA and other Mexican-American organizations sponsored a conference on the education of Hispanics." She writes, "In partnership with the Intercultural Development Research Association (IDRA) of San Antonio, MASBMA created and offered a program to train Mexican-American school board members in effective leadership. The program continued through 1987, with funding from IDRA, the Ford Foundation, the Carnegie Corporation of New York, the National Education Task Force *De La Raza*, and other groups."

Amancio Chapa, Jr., who served as MASBA President in 1987, remembers MASBA's annual conferences. Recalling his predecessor, Lydia M. Pérez, he says, "Lydia put together a great conference in Austin." He also recalls a MASBA conference in Odessa on a Father's Day weekend of an unknown year, likely between 1987 and 1999.

In the late 1990s, Juan Aguilera and Albert Martínez worked to organize an annual conference for the resurgent MASBA. For many years, Juan and his staff led the planning for this event. A decade later, Manuel Rodríguez of Houston ISD led the planning of MASBA's annual conference.

Existing records have enabled us to reconstruct the following history of MASBA conferences after the organization's resurgence.

First Annual MASBA Conference
1999
The University of Texas at San Antonio Downtown Campus

Second Annual MASBA Conference
"Hispanic Student Excellence: A Vision for the New Millennium"
In Memory of Senator Greg Luna (1932-1999)
January 28-30, 2000
The University of Texas at San Antonio Downtown Campus
Alberto "Albert" Martínez, San Diego ISD, President

Third Annual MASBA Conference
2001
The University of Texas at San Antonio Downtown Campus
Alberto "Albert" Martínez, San Diego ISD, President

Fourth Annual MASBA Conference
"Hispanic Educational Excellence: Education is Our Solution"
January 10-12, 2002
Co-hosted by the UTSA Office of K-16 Initiatives & Honors Programs
The University of Texas at San Antonio Downtown Campus
Jimmie Adame, Taft ISD, President

Fifth Annual MASBA Conference
"Hispanic Student Success for the New Millennium:
A Leadership & Issues Conference to
Address the Challenges of Our Mexican American Students in Texas"
January 17-19, 2003
Co-hosted by the UTSA Office of K-16 Initiatives & Honors Programs
and the Hispanic Border Leadership Institute
The University of Texas at San Antonio Downtown Campus
Jimmie Adame, Taft ISD, Outgoing President
Dr. Viola García, Aldine ISD, Incoming President

Sixth Annual MASBA Conference
January 16-18, 2004
Radisson Hotel, San Antonio
Dr. Viola García, Aldine ISD, Outgoing President
Óscar García, Ben Bolt-Palito Blanco ISD, Incoming President

Seventh Annual MASBA Conference
January 7-9, 2005
Radisson Hotel, San Antonio
Óscar García, Ben Bolt-Palito Blanco ISD, President

Eighth Annual MASBA Conference
January 13-15, 2006
"Reflejos del Mar / Reflections by the Sea"
Holiday Inn Emerald Beach Hotel, Corpus Christi
Dr. Manuel C. Flores, Corpus Christi ISD, President

Ninth Annual MASBA Conference
January 12-14, 2007
Omni Bayfront Hotel, Corpus Christi
Joe Muñoz, Hays CISD, Incoming President

Tenth Annual MASBA Conference
January 10-13, 2008
Austin Omni Hotel, Austin
Joe Muñoz, Hays CISD, President

Eleventh Annual MASBA Conference
2009
[Place currently unknown]
Joe Muñoz, Hays CISD, Outgoing President
María Leal, South Texas ISD, Incoming President

Twelfth Annual MASBA Conference
January 21-24, 2010
Hyatt San Antonio Riverwalk Hotel
María Leal, South Texas ISD, Outgoing President
Manuel Rodríguez, Houston ISD, Incoming President

Thirteenth Annual MASBA Conference
January 20-23, 2011
La Quinta San Antonio Riverwalk Hotel, San Antonio
Manuel Rodríguez, Houston ISD, Outgoing President
Joshua Cerna, Harlandale ISD, Incoming President

Fourteenth Annual MASBA Conference
January 19-22, 2012
[Place currently unknown]
Joshua Cerna, Harlandale ISD, Outgoing President
Juan Rangel, Fort Worth ISD, Incoming President

Fifteenth Annual MASBA Conference
January 17-20, 2013
Austin Doubletree Hotel, Austin, Texas
Juan Rangel, Fort Worth ISD, Outgoing President
Gloria Santillán Casas, La Feria ISD, Incoming President

Sixteenth Annual MASBA Conference
January 30 - February 2, 2014
McAllen Convention Center, McAllen, Texas
Gloria Santillán Casas, La Feria ISD, Outgoing President
Danny Bueno, Ben Bolt-Palito Blanco ISD, Incoming President

Seventeenth Annual MASBA Conference
January 22-24, 2015
Austin Doubletree Hotel, Austin, Texas
Danny Bueno, Ben Bolt-Palito Blanco ISD, Outgoing President
Louis Q. Reyes, III, Seguin ISD, Incoming President

Eighteenth Annual MASBA Conference
February 18-21, 2016
Hilton San Antonio Airport Hotel, San Antonio, Texas
Louis Q. Reyes, III, Seguin ISD, Outgoing President
Irene Galán-Rodríguez, Big Spring ISD, Incoming President

Nineteenth Annual MASBA Conference
February 23-25, 2017
La Quinta San Antonio Riverwalk Hotel
San Antonio, Texas
Irene Galán-Rodríguez, Big Spring ISD, Outgoing President
Armando "Mando" Rodríguez, Canutillo ISD, Incoming President

Twentieth Annual MASBA Conference
February 22-24, 2018
"¡MASBÁmonos!"
Hilton San Antonio Airport Hotel, San Antonio, Texas
Armando "Mando" Rodríguez, Canutillo ISD, Outgoing President
Homero García, South Texas ISD, Incoming President

Twenty-first Annual MASBA Conference
March 1-3, 2019
"¡Superhéroes for Kids!"
Renaissance Austin Hotel, Austin, Texas
Homero García, South Texas ISD, Outgoing President
Guillermo "Willie" Tenorio, Jr., Hays CISD, Incoming President

Twenty-second Annual MASBA Conference
February 20-23, 2020
"¡MASBAilemos! A Golden Jubilee Conference & Celebration"
Wyndham San Antonio Riverwalk Hotel, San Antonio, Texas
Guillermo "Willie" Tenorio, Jr., Hays CISD, Outgoing President
Jacinto "Cinto" Ramos, Jr., Fort Worth ISD, Incoming President

Appendix G

A History of MASBA Texas High School *Mariachi* Competitions

At the January 13, 2006 MASBA Member Assembly, Former Southwest ISD Trustee Juan Martínez, a MASBA Associate, proposed the following resolution, which was passed by the Assembly:

> Be it resolved that the leadership and membership of the Mexican American School Board Members Association of Texas petition the Texas University Interscholastic League to make *mariachi* music a full-fledged activity with regional and state competition, beginning with the 2007-2008 school year.

The rationale that accompanied the resolution read,

> Many high schools and middle schools in Texas have *mariachi* music programs, and they compete in a variety of non-school an non-UIL-sanctioned events. By making *mariachi* music a UIL event, it will allow students to letter in school-sponsored and state-sanctioned events. *Mariachi* music, like any other music or UIL program, becomes a reality only when a school district decides to implement such a program. This will increase cultural awareness when school districts opt to start *mariachi* music programs. It will raise the students' self-esteem and increase their cultural awareness.

In 2006 and 2007, various MASBA members testified at UIL board meetings in Austin, advocating for the sanctioning of *mariachi* music. They included MASBA President Dr. Manuel Flores, MASBA President Elect Joe Muñoz, MASBA Legal Counsel & Former MASBA Executive Director Juan Aguilera, and MASBA Board Member Manuel Rodríguez.

On January 12, 2008, MASBA President Joe Muñoz reported to the MASBA Member Assembly that he had hosted a press conference to announce that the UIL had accepted *mariachi* music as a sanctioned event, with competitions to begin in the Fall of 2008.

The following *mariachi* competitions were hosted by MASBA.

314

Year One

Texas High School *Mariachi* **Competition**
January 23, 2010
Edgewood ISD Performing Arts Theatre, Edgewood ISD

Year Two

Texas High School *Mariachi* **Competition**
January 22, 2011
Edgewood ISD Performing Arts Theatre, Edgewood ISD

Year Three

Texas High School *Mariachi* **Competition – East Area**
November 5, 2011
César Chávez High School, Houston ISD

Texas High School *Mariachi* **Competition – West Area**
November 12, 2011
Odessa Middle School, Ector County ISD

Texas High School *Mariachi* **Competition – 1A-3A Districts**
November 19, 2011
Southwest High School, Southwest ISD

Texas High School *Mariachi* **Competition – North Area**
December 3, 2011
Trimble Tech High School, Fort Worth ISD

Texas High School *Mariachi* **Competition – South Area**
December 10, 2011
Economedes High School, Edinburg CISD

Texas High School *Mariachi* **Competition – Central Area**
December 10, 2011
Southwest High School, Southwest ISD

Texas High School *Mariachi* **Competition – Finals**
January 28, 2012
Edgewood ISD Performing Arts Theatre, Edgewood ISD

Year Four

Texas High School *Mariachi* Competition – North Area
January 12, 2013
Trimble Tech High School, Fort Worth ISD

Texas High School *Mariachi* Competition – Central Area
January 12, 2013
Southwest High School Theatre of Performing Arts, Southwest ISD

Texas High School *Mariachi* Competition – South Area
January 19, 2013
Economedes High School, Edinburg CISD

Texas High School *Mariachi* Competition – Finals
February 9, 2013
Edgewood ISD Performing Arts Theatre, Edgewood ISD

Year Five

Texas High School *Mariachi* Competition – Central Area
January 18, 2014
Fox Tech High School, San Antonio ISD

Texas High School *Mariachi* Competition – North Area
January 25, 2014
Trimble Tech High School, Fort Worth ISD

Texas High School *Mariachi* Competition – South Area
January 25, 2014
Edinburg North High School Performing Arts Center, Edinburg CISD

Texas High School *Mariachi* Competition – Finals
February 8, 2014
Southwest High School Theatre of Performing Arts, Southwest ISD

Year Six

Texas High School *Mariachi* Competition – North Area
January 17, 2015
Trimble Tech High School, Fort Worth ISD

Texas High School *Mariachi* Competition – Central Area
January 17, 2015
Brackenridge High School, San Antonio ISD

Texas High School *Mariachi* Competition – South Area
January 24, 2015
Edinburg High School Performing Arts Center, Edinburg CISD

Texas High School *Mariachi* Competition – Finals
February 7, 2015
Southwest High School Auditorium, Southwest ISD

On October 18, 2014, the University Interscholastic League (UIL) Music Committee unanimously voted to sanction *mariachi* as a UIL event, beginning in the 2015-2016 school year.

Appendix H

MASBA *Mariachi* Competition Participants

Texas High School *Mariachi* Championship
January 23, 2010
Edgewood ISD Performing Arts Theatre

Participating Schools

Cotulla HS, Cotulla ISD	2A champion
Zapata HS, Zapata ISD	3A champion
Port Isabel HS, Point Isabel ISD	3A runner-up
Hidalgo HS, Hidalgo ISD	3A third place
Valley View HS, Valley View ISD (Hidalgo County)	4A champion
Roma HS, Roma ISD	4A runner-up
Lehman HS, Hays CISD	4A third place
C.C. Winn HS, Eagle Pass ISD	5A champion
Eagle Pass HS, Eagle Pass ISD	5A runner-up

Texas High School *Mariachi* Championship
January 22, 2011
Edgewood ISD Performing Arts Theatre

Participating School	Director
Hebbronville HS, Jim Hogg County ISD (2A champion)	
Cotulla HS, Cotulla ISD (2A runner-up)	Manuel "Elio" Ramírez, Jr.
	José Ángel Soliz & Miguel Cabrera
Zapata HS, Zapata ISD (3A champion)	Adrián Padilla
Roma HS, Roma ISD (4A champion)	Noé Sánchez
H.M. King HS, Kingsville ISD (4A runner-up)	Rolando Molina
North Side HS, Fort Worth ISD (4A third place)	Ramón Niño, III
Palmview HS, La Joya ISD (5A champion)	Mayra García
Economedes HS, Edinburg CISD (5A runner-up)	Ignacio A. López
Odessa HS, Ector County ISD (5A third place)	Gabriel García
La Joya HS, La Joya ISD (5A)	Emilio César Cantú
Eagle Pass HS, EPISD (5A)	Gregorio Cavazos & David M. Solís

Texas High School *Mariachi* Championship
January 28, 2012
Edgewood ISD Performing Arts Theatre

Participating School	Director
San Diego HS, San Diego ISD (2A champion)	John A. Vela
Grulla HS, *Río Grande* City CISD (3A champion)	Alfonso Rodríguez
Zapata HS, Zapata ISD (3A)	Adrián Padilla
Polytechnic HS, Fort Worth ISD (3A)	Marta O. Ocampo
Roma HS, Roma ISD (4A winner)	Noé Sánchez
Edcouch-Elsa HS, Edcouch-Elsa ISD (4A)	
Homero Gutiérrez, Marcos Zarate & Marcos García	
North Side HS, Fort Worth ISD (4A)	Ramón Niño, III
H.M. King HS, Kingsville ISD (4A)	Rolando Molina
Fox Tech HS, San Antonio ISD (4A)	David Zamarripa & R. García
Brackenridge HS, San Antonio ISD (4A)	John P. Nieto
Southwest HS, Southwest ISD (5A)	Eddie Perales & J. Porras
Palmview HS, La Joya ISD (5A)	Mayra García
Edinburg North HS, Edinburg CISD (5A)	Abel Acuña
Odessa HS, Ector County ISD (5A)	Gabriel García
Economedes HS, Edinburg CISD (5A)	Ignacio A. López

Texas High School *Mariachi* Championship
February 9, 2013
Edgewood ISD Performing Arts Theatre

Participating School	Director
Ben Bolt HS, Ben Bolt-Palito Blanco ISD (1A)	José Ángel Soliz
Premont HS, Premont ISD (1A)	Héctor M. Cantú & Ernesto Cortez
Mathis HS, Mathis ISD (2A winner)	Miguel Cabrera
Grulla HS, *Río Grande* City CISD (3A champion)	Alfonso Rodríguez
H.M. King HS, Kingsville ISD (3A)	Rolando Molina
Hidalgo Early College HS, Hidalgo ISD (3A)	Víctor Galván
Zapata HS, Zapata ISD (3A)	Óscar Martínez
Río Grande City HS, *Río Grande* City CISD (4A champion)	
	Alex Rodríguez
Brackenridge HS, San Antonio ISD (4A)	John P. Nieto
Roma HS, Roma ISD (4A)	Noé Sánchez
Valley View HS, Valley View ISD (Hidalgo County) (4A)	
	Juan M. Vázquez & Guillermo Rodríguez
North Side HS, Fort Worth ISD (4A)	Ramón Niño, III
Edinburg North HS, Edinburg CISD (5A champion)	Abel Acuña
Martin HS, Laredo ISD (5A)	Rubén Guadián
Southwest HS, Southwest ISD (5A)	Eddie Perales
Vela HS, Edinburg CISD (5A)	Karina A. López

Texas High School *Mariachi* **Championship**
February 8, 2014
Southwest High School Auditorium

Participating School	Director
Premont HS, Premont ISD (1A)	Ernesto Cortez
Ben Bolt HS, Ben Bolt-Palito Blanco ISD (1A)	José Ángel Soliz
Mathis HS, Mathis ISD (2A)	Miguel Cabrera
Cotulla HS, Cotulla ISD (2A)	Jaime Martínez
Grulla HS, *Río Grande* City CISD (3A)	Alfonso Rodríguez
Port Isabel HS, Point Isabel ISD (3A)	Obed Salas
H.M. King HS, Kingsville ISD (3A)	Rolando Molina
Hidalgo Early College HS, Hidalgo ISD (3A)	Adrián Padilla
Zapata HS, Zapata ISD (3A)	Óscar Martínez
Brackenridge HS, San Antonio ISD (4A)	John P. Nieto
Roma HS, Roma ISD (4A)	Eloy Garza
Polytechnic HS, Fort Worth ISD (4A)	Michael A. Cruz
Fox Tech HS, San Antonio ISD (4A)	David Zamarripa
Río Grande City HS, *Río Grande* City CISD (4A)	Alex Rodríguez
Edcouch-Elsa HS, Edcouch-Elsa ISD (4A)	
	Marcos García, Mario Ferrer & Michael Sital
Vela HS, Edinburg CISD (5A)	Karina A. López
Palmview HS, La Joya ISD (5A)	Mayra García
Edinburg North HS, Edinburg CISD (5A)	Abel Acuña
Grand Prairie Fine Arts Academy, GPISD (5A)	Marta O. Ocampo
Sharyland HS, Sharyland ISD (5A)	
	Juan C. López & Juan G. Vázquez
Eagle Pass HS, Eagle Pass ISD (5A)	David M. Solís
Southwest HS, Southwest ISD (5A)	Eddie Perales
McAllen HS, McAllen ISD (5A)	Alex Treviño
North Side HS, Fort Worth ISD (5A)	
	Ramón Niño, III, Wendy I. Martínez & Dr. William Gradante

Texas High School *Mariachi* **Championship**
February 7, 2015
Southwest High School Auditorium

Participating School	Director
Ben Bolt HS, Ben Bolt-Palito Blanco ISD (1A)	José Ángel Soliz
Premont HS, Premont ISD (1A)	Ernesto Cortez
Mathis HS, Mathis ISD (2A)	Miguel Cabrera
Falfurrias HS, Brooks County ISD (2A)	Roel Sáenz
San Diego HS, San Diego ISD (2A)	Héctor M. Cantú
Cotulla HS, Cotulla ISD (2A)	Francisco C. Ramírez, Jr.
Port Isabel HS, Point Isabel ISD (3A)	Obed Salas
H.M. King HS, Kingsville ISD (3A)	Rolando Molina
Grulla HS, *Río Grande* City CISD (3A)	Alfonso Rodríguez
Hidalgo ECHS, Hidalgo ISD (3A)	Adrián Padilla & Víctor Galván
Zapata HS, Zapata ISD (3A)	Óscar Martínez
Brackenridge HS, San Antonio ISD (5A)	John P. Nieto
Valley View HS, Valley View ISD (Hidalgo Co.) (5A)	Juan J. López
Edcouch-Elsa HS, Edcouch-Elsa ISD (5A)	
	Marcos García, Mario Ferrer & Michael Sital
Nixon HS, Laredo ISD (5A)	John Spillane
Martin HS, Laredo ISD (5A)	Rubén Guadián
Cigarroa HS, Laredo ISD (5A)	Servando Serna
Roma HS, Roma ISD (5A)	Eloy Garza
Río Grande City HS, *Río Grande* City CISD (5A)	Daniel E. Rentería
North Side HS, Fort Worth ISD (5A)	
	Ramón Niño, III & Wendy I. Martínez
Sharyland HS, Sharyland ISD (5A)	Juan G. Vázquez & Martin Cantú
Donna North HS, Donna ISD (5A)	Víctor Cárdenas
Veterans Memorial HS, Mission CISD (5A)	Francisco Vela, Jr.
Grand Prairie Fine Arts Academy, GPISD (6A)	Marta O. Ocampo
Eagle Pass HS, Eagle Pass ISD (6A)	David M. Solís
Edinburg HS, Edinburg CISD (6A)	Lorena López
Lehman HS, Hays CISD (6A)	Joseph Baird
McAllen HS, McAllen ISD (6A)	Alex Treviño

Juárez-Lincoln HS, La Joya ISD (6A)	Emilio César Cantú
Palmview HS, La Joya ISD (6A)	Mayra García
South Grand Prairie HS, GPISD (6A)	Felipe Díaz, Jr.
Edinburg North HS, Edinburg CISD (6A)	Abel Acuña
John Jay HS, Northside ISD (6A)	Alexandra Velásquez
La Joya HS, La Joya ISD (6A)	Juan Carlos López
Southwest HS, Southwest ISD (6A)	Eddie Perales
Fox Tech HS, San Antonio ISD (4A)	David Zamarripa

Index

334

338

Do you have any comments on this work? Any memories you'd like to share? Any MASBA meeting agendas and/or minutes, conference programs, photos, and/or other materials that might assist us in reconstructing MASBA's history?

Please email info@masbatx.org or call (512) 826-0280.

¡Gracias!

Made in the USA
Middletown, DE
07 February 2020